RAIN MAKING

The Professional's Guide to Attracting New Clients

RAIN MAKING

The Professional's Guide to Attracting New Clients

FORD HARDING, CMC

BOB ADAMS, INC.
Holbrook, Massachusetts

Published by Bob Adams, Inc.
260 Center Street, Holbrook, MA 02343

ISBN: 1-55850-420-6

Printed in the United States of America.

J I H G F E D C B

Library of Congress Cataloging-in-Publication Data
Harding, Ford.
    Rain making : the professional's guide to attracting new clients / Ford Harding.
      p.   cm.
    Includes bibliographical references and index.
    ISBN 1-55850-420-6
    1. Professions—Marketing. I. Title.
    HD8038.A1H37   1994
    658.8–dc20
                                     94-32884
                                        CIP

This book is available at quantity discounts for bulk purchases.
For information, call 1-800-872-5627.

Contents

Part I
Marketing Tactics:
How Professionals Generate Leads

Part II
Sales Tactics: How Professionals
Advance and Close a Sale

Part III
From Tactics to Strategy:
What Works and What Doesn't

Acknowledgments

This book is the result of almost twenty years of learning and teaching the marketing and sale of professional services. During that time hundreds of prospects, clients, colleagues, and friends contributed to my education and, indirectly, to this book. I cannot name them all.

I wish to express my thanks to Maurice Fulton, who gave me my first opportunity in consulting and had the strength to let me stumble many times as I learned to succeed. Also to Jim Keane, who gave me my first opportunity to manage a consulting office and taught me so much about management. And to Bob Hillier, who introduced me to architecture.

Several organizations have been particularly helpful. These include IBM Executive Consulting Institute; the Institute of Management Consultants; and The Society for Marketing Professional Services. Participation in ACME Inc., the association of management consulting firms, played an important part in my education, and its president, Ed Hendricks, has been a valued friend and advisor. It has been both an honor and a pleasure to be a part of the Network of Opportunity. Its members have been a source of motivation and practical help. Several, including David Gensler of Madison Pension Services, Norman Kallen of Ravin, Sarasohn, Cook, Baumgarten, Fisch & Baime, and Michael Seltzer of Insurance Planning Concepts, contributed their experiences to this book.

I have benefited from the example of many people. These include Linda Lukas, an exceptional business developer in the field of architecture; Joan Jorgenson of Executive Resource Group, an entrepreneurial executive recruiter; and Robert Leisk of Cagley, Harman & Leisk, the cheeriest engineer I know. Michael Paris of Michael Paris Associates, Ltd. has provided thoughtful advice over the years. Judy Koblentz of Jannotta Bray & Associates has been a source of so many ideas, introductions, and uplifting comments that I have lost count. Steve DePalma of The Schoor DePalma & Canger Group Inc. saw his consulting engineering firm through a major turnaround under the toughest personal circumstances. His resolution and current success can provide a lesson to us all. It is hard to know how to thank Gail Atlas, who taught me so much in so little time. My life is better for her help. I wish Oscar Megerdichian were alive to thank for his mentoring and guidance. I miss him.

Of special help in providing insights into specific professional practices were Ed Greene of Cleary, Gottlieb, Steen & Hamilton, whom I am fortunate enough to have as my brother-in-law; Mike Schell of Skadden, Arps, Slate, Meagher & Flom, with whom I built a tree house long ago; Charles O'Neill of O'Neill & Neylon; Terry Meginniss of Gladstein, Reif & Meginniss; Dennis Yaeger; Bruce Pritkin of Robbins, Spielman, Slayton & Halfon, who has probably given up camping for life after our last shared experience with our sons; Paul Taenzler; and Emad Youssef of Paulus Sokolowski & Sartor. The partners of the firm Herman Yula Schwartz and Lagomarsino have provided help either directly or indirectly. The questions and comments of students and clients at classes I have taught have sharpened and expanded my thinking. Thank you all.

Several times during the writing of this book I found I needed to discuss ideas with someone with a fresh perspective. Many people helped in this way. Particular patience was shown by Bill Shapiro of Price Waterhouse. Mary Wisnovsky, the most thorough of conference organizers, kindly commented on the chapter on seminars and conferences.

Edith Poor and Ed Meier, both authors, and Don Cleary taught me much about getting a book published. My agent, Jeffrey Herman of the Jeff Herman Agency, Inc., proved a faithful guide through the rigors of finding a publisher for a first book. Dick Staron, my editor, pushed me to make the book longer and better. Without him it would have had several gaps. I want to thank the *Journal of Management Consulting* both for originally publishing several of my articles and for permission to adapt and reprint them here. Chapter 3 originally appeared in the *Journal* under the title "Ten Rules for Better Networking," 1990, volume 6, number 1; chapter 1 as "Make Yourself an Efficient Writer," 1991, volume 6, number 4; and chapter 19 as "Rain Making," 1992, volume 7, number 1. Deborah Baxley's appendix on bios originally appeared in *The Professional Consultant* (July 1993). I also wish to thank that publication. Portions of chapter 6 originally appeared in *National Business Employment Weekly*.

Finally, and most importantly, I want to thank my parents for teaching me to love books and Dinny and Judy and Jon for the close friendship that only family can give. My sister Dinny, a lawyer, also contributed directly to this book in several ways. Jon gave editing advice. My son, Charek, has inspired and motivated me and given up many hours with me while I wrote. I dedicate this book to my wife, Liz, for her tolerance and kindness and support, and because she is the love of my life.

Introduction

You must sell yourself to sell your firm. This is true of accountants, architects, consultants, engineers, and lawyers. It is also true of actuaries, executive recruiters, interior designers, public relations specialists, real estate brokers, and, increasingly, doctors. Though a buyer of manufactured goods seldom thinks about those who produced them, one who buys professional services almost always does. Unable to try out or even look at a service before buying it, the buyer does the next best thing by assessing what it would be like to work with the professional who delivers it. This means that, sooner or later, all professionals must market if they want to advance their careers and grow their firms.

This book is written for the professional in a firm who must make the transition from doing and managing work to marketing and selling it, as well as for the professional who is already marketing and who wants to enhance his or her skills. It is also for the sole practitioner who must sell to stay in business. These are the people who must face the implications of what Warren J. Wittrech noted long ago is the buyer's desire to deal with a professional who sells rather than a professional salesman.[1]

Historically, development of professionals toward winning new clients has been haphazard. Law, accounting, engineering, medical, and architectural schools teach nothing about marketing and selling. Many professional associations require education credits each year to maintain certification, but to qualify the education must be technical. Many firms offer in-house education on technical issues, and almost all provide such training on the job, but marketing and sales training is spotty and often limited to training in presentation skills.

Stories about marketing and sales training that would seem pathetic and even cruel in other industries abound in the professions. The head of professional development at a Big Six accounting firm admitted to me that "we promote our people on the basis of their technical ability, and then it's sink or swim on whether or not they can bring in business. It causes a lot of turnover." At a major architectural firm

9

the concept of selling was so misunderstood that the term "sales training" was used to refer to presentation training, as if there were no other skills involved. My seat mate on a plane trip recently had just been made a partner at a large law firm. He told me he had not expected to be made a partner because he hadn't sold enough business, and now he was afraid for his job because he didn't now how to bring business in but was expected to do so. And not long ago, one of Wall Street's largest law firms terminated partners who thought they had jobs for life. They weren't bringing in new business, and their high salaries could not be justified on the basis of billable work alone. Most had never expected to have to sell; nor had they received any sales training.

This book is a self-help manual for professionals wanting to enhance their sales and marketing skills. In creating it I have drawn on several sources, beginning with my own experiences from the time I developed as a marketer and salesperson at a consulting firm. This process, largely one of trial and error, convinced me that a more efficient approach must be possible, and eventually led to my current practice. I have also drawn on my work with hundreds of professionals—architects, accountants, engineers, consultants, and lawyers, both in one-on-one training sessions and in classrooms. This experience is supplemented by surveys and studies conducted by me and others, and, of course, by literature on the subject.

Many professionals make the transition to marketing slowly, and others never make it at all, at great cost to their own careers and their firms' bottom lines. The fact is, having professional skills and training just isn't enough to advance in most firms in today's world. To succeed you must learn to market and sell.

Sales mean survival
The sole practitioner who cannot sell will lose his independence and have to go back to work for someone else. The professional within a firm who does not market and sell has a far higher probability of seeing his career plateau than one who brings in new business. When times are tough, a company will hang onto those who bring in business longer than those who provide technical support. You may know this, but if you aren't doing something about it now, you are endangering your career. The professional career path is strewn with the bodies of those who meant to get around to marketing someday.

Lack of time is no excuse
The economics of the professional services compel firms to keep their employees billed to clients for as high a percentage of their time as possible. This is especially obvious in project-oriented fields such as management consulting and architecture, fields in which most project revenues extend for only a few months; such firms are also notoriously reluctant to hire new employees unless work is overwhelming the current staff even when they are putting in many hours of overtime. I know and your management knows that you simply don't have much time for marketing.

But that is no excuse. This is not a value judgment; it is a statement of fact. Yes, during good times management will cut you some slack because you have not had time to market. When times get tough, however, and the boss has to make lay-off decisions, who will he hang on to? His marketers. And what about when promotions are handed out? Then again, marketers will get the lion's share.

The consulting firm I used to work for went through an annual ritual that is common in many of the professions with the same results. At the beginning of each year everyone was asked for a marketing plan. Each practice had to have a plan, and each practice's plan was, in essence, the composite of the individual plans of its professionals. At the end of every year the results were always the same. Most professionals had failed to complete the marketing tasks they had promised, always with the same excuse—they were too busy. And by any fair measure they *were* busy. But so were the few who did market and who did meet the objectives they had set. It was always the same few, and they were no less busy than those who had made excuses. Somehow they had found a way. The executive committee noticed this, and rewards went to those who marketed. This book is designed to help you find a way, busy as you are.

If you are a sole practitioner, the belief that you are too busy serving one client to market to others will not save you when work for that client runs out and you have no business to replace it.

This book provides tips on how to fit marketing into a busy schedule.

You must take responsibility for your own development
I have already noted that professional firms do a poor job of training their employees to market and sell. This is unfortunate and perhaps unfair, but it is the way things are. If you do not take responsibility for your own development, no one will. Be thankful for whatever help you can get and then go out and take care of yourself.

There are reasons why firms have effective technical but few marketing mentors. Technical mentors tend to manage projects. They must work closely with junior personnel to get their own jobs done, and often their work is made easier if the junior personnel perform better. This gives them an incentive to mentor.

The best marketers, on the other hand, are focused *outside* the firm—on the market. The things they do to develop new business are often done alone. Moreover, time spent on mentoring can reduce their immediate contribution to the firm and create competition for scarce prospects. Skilled marketers are also aware of the risk that taking an unproven associate along creates, when one ill-chosen word can destroy an opportunity that has taken months to create. All in all, they have little incentive to mentor.

This book provides some of the knowledge a good marketing mentor might offer, but it cannot replace the personalized and personal attention of a true mentor. Most people have to learn on their own. You cannot let this stop you.

You have to get over the hump before it starts to be fun
You probably did not become a professional in order to market. More likely you wanted to serve, to interesting work, and earn a good living. You have prospered because you are client-focused, enjoying the recognition and power clients give to professionals who serve them well. You have come to enjoy the influence you exer-

cise based on specialized knowledge and skillful management of the client relationship. It's not easy, and it's rewarding when you succeed.

Initially, marketing can seem like a comedown from this heady status. Clients almost always return phone calls; prospects often don't. Clients listen respectfully to what you say because they are paying for it; prospects aren't always sure they should listen to you at all. To a client you are an authority; to a prospect, a vendor. The hard work and adept application of technical, managerial, and client relations skills that can pull you out of a fix on almost any project may have no impact at all on a prospect. This sudden change makes many professionals feel that they have lost control. The lack of prospect response can make you feel unprofessional and embarrassed. Surely you must be doing something wrong. Faced with this situation, many professionals quickly—too quickly—conclude that they aren't any good at marketing and that they don't like it.

Don't let this happen to you. You have to develop new skills and go through the discomfort of gaining some marketing and sales experience, but once you do, it will enhance your sense of control over your own fate, add to your recognition with clients and among your peers, and become a source of well-founded pride and pleasure. An actuary friend of mine who made the transition said to me recently, "I suppose I was happy before when I was managing projects, but I would never go back. I'm having so much greater impact now."

My son learned to ride a bicycle a year after most of his friends. His inability embarrassed him and cut him off from one social activity. On the morning of the day he finally learned, he insisted, "I can't do it. I hate bike riding. I hated it last year and I hate it this year." But on the way home from the parking lot where he finally got the hang of it, he chirped "What a great day! I love bike riding. It's my favorite sport." It can be the same with marketing; you have to get over the hump and you have to fall a couple of times before it starts to be fun.

You must adopt new measures of productivity and success

This is a major obstacle for many professionals, though I have not seen it mentioned anywhere in the literature. If you have worked in a firm as a doer and manager, you have been inculcated with certain beliefs about productivity and success that can obstruct your ability to market. Among them are:

- *I must maximize billable time.* Although it is true you must do this early in your career, you cannot let this principle stop you from marketing. At times it is essential to expend time that could have been billed to a client on marketing efforts.

  When you catch yourself using this phrase as a reason for not marketing, replace it with, *I must optimize billable time and meet firm standards. I must also make time to market.*

- *Nonbillable time is wasted time.* In their efforts to maximize profits, good project managers often instill this belief with statements like, "Don't waste your time on that; it isn't billable." Although true of many activities, it is not true of marketing. Time spent on ten unreturned phone calls may seem wasted to someone with a production mind-set; to a marketer, it is a necessary investment.

- *Sales people are pests.* Professionals trying to maximize billable hours may perceive frequent calls from vendors as a nuisance. After all, time spent with vendors is not billable. Abstracting from this, they often feel that they, too, become pests when they call a prospect.

   There are several fallacies in this logic. First, it is doubtful that you see vendors who add value as pests. Second, the fact that you feel a call at this moment is inconvenient is far different from perceiving the caller himself as a nuisance. Persistence is okay so long as it is courteous. Third, people react to calls in different ways. Many will not be troubled by your calls at all, even if they don't return them.

   If you view yourself as a pest, you will have difficulty developing new business. It will undermine your persistence, and you will become one of the many professionals who make three calls and then give up. Those are the ones who never become marketers. This book will help you find ways to ensure that your calls do have value and to get through to the people you want to talk to.

- *I can get the outcome I want on a project if I just work harder.* When you face a production crunch, you work harder and longer, more work gets done, and your problem is solved. This isn't necessarily true in marketing, where the one-to-one correlation between effort and results is lost.

   Marketing is a numbers game. You have to pursue ten or fifteen or twenty jobs to win one. On average, if you work longer and smarter, you will win more jobs, but this is not always so. Market conditions and other factors can offset all your hard work.

   In baseball, some players have higher batting averages than others, but all strike out a lot of the time. It's the same in marketing. If you go to the plate, there is a good chance you will strike out, but you must go to the plate to get a hit, and the more often you go, the better your chances of getting one. This book will help increase your batting average, but it cannot save you from striking out some of the time. Like a good batter, you must prepare yourself mentally for this kind of game.

- *Whenever my work doesn't produce results, I have failed.* When doing client work this is generally true. Any professional working on a project who runs up a lot of hours without producing a tangible result either runs down profitability or is doing his client a disservice.

   Just before writing this section I finally reached a prospect I have wanted to talk to for several months. It took me thirty-seven calls spread among seven different people to get to this point, and I still haven't got any business to show for it. This isn't failure. It's how marketing works. Marketing is a numbers game. Each call was like a drawing a card from a deck in a game where the high card wins. When I spoke to someone and the information I received got me closer to the person I wanted to talk to, I had drawn a face card. When I hit a dead end, I had drawn a two. Unreturned calls aren't failures; they are like jokers—they simply don't count in this game. There may be a lot of jokers in the deck, but it doesn't matter, because you can draw as often as you want.

In marketing you must learn not to see efforts that produce no results as failures, or you will become demoralized and you *will* fail. Marketing requires bouncing back from adversity.

The production mind-set can deeply permeate a professional's thinking, so that even when you accept a marketing setback at a logical level, emotionally you take it as a loss. When you market, you must guard against this. Remind yourself that marketing is a numbers game. Next time you may win.

Marketing is an emotional roller coaster

In most firms rain makers are seen as more emotional than the staid individuals who manage projects. They are. They work in a win/lose environment where a misstep or bit of bad luck can wipe out months or even years of work, but where skill and good luck can have incredible impact on the firm and their own careers.

Someone who has not marketed much in the past can find the emotional swings disturbing, especially if they do not understand them fully and are not prepared for them. You must prepare yourself, or you will decide you don't like marketing before you give it a chance. It's okay to feel a little bad when you lose a job or frustrated when you can't make the progress you want with a particular prospect. But you must develop the ability to bounce back and try again. Eventually you will win, and it will probably happen sooner rather than later. Oh, how good it feels when you do win! It can produce the biggest highs you have felt in your business career.

You can gain a sense of control in marketing

Feelings of stress are highly correlated with a sense of lost control over important things that happen to us. Marketing operates by such different rules from client work that many professionals feel a tremendous loss of control when they first begin to market. When this happens, stress levels rise.

As a structural engineer who was pushed cold-turkey into full-time marketing once put it, "I had never had any marketing training. I thought my boss would mentor me, but he didn't. Later, I realized it was because he didn't really know how to do it himself. No one told me anything about how to do it. I couldn't quantify anything I was doing. The first six months were hell." After fourteen years performing and managing engagements, where he knew exactly what to do when, no wonder he felt a loss of control. No wonder he felt stressed! Though most transitions are less abrupt, most professionals feel the same way about their early marketing efforts.

As with learning to ride a bicycle, if your fear of falling stops you from pedaling, you will never learn. You won't go very far or very fast at first, and sometimes you will fail. But you will gain ability and confidence. My friend the structural engineer brought two million dollars of new business into his firm this year.

It is always better to be doing some marketing than none

When doing client work, a little planning can save a lot of trouble later. This is true of marketing, too, with the big difference that planning does not assure results. Effective planning can reduce risks on an engagement to minor proportions, but marketing is a numbers game. All that can be said is that the better your marketing planning and execution, the higher your *probability* of success. Planning cannot eliminate risk.

A client of mine who provides litigation support in a technical area fell into a common trap. We had discussed repeatedly his need to develop stronger credentials through article writing and speech making. Wishing to pick the best subject, he analyzed litigation trends, and analyzed and analyzed. He wanted to be sure that he picked a hot emerging area so that he would reap the biggest results from his efforts. The problem was that beyond a certain point, he could not know what the emerging trend would be. No amount of analysis will let us divine the future. Rather, he needed to make an educated guess and then get into the market place. You too must realize that analysis in marketing will not reduce risk to the same degree it does in client work; therefore almost any reasonable *action* is better than none.

Simply put, the professionals who succeed at marketing are the ones who market. They always have some marketing activity underway. That activity may not be original or brilliant, and it may not be the best marketing activity they could be doing, but unlike most of their peers, they are doing something, and eventually they get results. Marketers market.

That is not to say that marketers want to give up client work completely. Few do. Rather, they realize that making progress on marketing is as urgent as making progress on a client's project. They become as uncomfortable when they do not have some marketing effort underway as you do when you have a shortage of project work. At least once each day you need to remind yourself that marketers market and that you should be working on something.

You need to get face to face with a prospect to make a sale

Brochures, newsletters, mailings, advertisements, press releases, and articles can strengthen your marketing, but they will not help you unless they or some other technique in your marketing mix get you face to face with a prospect to talk about his needs.

If you have not sold before and lack basic selling skills, getting face to face with a prospect may feel uncomfortable and even scary. This book will help you develop the skills to get over this discomfort and succeed, but you must ensure that your marketing mix includes activities that will get you face to face. Marketing mixes are addressed in the chapters on strategy.

When you find yourself wanting a brochure, ask yourself whether you really need it or whether you are avoiding the hard work of engaging prospects in a dialogue.

Everyone can make a contribution

There is no one right way to market. Whatever your particular skills and interests, you can make a contribution. If you don't want to write, you can speak. If you don't want to speak, you can network. This book provides you with a wide array of activities to consider as well as guidance on choosing among them.

This is important not just for you but also for your firm. The organization that can mobilize the most resources has a significant advantage over its competitors. Lincoln realized this during the Civil War when he directed his commander in chief, General Grant, to get all his generals to apply pressure on the Confederacy. "Those not skinning can hold a leg," he wrote.[2]

I was once asked to turn around a troubled consulting operation, and noticed that the most troublesome competitor operated on the star system, with one individual doing virtually all the marketing. Borrowing from Lincoln, I reasoned that if we could mobilize numerous marketers, even if many made a smaller individual contribution to our firm than this competitor did to his, we would beat him. It worked. If you're not skinning, hold a leg.

When you win, celebrate

Companies with large sales organizations spend fortunes motivating their sales forces. They recognize how crucial motivation is to sales success. Professional firms are often less effective in this area. If your firm doesn't celebrate a major success, do it yourself. Take your spouse to dinner or buy something that can serve as a trophy. You should certainly do this when you close a major sale. Landmark accomplishments such as your first publication or getting yourself invited to speak to an important audience also warrant a reward.

If motivation doesn't come from the firm, you must provide it yourself.

Now is the time to start

If you have not begun to market yet, now is the time to start. Every day you delay will make it more difficult. Every week that passes is an opportunity missed to make a contribution to the firm.

This book is organized into three parts. Part I shows how to get leads. It will teach you methods you can use to find prospects and to make it easy for prospects to find you. Part II shows how to advance and close a sale once you have a prospect. Part III shows how to build a marketing strategy that is appropriate for you and your firm. It comes last, because you must understand something of the tactics at your disposal before you select a strategy.

Finally, a series of appendices covers four subjects that I felt it best to let others write about. In each case I have chosen an expert who has worked with professionals to address an area he or she knows well.

You will probably want to use the book in two ways. First, read it all the way through to gain the understanding of the subject matter required to begin to market. Later, you can refer to specific chapters as needed, in reference manual style. Knowing that the book would be used for this second purpose has required me to repeat some concepts and information so that individual chapters can stand on their own. I have tried to minimize redundancy by referring readers to other chapters when appropriate, but some has been unavoidable.

Because professionals must sell themselves in order to sell their firms, I have written about career as well as marketing strategies—about selling yourself as well as selling your firm. You must find the appropriate balance between the two, but you cannot do one without also doing the other.

I have tried throughout to give simple, practical advice, believing that professionals learn best when offered a mix of concept and how-to instruction. Most of the content has been tested in training and one-on-one coaching sessions at a variety of organizations. I will know I have succeeded if those who read this book and follow its guidelines can say, "I tried it and it works."

Part I

Marketing Tactics: How Professionals Generate Leads

The founder of a civil and environmental engineering firm that today does $20 million worth of business each year told me how he became a marketer. "I never planned it. I started my own company because one client said he would give me all his business. A week later he died. I had a wife, kids, and a mortgage. That's how I became a marketer."

Most professionals who succeed as marketers begin by doing. They don't have a grand design. They aren't trying to build a firm. They're just trying to find a client. Such people are doers first and planners second. They are either trying to squeeze some marketing in amidst demands from paying clients or struggling to stay in business.

For the beginning marketer, doing before planning offers several advantages. It builds your self-confidence. It increases your knowledge, without which you will find it hard to plan. It puts you in contact with the market, the best teacher you will ever have. When you have developed basic skills, you can then create a more deliberate marketing strategy.

When you start, each marketing effort is a test. Even if the speech you give doesn't bring in a job, it will help you learn what works and what doesn't. Most professionals learn to market that way. I certainly did. I had worked as a management consultant for over ten years and sold many assignments before I received even an hour of formal training.

This portion of the book will help you learn to generate leads. It will reduce trial-and-error learning by providing practical advice on how to write an article, get an opportunity to speak, develop a network, work a trade association, establish a lasting relationship with a client, make a cold call, hold a seminar, send a mailing and get quoted in the press. It is based on my long-term commitment to spare others the waste and frustration that I experienced when teaching myself. In one-on-

one coaching sessions and in classrooms, as a manager of professionals and as a marketing consultant, I have analyzed what keeps professionals from succeeding at generating leads. I have used these analyses in developing the how-to advice found in the succeeding chapters.

While working with this portion of the book, please note the following.

Your success as a marketer and salesperson will depend on the development of four core skills

All of the techniques to generate leads described in part I and the techniques for advancing and closing a sale described in part II require a combination of four key skills (see exhibit 0.1): relationship building, presenting, writing, and organizing. Each of these core skills is in turn made up of subsidiary skills. The ease with which you learn a specific marketing task, such as writing an article or working a trade association, will depend in part on your natural abilities and prior training in these core skills. All marketers are better at some activities than others, because some of their skills are stronger than others. The best marketers have developed at least a fundamental competence in all of them.

I recommend that you work at becoming competent in one kind of task and its underlying skills first. As you gain confidence in that one area, you will naturally broaden your activities. Each chapter in part I begins with a vignette about a professional who became a successful marketer. Most started by becoming skillful in one area first.

Because each of the core skills is crucial to several marketing techniques, the chapters in part I are interlinked. The chapter on networking (chapter 3) provides fundamental guidance on relationship-building skills and should be read before the chapters on working a trade association (chapter 4), relationship marketing (chapter 5), cold calling (chapter 6) or publicity (chapter 9). The chapter on article writing (chapter 1) provides concepts applicable to giving speeches (chapter 2). If you are giving speeches or holding seminars, you should also read the chapter on making sales presentations to prospects (chapter 11). Indeed, you may find it helpful to read all of parts I and II before focusing on a specific marketing task.

I have assumed you have a basic level of skill in all areas. This book does not, for example, provide guidance in English composition, though that skill is essential to writing. Appendix E offers a list of references to other sources on subjects not addressed in this book.

You will learn more if you complete the exercises in each chapter

People learn more by doing than by reading. The text will guide you on what to do; the exercises provide a means to try out what you have read and help you internalize it.

You can't sell until you have a lead

As a successful interior designer said to me, "It all starts with a lead. You have to have a lead to get a client." Some firms forget this. When a professional says, "I sold the XYZ job," he may mean that he generated the lead and then sold the en-

Exhibit 0.1
The Four Core Marketing Skills

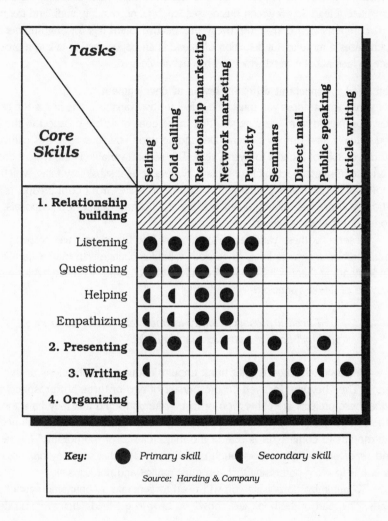

Tasks / Core Skills	Selling	Cold calling	Relationship marketing	Network marketing	Publicity	Seminars	Direct mail	Public speaking	Article writing
1. Relationship building									
Listening	●	●	●	●	●				
Questioning	●	●	●	●	●				
Helping	◖	◖	●	●					
Empathizing	◖	◖	●	●					
2. Presenting	●	●	◖	◖	◖	●		●	
3. Writing	◖				●	◖	●	◖	●
4. Organizing		◖	◖			●	●		

Key: ● Primary skill   ◖ Secondary skill

Source: Harding & Company

gagement, or he may be thinking only of the accomplishment of having sold the job, forgetting the hard work that went into giving him the opportunity to do so. You should make a clear distinction: The first step is to get a lead, the second is to advance and close a sale.

This, of course, implies that you know what "a lead" is. It's not so simple, because the term is used loosely to refer to everything from a piece of information about a prospective client's needs to an invitation to talk about your services. A useful definition depends, in part, on the nature of your services. In event-driven businesses, like disaster recovery consulting, litigation support, or architecture, information that a specific prospect has a need has high value and may legitimately constitute a lead. In evergreen businesses, such as accounting, audit and tax work, and compensation consulting, every prospective client has an ongoing need. In such cases a more useful definition of a lead is an opportunity to talk to a prospect face to face about a need which he has acknowledged.

You need prospects at different levels of development

For your own business you must gain a feel for two variables. The first is the typical gestation period from the time you first make contact with a prospect to the time you actually sign him as a client. Depending upon your business, this can range from a couple of months to over a year. The second variable is the typical conversion rate from prospect to client. This may have several subsidiary rates, which you should also understand, such as the conversion rates from cool prospects with whom you are just talking to hot prospects who have requested proposals, and from hot prospects to clients.

A sense of these variables will suffice, at first, though you will probably want more precise measures later, since both variables change with market conditions. Understanding them will help you complete the following sentence, which underlies one of the key principles of marketing:

> *I need x prospects today to have reasonable assurance*
> *that I will have a new client in y months.*

Professionals often do not think enough about the implications of this sentence. They become focused on the pursuit of two or three hot prospects, and once these projects are either won or lost, wake up to find that they have too few others in the early stages of development to generate the business they will need in the months to come. This is one of the major causes of "porpoising," the radical and repeated swing from too much work to too little that so many organizations face. It is to avoid porpoising that you must market and not just sell.

To minimize porpoising you will need to generate a continuing flow of new leads. This part of the book will show you how to get leads, however you define them.

1

Writing and Publishing Your Article

Case example: The Author
John liked to write. It helped internalize and organize things he learned, and he liked to see his name in print. Early in his consulting career he wrote an article that was published in a major business periodical and found that by doing so he had become the firm's expert in one of its small practices. He wrote more and soon developed a personal plan to produce articles for trade journals addressed to each of the major industries his firm did business with, and to each of the functional areas within corporations that his firm's consulting services supported. The exposure and increased stature the articles gave him made it easy for senior managers to market him for major projects. When they needed an expert on the insurance industry or on labor issues, John's articles gave him the credentials. Frequently in front of clients, he soon began to get opportunities to sell as well. He leveraged his article writing time by modifying the same piece for more than one publication and by using his articles as the basis for speeches. He rose to become the leader of a regional office and a national practice for his firm.

When I hire a professional, I want an expert. I know from the start that it's going to cost me a lot of money; indeed, if my need weren't urgent, I wouldn't be hiring at all. But my need *is* urgent, and I am going to pay—only I want someone really good for my money. That's where my problem begins. I know little about law or accounting or many other fields where I might have a need, which makes it difficult for me to distinguish who is really good and who isn't. My cynical nature makes me suspect that many more will claim to be experts than really are. They all want my money.

Publications provide one proof of who is real and who isn't. Whether I see an article in a magazine or have a reprint handed to me by the author, published work tells me that the author must have substantial experience, and that she has reflected more deeply on her business than some. That the editors of the journal in which it appeared thought enough of it to print it also counts for something. Maybe someone else does know more about the subject, but I have to base my decision about who to hire on evidence. All other things being equal, the article will weigh more heavily than someone's self acclamation.

This scenario explains why publishing an article is a logical first step in marketing. Professionals first beginning to market need to build their stature, develop name recognition, and flesh out a resume. Articles do all of these things. Although they are not especially effective in generating leads, they do sometimes result in direct queries from prospective clients. Over a long consulting career I have known articles of mine to lead to contacts that in turn resulted in jobs at companies like IBM and Ford Motor Company. As reprints my writings serve as proof of expertise. A future client from a major financial institution put it to me succinctly while holding up a reprint from a major business publication I had sent him: "Here's your credibility right here!" Reprints can also serve as mailers to remind past clients of your continued existence.

In spite of these benefits, professionals plan far more articles than ever get written. I have participated in so many discussions about articles that died aborning that I have come to believe professionals need more than an admonishment to go forth and publish. Additional guidance is called for.

Ask a group of professionals and they will tell you that they don't write articles because they don't have time. It is axiomatic in professional service firms that production and sales pressures drive out marketing time. This is untenable. Firm management and individual professionals simply must preserve time for marketing, and at the same time find ways to make as efficient use of their marketing time as they do their billable project time. It's not as difficult as it sounds. By learning some basic techniques, professionals can greatly reduce the time required to write articles while enhancing the probability of getting published.

In my experience most professionals spend their article-writing time unproductively. Lacking confidence, they waste too much time thinking in an unstructured way about what they will write. If an article gets beyond this point, too often it is constructed as a report or dissertation, and the resulting draft ends up long, ponderous, and dull. This means the author must rewrite it, a process it seldom survives. Discouraged, he places it in a file intending to return to it when the workload lightens, and never puts hand to it again. You can avoid this outcome.

It starts with an idea

One way to increase your article-writing effectiveness is to know what you want to write about when you find the time to do it. Whenever I have an idea for an article, I write it down on a slip of paper and put it in a file entitled "Article Ideas." As other thoughts come to me on the same subject, I note them in the same place. I will clip articles, write down quotes that I hear, and make copies of data that pertain to the subject. They all go into the same file. When I do get time to write, I have a packet of materials ready to work from. The file always has five to ten ideas in it, rising like dough in an oven, until I am ready to work with them.

If you do not have such a file, start one now. Take a few minutes and write down whatever ideas you have. Discipline yourself to write down additional thoughts on the subject as they come to you. It only takes a moment and will save time later.

Most articles run between eight and twelve double-spaced, typewritten pages. A short opinion piece might run six, and a long, more academic one, over twenty. If you have an unexpected free morning or even a full day when you can write, you will find you can spend the time far more productively if some light research and many of the ideas are waiting for you in a file.

Know thy market
Professionals often attempt to write articles without a specific journal in mind, viewing placement as secondary. This is akin to writing a report and then seeking a client to sell it to, a task few professionals would undertake. By picking a target journal, you permit yourself to study several copies in advance, researching the journal the way you would any other prospect before attempting a sale. When reviewing a target publication, first determine who your audience will be. What is the editorial approach? Is it geared toward news items? Professional practices? In-depth case analyses? The article you submit must address the appropriate audience in a manner consistent with the journal's editorial policy.

Stop reading now and collect four or five periodicals—the more diverse the better. Leaf through them, looking at each as a market rather than reading material. Which periodicals are written by staff and which by contributors? This is an important difference. Staff-written magazines (*Business Week, Fortune, Forbes*, etc.) will take no contributor-written articles, except (rarely) for a few specific purposes, such as a guest contributor column. If this is your target, your article must comply with the strictures of the column concerning length, format, and content. Occasionally a staff-written periodical will accept a piece in interview format or use a contributed article as a foundation for a staff-written one, in which case portions of your article will appear as quotes attributed to you.

Your best bet, however, is contributor-written journals (*Association Management, Best's Review, Urban Land,* etc.). Again, be sure to study past issues to identify the audience and determine editorial policies. Many will send you free "Contributors' Guidelines" upon request, spelling out their requirements in detail. Media kits, used to market the journal to potential advertisers, are usually available for free and can provide useful information about circulation and editorial calendars. You can also query the editor by phone or mail about whether a subject would be of interest. Editors will state clearly if you are far off the mark but are otherwise cautious before seeing anything in writing. So save queries, unless your question clearly cannot be answered by studying copies of the magazine or reading the contributors' guidelines.

"Refereed journals" (*Harvard Business Review, Journal of Management Consulting,* etc.) are those that submit articles for review to two or three experts. The decision to print will depend more on the votes of these reviewers than on the staff editor. Such journals tend to be academically oriented and usually require footnotes. The turnaround time between submission and publication tends to be long, often a year or more.

Reviewing journals is essential to selecting your market. It does not take long, and once done requires only brief refreshers. If you'd like some extra guidance, *Bacon's Publicity Checker, Magazines, Vol. 1*[1] is an annual publication that provides brief information on many magazines, including an indication of whether they are staff or contributor-written.

What every journalist knows

Once you have a publication in mind, you next need to pick an angle, the point of view you adopt in writing about a subject. Choosing a clear point of view allows you to:

- address the article to a specific audience
- screen information in and out of the article
- provide focus, interest, and purpose
- develop an initial structure

You should be able to state your angle in a single sentence. In this chapter, for example, I stated, "by learning some basic techniques, professionals can greatly reduce the time required to write articles while enhancing the probability of getting published." My audience is apparent—professionals who have difficulty getting articles written and those who are concerned about this problem, such as firm managers. The theme is circumscribed, greatly simplifying both my research and my writing tasks. Why? Because specific supporting information is called for. An article stating, "Evidence shows that professionals who write articles bring more business into their firms than those who don't" would require a different set of material.

Note how the sentence summarizing the angle for this article helps structure the piece. It cries out for an introductory paragraph or two on why article writing is important to professionals, followed by a description of why article writing usually takes so much time. It dictates a brief description of the required techniques. A good angle should provide this simple benefit to the author. Exhibit 1.1 lists some subjects and possible angles for articles.

Once you have picked a journal, you can test an angle against its audience by asking yourself whether it is really targeted to them. If it is too broad or too narrow, rewrite it to focus your piece and you will improve the probability of being published. Many professionals have frustrated themselves and nipped writing careers in the bud by producing articles that were too broad or too narrow to appeal to the editor of any identifiable journal. Discouraged by working so hard for nothing, these professionals often give up article writing completely as something they aren't good at. Review the angles you prepared based on Exhibit 1.1 and ask yourself whether they

Exhibit 1.1
Subjects and Angles

Review the exhibit and then, in the bottom portion, list a subject you want to write about, plus three alternative angles.

Subject	**Angles**
Library design	1. Ten common mistakes in library design can be avoided by skilled planning and programming.
	2. New technologies are radically altering the way that libraries should be designed.
	3. Libraries can serve different functions that require radically different designs.
Wills	1. You should review your will and possibly rewrite it when certain key events happen in your like.
	2. When a will is poorly written, it can stimulate the events the deceased specifically wanted to avoid.
	3. Preparing a good will should begin with a clear understanding of your values and goals.

Your subject: *Your angles:*

Cost Control
1. How it differs from cost analysis
2. Why its important today
3. Benefits of Cost Control to any business.

are well targeted to the specific journal you would like to be published in. Adjust them as needed.

Once you formulate an angle, you must write within its constraints or reformulate it. Reformulating is usually required when the first angle does not truly encapsulate what you want to say. Be sure to check any revised angle against your target audience to make sure it still fits. In my experience teaching professionals to write articles, a common mistake is to forget the limits and focus that a good angle requires of an author. Those who forget end up with wordy, rambling pieces. If you are having trouble with an article, check to see whether this is happening to you. Beware of "angle creep." Every author, including this one, has ideas and stories he falls in love with, even though they don't quite fit the angle he is writing about. Part of the discipline of writing a publishable piece is to delete such items from your work. Save them for another article in which they would be more appropriate. Take the time to develop a good angle up front and then write the article to elaborate on it and it only.

Exhibit 1.2 provides a second exercise to help you understand angles.

Exhibit 1.2

Incomplete and Complete Angles

What is wrong with this angle?

Quality Assurance in the Property & Casualty Industry

Answer:

It is a subject, not an angle. It is not a complete sentence. A complete angle is "Quality assurance offers a means for property and casualty insurers to differentiate their services." This angle makes it clear that the author plans a marketing article rather than an operational/how-to or financial/cost-savings one. It clearly focuses on a specific audience and set of issues.

Artful use of angles also permits you to place an article where you might not otherwise be able to. A colleague and I once sought to place an article on research lab location in a trade journal read by many researchers. Therein lay the problem: The editor only wanted articles addressed to actual researchers, while the audience we had in mind was management. The angle we chose was: "As part of your career planning, you should understand how corporations select research lab locations so that you can improve your chances of living where you most want to." It became an article suitable to both audiences and was accepted.

With a little practice, sitting down and listing two or three possible angles on a subject that will make it attractive to a specific periodical should not take long. Once you choose a clearly stated angle, your writing job will be easier, because the temptation to include too much information in a clumsy structure will be reduced. This focus also reduces research requirements.

Formula power

A formula is a set pattern for expressing ideas. It helps you determine the components of your article and the relationship of the components to each other. This chapter uses one of the most common formulas found in professional and trade journals, the How-To Formula.

Though many professional writers use formulas unhesitatingly, I have found it necessary to convince my clients of their true value. Many feel that writing based on a formula is inherently of lower quality than other writing. This belief is simply not so. It is based on the knowledge that most high-volume producers of popular fiction rely heavily on formulas, and a feeling that this fiction, because it is popular, cannot be good.

This outlook ignores the many examples of formula writing of the highest quality. P.G. Wodehouse, who wrote over a hundred books and has been praised by such authors as Evelyn Waugh, is but one example. The formula used by John Mortimer for his delightful stories about Rumpole, barrister of the Old Bailey, which have been dramatized on television, has been neatly summarized by Donald E. Westlake, an author of comic mystery novels:

> This is the Rumpole formula: A mystery is presented that contains the possibility of a subject to ponder—the workman's right to withhold his labor, say, or the citizen's right to remain silent when charged with an offense. Several of the other recurring characters in the series will then turn out to be engaged in activities containing variants on the same matter (for instance, shall Mrs. Rumpole withhold her labor from Mr. Rumpole's house?), allowing Rumpole's ruminations broader scope. Partway along, someone coincidentally will just happen to tell Rumpole the fact that solves the initial mystery. Once the theme and variations are complete, Rumpole will take that fact to court, confound the prosecution and judge and retire triumphant, with a wry parting summation directed at us, his audience.
>
> No variation on the above is permitted, or even considered. If the subject is the citizen's right to remain silent, for instance, you may be sure no character in that particular story will be so inattentive as to be found withholding his labor instead. He will dutifully wait for the withholding-his-labor story.[2]

The use of formulas is not restricted to light or popular fiction. The formulaic components of Shakespeare's plays have been carefully described by Mark Rose of Yale University.[3] The gripping speeches of Dr. Martin Luther King, Jr. utilize formulas for sermons he learned in seminary.[4]

The power of the formula lies in productivity. I have illustrated this point in my consulting assignments by asking clients to say something funny, with the restrictions that they must not use something they have said or heard before and that they have only two minutes. Not surprisingly, most are struck dumb by this request. I then ask them to do the same thing with the following additional restrictions: They must make their funny statements in five anapestic lines with the rhyme scheme aabba. The first, second and fifth lines must have three feet and the third and fourth two feet. The first line must be "There was once a consultant named Ford." Once the participants realize that they are being requested to create a limerick, they are usually able to struggle through the exercise. Votes after the exercise show that my clients unanimously prefer the second exercise to the first.

This demonstration shows that it can be much easier and faster to create within the confines of a formula than with total freedom. The formula liberates you from many of the requirements to structure your writing, allowing you to focus on

2. content. Formulas for articles are less rigid than those for a limerick but benefit the writer in the same way structured verse does the poet. There is no shortage of formulas to choose from. Some of the most common are:

- **The List** This is the most basic of formulas and one of the easiest to use. Commonly used in articles reporting trends, this formula provides brief write-ups on each of a list of items tied together by an overall theme. An article entitled "The Real Estate Industry in the Year 2000" might use such an approach, with descriptions of such listed factors as the changing roles of developers, the tendency for brokerage commission discounts, the increased focus on build-to-suit, and so on. The list of formula types you are now reading is another example, although shortened and simplified so that it can be subsumed within the How-To Formula of the whole chapter.

- **The Straw Man** A premise is set up and then knocked down, showing the benefits of a different point of view or approach. This formula is commonly used when new practices sweep an industry. A piece showing why an accepted method of cost accounting can be misleading and proposing an alternative one might use this formula.

- **The Miniature Case Study** A question is raised and then answered through three or four brief case studies (roughly one and a half or two double-spaced, typewritten pages each). An article answering the question "Does quick response provide competitive advantage?" might use this formula. One case study could show how quick response can lower unit cost, another how it increases customer perceptions of quality, still another how it permits premium pricing, and so forth. Anecdotes, strong selling tools in any profession, are used to make the case.

- **The Interview** On three occasions I have interviewed others in the firm I was working for and on one I sat at my word processor and silently interviewed myself. Another time I provided a list of questions to a compatriot who then wrote out responses. All four articles were printed in reputable journals. This approach is particularly useful with staff-written trade journals. An interview can have higher value than a bylined article in building your reputation, because the format implies you were sought out by the journal as an expert.

- **The Fad** Fads sweep professions like fashions. Whenever one does, articles explaining the fad to different audiences appear all over the place the way a trendy color suddenly shows up on everything from dresses to automobiles. Articles on reengineering can and undoubtedly have been written to explain the process to metal stampers, discount retailers, bankers and many other groups. Articles on the latest tax shelter and investment approach appear in magazines targeted at doctors, lawyers, yuppies, and almost any other identifiable group that might provide a market. These articles tell what the fad is and what its benefits are and provide a hint of how-to.

- **More and More** or **Fewer and Fewer** These articles report findings of a survey or other study. Almost any survey provides grist for an article. A piece entitled "Corporations Are More Concerned about Flexibility in Office Design Than Ever Before" might show how corporations require designs that allow them to adopt new technologies, down-size and sub-lease, move business units frequently, and so forth.

There are other formulas, but these examples should suffice to get you started. Different formulas lend themselves to different objectives.

I have found that my clients understand the concept of formulas better if I show them how a subject must be adapted to each formula. Take the admittedly trivial subject (but one that everyone can understand), picking up dates in bars. An article entitled, "How to Pick Up a Date in Bars" would use the How-to Formula to provide step-by-step instructions on technique. One entitled "Are Bars the Best Places to Pick up a Date?" might be a Straw-Man article written by someone who is against this practice. It would first describe the reasons why people pick up dates in bars, then knock them down by pointing out risks or faulty reasoning. Finally, it would point out that people have much better success meeting by taking French classes, joining an athletic club, signing up with a computer dating service or (ig-noring the risk of a sexual harassment charge) attending office parties. "Should You Pick People up in Bars?" might be a Miniature Case Study article. After posing the question in the title and citing a few statistics about the number of people who do pick up dates in bars, it would describe four specific cases. If it is an article op-posed to the practice, each case might show a different and progressively more horrible outcome. "What's Happening in the Bar Scene?" might be a List article in a magazine devoted to the subject of dating. It would describe the latest trends at bars, in list format, which might include virtual reality games, a return to the ethnic bar, and who knows what else. The discussion of each item would include a com-ment on its implications for the individual seeking to pick up a date. "An Interview with Mr. (or Ms.) Pick-Up" would be just that, covering an expert's experiences and asking for advice and his or her vision of the future, given changes that are occur-ring in the bar world. "More and More People Are Picking up Dates in Bars" would be an article reporting survey findings on dating habits and the habits of people who hang out in bars.

Now pick a subject more substantive and pertinent to your business than the one than in the preceding example and see how it would change by using different angles and formulas. You will probably find that one or two really do have potential for a real article.

Once you have mastered formulas at this level, you will begin to see others in the articles you read; or you can develop your own. Use of formulas provides you with instant structure, allowing you to write an article surprisingly quickly. This matters in an environment where writing time must be squeezed in among hours devoted to billable projects.

When you have chosen a formula and angle, list all the points you want to make. Then rewrite the list, organizing it within the structure that the formula dictates. Delete and add points, as needed. Now you are ready to start writing.

If you wish to see how research, angles, and formulas can combine to make article writing easy, try this experiment. Review several journals in your field and select one that is contributor-written. Develop an angle for an article to be submitted to this journal that is a variation on the theme "Professionals in (your area of expertise) Provide Great Value in Certain Identifiable Situations." Outline an article based on this angle using the Miniature Case-Study Formula. From your own experience or those of your associates, pick three or four cases, each illustrating a situation in which a professional provided a specific, identifiable benefit (confidentiality, objectivity, issue resolution, and diagnostic insight, for example). Then sit down and write your article and see now long it takes. The conclusion should reiterate your angle.

What editors like

Articles will have a better chance of being accepted if they are submitted in a way that makes working with them easy for the editor. This means...

- ...*leaving wide margins* (1¼ inches) and extra space at the beginning of the manuscript (⅓ of page). These allow the editor to make notations easily. All articles should be double-spaced for the same reason.

- ...*using a paper clip rather than staple.* Editors work from loose sheets. They don't like staples.

- ...*placing your last name, the article's title, and the page number in a header* at the top of each page. If a pile of unstapled manuscripts is dropped, yours will be easy to reassemble.

- ...*providing an approximate word count on the last page.* The editor will have to do this if you don't. Most word processing programs make this easy.

- ...*including charts, tables, diagrams, checklists, photos, or side bars* to enliven the text. Some journals require or prefer camera-ready copy.

- ...*providing headings where appropriate.* Good headings do not just help the logical flow of a piece but also engage the reader (and the editor) by catching his or her eye. Thus, "Avoid Overcharging" has less catching power than "Greed" or "Like Pigs at a Trough" and so is an inferior heading.

- ...*stating in a cover letter that the article is being offered exclusively*, so that the editor does not have to worry about accepting it for publication and then finding it in print in a competing journal.

- ...*in the same letter, providing a one-sentence statement of why the article is pertinent* to the journal's readers. Don't place the burden of figuring this out on the editor.

- ...*describing the article in two or three sentences,* showing the main points you will make.

- ...*including a suggested author's description,* consistent in length, format, and content with those the journal typically provides. This will increase the odds that the description says what you want it to.

- ...*complying with any other submission instructions* noted in the magazine or its writers' guidelines.

By following the approaches I have described, you will find that article writing becomes easier and faster and publication more frequent.

Getting leads from articles

Articles should not be relied on to generate leads. Although they can occasionally do so, they will never provide the predictable, steady supply of prospects that a primary lead-generating activity must.

There are, however, a few things you can do to increase their lead-generating power. First, you should be sure that your name, firm, and the name of the city your firm is located in appear with the article. This can usually be done in the author's description. A few journals will not reference the city from which you do business. In such cases it may be possible to mention it in the text of the article. Do so carefully, since most journals will not accept articles that are patently self-promotional, rather than educational.

Some journals, especially trade journals, will be happy to reference an offer you make to readers to send something of value to them. This is usually a report of some sort that you have prepared. By requesting the report, a reader identifies himself as a prospect. The editor will usually want to see a copy of the report to make sure that it is not simply a brochure or something that would embarrass him, like a reprint from another publication. Sometimes offers must be made in a letter to the editor following publication of your article. It is worth asking the editor whether an offer will be printed if you are interested in this approach.

Research, angles and formulas can be as important to this aspect of your marketing effort as the technical tools of your trade are to providing professional services efficiently. They help ensure that articles are not just planned but also produced and published.

2

Finding a Podium

Case example: The Speaker

After teaching for two years at a law school and working for several more at a large law firm, Frank accepted a government appointment at a regulatory agency. Because of his new position, bar associations and universities frequently invited him to speak. Frank had noticed at a recent conference how ill-prepared many of the speakers were and decided that audiences deserved better. Though he had not made many speeches previously, he brushed up the skill he had developed as a teacher, spent hours developing a speech that would have value to his audience, and rehearsed. The audience clearly liked his speech, and he was invited to make others.

As his speaking reputation developed, Frank continued to prepare carefully, seeking out new material to keep his content fresh. He sought to develop a relationship with members of his audience and with those who had arranged for him to speak. After each speech he reviewed the evaluation forms the audience had filled out to see what he could learn that might help him get better. He also followed up with as many people as he could by writing letters. He developed a reputation as a reliable speaker.

When Frank returned to private practice as a partner at a major firm, the invitations continued. Increasingly seen as an expert in his field, he began to receive leads from people who had heard him speak. As he learned about the power of the podium, he enhanced his efforts in several ways. He would convert speeches into articles, gaining added exposure for little extra work, and he began developing speeches on a specialized area of his field not often touched on by others, increasing the probability that he would be invited to round out panels and conferences. Because he was a successful speaker, others often sought his ideas for fresh content at conferences. Such discussions often resulted in additional invitations. Leads continued to come, and others in his firm also found it easy to sell him to their clients as an expert in his field. He became a recognized rain maker at his firm.

Case example: The Raconteur

Wendy loved to tell stories, and she told them well. Events that passed unnoticed by others became hilarious when she recounted them. People sought her out at gatherings and afterward remembered her. When they called, she remembered them and reminded them of an event that made them laugh. She was fun to be with.

Wendy translated this social ability into a personal marketing strategy. She sold consulting services to public sector and not-for-profit community groups, of which there were thousands spread across the country. Associations of these groups met annually in each state and region, and there were several national organizations, as well. They were always looking for good speakers. On the basis of her storytelling ability Wendy was invited to speak at these events, and soon proved as entertaining at the podium as she was in the conference room and over the dinner table. Better yet, her stories delivered a message.

In time her speaking reputation brought her more invitations than she could handle. What had begun as an occasional, informal marketing task evolved into a central strategy. As this transformation occurred, she...

- *...began to charge fees for speaking, turning this activity into a financially self-supporting marketing campaign.*
- *...focused on selected key messages that supported the firm's central marketing positions.*
- *...leveraged the time she invested in speaking by reusing the same speeches many times, converting them to articles and book chapters and collecting names from her audiences so that she could follow up with them by mail.*

Eventually she developed a two-day seminar, which prospective customers paid to attend. Her career prospered, and on the basis of these and other activities she rose to become the president of her company.

Speeches are articles with faces. Like article writing, public speaking helps build your reputation as an expert. The audiences are smaller, but the impression you leave is stronger. You are more likely to be remembered by someone who has heard you speak than by someone who has read an article you have written, because they have seen you. Face to face with your audience you can develop an emotional linkage not possible with an article, and so increase their comfort with calling you later. Your chances of conversing directly with the audience, and of obtaining names and phone numbers so that you can follow up, are greatly increased.

Like the speaker and the raconteur, some professionals speak frequently. They develop reputations as speakers, find platforms, and, if they are good at it, bring in a steady flow of leads for their firms. Other professionals speak seldom or never, for one of three reasons: fear of public speaking, uncertainty about their own speaking abilities, or lack of a podium.

Fear of public speaking

Fear of public speaking is a common complaint. If you feel this way, it may help to understand that your fear is shared by thousands of others, including those who speak frequently. Even the most accomplished speaker will have a queasy stomach when standing before a group larger or more important than he is accustomed to. Frequent speakers learn to handle the fear and counter it with confidence in their own abilities. They do not let their fear stand in the way of their careers.

If you lack confidence in your speaking abilities, I recommend taking one of the professional training courses available from a variety of organizations. Even skilled speakers can benefit from such programs. Pam Yardis, Chair of the Institute of Management Consultants and a successful professional, once told me that she tries to take a presentation skills course at least once a year. Successful public speaking results from your appearance, movements, and tone of voice as much as it does from content. You can control all of these, and the courses teach you to manage them effectively, taping your performances so that you can see the effects as you change behavior. I have seen many individuals dramatically increase both their skills and confidence through such programs.

If you are unable to attend such a program, there are several good books on the subject; I have listed several in appendix E. You should also study effective speakers every chance you get and emulate them. And don't forget to read chapter 11 of this book.

Whenever I attend a conference, I learn from watching other speakers. I not only learn from those who do well, I also find out how abysmal the average speaker is. Long ago I realized that one didn't have to have the oratorical power of Winston Churchill or Dr. Martin Luther King, Jr. to outperform most of the speakers on the trade-show circuit. I became convinced that through preparation and rehearsal I could outdo most of the speakers I would be compared to. Formal ratings by my audiences have proved this true. Most speakers do not prepare adequately, and fewer still really rehearse; rather, they review their notes silently or read scripts. I will deal with this issue later.

Finding a podium

Some platforms are more competitive than others, but there is ample opportunity for everyone. Most organizations hunger for speakers and will be willing to give you a chance if you present your case properly. Developing a reputation usually requires building from small audiences to large and from humble to prestigious ones. Even Martin Luther King, the preeminent American orator of the latter half of the twentieth century, practiced before peers in seminary and at church congregations before earning the chance to speak to larger groups.[1] Early on you should accept almost any opportunity offered for the practice. Some people I know have joined Toastmasters, an organization dedicated to improving members' speaking skills, in order to get this experience.[2]

36

You will have more opportunity more quickly if you seek it out. This means identifying and researching organizations that can offer you an audience. You may already know many of the groups you want to address from your work. If not, you can...

- *...ask others who would know.* I once wanted to speak to senior human resource officers and found that meetings of the largest trade association tended to draw lower level managers. By asking around I learned that there was no single organization that fit my purpose. In each major metropolitan area some smaller group served as the gathering place of my target market. These groups had to be identified on a city-by-city basis.

- *...identify groups by consulting the* Encyclopedia of Associations.[3] This publication, available in most libraries, provides concise information on thousands of associations, their purpose, membership, meetings, and publications.

Once you have identified a group to speak to, try to attend a few meetings. Speaking formats differ from organization to organization. Some prefer individual speakers; others, panels. One organization I know almost always pairs a corporate employee with a consultant he has worked with. By going to a meeting you will find out what formats are available, as well as what subjects attract the most interest; you can also meet members and staff. If possible, review an organization's publications to get a sense of members' interests. Speeches made at conferences often appear later in article form in an organization's publications.

Staff and committee members can tell you about procedures for selecting speakers and what kinds of speakers they are looking for. However, most organizations are looking for two things: strong speaking ability and strong content. Most will sacrifice some content for a speaker able to excite or entertain an audience, because they have seen the effects of the expert bore on attendance. This means that you will want to demonstrate both your speaking ability and subject knowledge when offering yourself.

The two most common approaches to selection are often used in combination. The first is referrals. Members or other contacts are asked for suggestions. In such cases you must know who to contact to request consideration. I would recommend a low-key phone call to the appropriate person, stating that you had heard the group is seeking speakers and that you are available to speak on a specific subject. Ask whether you could send a summary of what you would like to talk about, plus a little information about yourself, and then get off the phone. Once the person has reviewed your materials, you can make a stronger pitch.

A second approach to selecting speakers is to solicit proposals with an application form. These forms usually request a concise summary of your speech and proof of your credentials.

Whether you are sending a letter or a completing a form, you should include the following:

- *A statement of relevance.* You should state why the subject you wish to present is important to the audience. You may also be able to tie the subject to the theme that many trade associations have for their annual meetings. The ability to adapt a standard speech to a specific situation often makes the difference between acceptance and rejection.

- *A concise summary.* A three- or four-sentence description focusing on benefits the audience will receive is usually adequate, though some organizations require more.

- *Expert's credentials.* The reader will want to know why you are qualified to present. A reduced version of your bio, focusing on your knowledge of the subject you wish to address, is the most obvious proof. Reprints of articles you have written and lists of other audiences you have spoken to on the subject are good supplements.

- *Speaking Credentials.* By providing proof of your speaking credentials, you will distinguish yourself from the overwhelming majority of applicants. This subject is so important that it warrants special attention.

    Finding someone who will stimulate an audience is a most difficult task. Ask anyone who has tried to line up a series of speakers. A person scintillating and vibrant in one-on-one conversation can turn into a wooden mannequin on the platform. Program committees dread inflicting such a person on their fellow members. Anyone who can demonstrate an ability to speak well will have a strong advantage in getting selected. As in most selection processes, the one who presents himself best will usually win, whether or not his actual performance is superior. Anyone who aspires to be a speaker should develop a file of speaking credentials. These should include:

    □ *References.* You can supply two or three references for your speaking abilities from others who have heard you speak. Staff or elected officers of organizations you have spoken to are best, but the references can be from anyone who has heard you.

    □ *Lists of podiums.* Lists of organizations you have spoken to also constitute a proof, evaluators commonly making the assumption that if you have spoken often you must speak well.

    □ *Testimonial letters.* Thank-you letters are often sent to speakers. Any that say good things about your effect on the audience should be saved, so that copies can be sent with future requests for a podium. Better still, you can solicit testimonial letters and request that they make specific reference to your speaking abilities.

    □ *Speaker evaluations.* Many organizations ask attendees to fill out speaker evaluation forms. Always request a copy of the results. These are especially valuable if they show you in comparison with other speakers rather than in isolation. In cases where evaluation forms are not used, I often prepare my own. This has allowed me to demonstrate my abilities in forums not usually evaluated, such as in-house training courses. A typical form is provided in exhibit 2.1. Results should, of course, be summarized. Reviewing evaluations will help you polish a speech. If necessary, edit your summary to focus on positive commentary.

Exhibit 2.1
Sample Speaker Evaluation Form

Event: _____

Date: _____

Location: _____

Speech title: _____

Speaker: _____

Please help us by completing the following evaluation:

Topic

Excellent	Very Good	Good	Fair	Poor
5	4	3	2	1

Speaker

Excellent	Very Good	Good	Fair	Poor
5	4	3	2	1

General comments:

_____

_____

_____

What did you find most helpful?

_____

_____

What could be improved?

_____

_____

Name: _____   Company: _____

Use these proofs of your speaking abilities selectively. No one performs equally well on all occasions. Ratings will vary with the nature of the audience, the frequency with which you have given a particular speech in the past, and other speakers' abilities; if you follow a four-star orator, your ratings will not be as good as when you follow a dud. I have many ratings I am proud of and a few I am not proud of; I only use the former when I am making an application.

All letters and applications should be treated with the same attention that you would give to a proposal to a prospective client. They should be thorough, neat, clear, and attractively formatted to make life as easy as possible for the reviewer. This will communicate the seriousness of your interest. You would be surprised at how many sloppy applications are submitted.

To talk of many things

Once you are invited to speak, you must prepare for the event. A few guidelines follow; however, this chapter is less about the preparation and delivery of a speech than on gaining the opportunity to speak in the first place, and using that opportunity as a vehicle to build your reputation and develop leads for new business. Several good books on speech preparation and delivery are listed in appendix E, and most of the material in chapter 1 on angles and formulas in article writing applies equally to the construction of speeches. Formulas, for example, are commonly used in speeches. I have heard excellent speeches entitled "Ten Things You Should Do to Improve Your Public Relations" and "Ten Steps to Hiring Better Employees." In both cases the audiences dutifully wrote down the ten points, the formula giving them a simple structure they could follow easily.

A few guidelines on the nature of speaking engagements not found elsewhere are offered here.

1. **Don't speak too long.** The most common formats for speeches before associations are the single speaker and the panel. Time allocations for both vary, but most run between an hour and an hour and a half total. Single speakers should seldom talk for more than thirty minutes, leaving half an hour for questions. If you use slides or transparencies, controlling the number you use is one good way to regulate the length of time you speak. I know that I cannot present more than fifteen transparencies in half an hour. When that is my time limit, I force myself to use no more than this number. This, in turn, forces me to make decisions about the content to be presented. (See appendix B for guidelines on preparing visuals.) Panel speakers usually have between ten and twenty minutes each for their presentations. If they fail to control themselves they risk appearing insensitive to other speakers and to the audience.

2. **Be conversational**. Today's most successful speakers use a conversational style, as opposed to one of the more formal alternatives. Many people find it hard to retain an informal tone when standing before an audience. To do so requires that you carefully avoid using long and for-

40

mal words when simple ones will do. As you rehearse, listen to what you say, or have someone critique you, so that you can replace phrases like, "They were impressed with our method" with "They liked what we did." Beginning your presentation with a direct question to the audience may help you to retain a conversational style. Ask for a show of hands or a few comments in response. This brief dialogue with your listeners will help get you started with the right tone.

3. **Rehearse without a script.** I usually write a speech prior to rehearsing it, but once the rehearsals start I set it aside. At most I retain a four- or five-point outline and notes on any facts and figures I might not remember. The purpose of writing out a speech is to organize my thoughts, not to develop a script. Because starting off and finishing are difficult, I will sometimes memorize the first and last lines. For the rest, I count on rehearsals to make me facile with the material so that it will come to me as I need it. Be sure the opening line is conversational in tone. One architect and programmer I know was able to transform a stiff and stilted style to a quite charming one by beginning with a disarming claim for his own expertise: "By some strange quirk of fate I have programmed more conference centers than anyone else in the world."

If possible, rehearse with a coach who will critique you. Ask this person to interrupt whenever he finds his mind wandering. Many coaches are too polite to do this unless asked, feeling that it is their responsibility to pay attention rather than yours to hold it. When stopped for this reason, review your content and the words you are using to see what is causing the presentation to drag. Are you giving more detail than is needed? Will an anecdote illustrate a point better than a description? Is the value of what you are saying clear to the listener? Do you need to change your tone of voice, increase your volume, or inject more emotion into your delivery?

Don't expect to feel good during a rehearsal. They seldom provide the adrenaline lift of the real thing, but two or three real rehearsals during which you sand up and speak aloud will help make the real thing better.

Knowing the size of the audience and layout of the room will also help you prepare. The host can usually give you an estimate of the former and almost always describe the latter.

Further guidance on presenting and coaching can be found in chapter 11.

Generating leads

Generating new business leads is the main reason for seeking a speaking engagement. You will be more successful at doing so if you are deliberate about it. Though you may be willing to speak to a wide array of organizations at first to gain experience, once you have established a reputation you will want to be more selective, focusing only on audiences likely to be productive. Evaluation factors include audience size, the percent of potential clients as opposed to other attendees, and the cost in time and money of attending. I once accepted an invitation to speak to a group without conducting proper research, only to find that I had wasted two days, including travel time, to address a group that had not a single potential client. I never made that mistake again.

You should also plan to attend the whole event you are speaking at, whether it lasts for only an evening or for several days. This allows you to...

- ...stir up interest in your presentation, increasing attendance.
- ...assess your audience in advance.
- ...meet with members of your audience after the presentation. Build off your presentation. Informal discussions can build rapport that turns into leads later.
- ...reinforce your stature as a speaker in casual meetings.

Your ability to generate leads also depends on your subject and content. A tax accountant who built the largest practice in his firm and is a frequent speaker says, "I usually average one new account per presentation. You have to have a hook. It helps if you can show special expertise at solving a nagging problem or avoiding a painful one. A lot of speeches don't do that."

Most leads come when you follow up with your audience after the speech. This means you must obtain their names, addresses, and phone numbers. There are several ways to do this. One is to circulate a sign-in sheet. This is not always practical, and the resulting list will have to be shared with any competitors on your panel. It also creates a minor distraction as it is passed around. When it works, it is efficient.

A second approach is to offer copies of your presentation materials to all who leave you their business cards at the end of the presentation. This is a common and effective technique, but deprives the audience of take-home copies that many would like to have. As an alternative, you can offer something else—a report on a study, for example. This approach creates the extra burden of coming up with the something else. A final approach I have used with large audiences is to ask them to fill in a survey form, offering to send copies of the findings to all who also fill in a name and address section.

Follow-up should occur between one and three weeks after the presentation. A brief letter thanking the recipient for his interest will personalize the mailing and refresh fading memories of who you are. You can then follow up by phone, taking the opportunity to inquire about the need for your services.

Speech making can be among the most effective ways to develop leads for a professional practice. It also builds your reputation and that of your firm. No wonder it is among the most common marketing tools used by professionals.

3

Networking, the Alternative to Cold Calling

Case example: The Man Who Knew Everyone

Oscar Megerdichian grew up in the rough-and-tumble moving industry in New York City and never went to college. Combining social skill with business acumen, he built a consulting firm specializing in move management. A self-educated, intelligent man, he liked people. He liked talking and was always on the phone. He honestly cared about his business friends and tried to help them whenever he could. He knew thousands of people. I once introduced him to a client. As we toured the building, we met five different people. During five-minute conversations, he identified mutual friends with each. "What a small world," he would say each time with a quizzical smile. When this happened a month later at another company, I knew I was dealing with something special.

Once you met Oscar, he didn't forget you. He would call periodically to see how you were doing. Better still, he often offered useful pieces of information. His real help came from introductions. He was always introducing people who could help each other. He introduced me to several people who later gave me large consulting assignments. His calls, needless to say, were always welcome, though they did sometimes make me a little uncomfortable that I had not done enough for this nice man who was working so hard for my benefit. I sought ways to return his help in kind.

By the time Oscar died, he had built a substantial firm. More importantly, his life had been warmed by many friendships, and those of us who knew him reflect on him often with affection.

One key to successful marketing is gaining access to a decision maker while he has a high concern about confidentiality and is still formulating his needs around a specific problem. This means knowing him so well that he confides in you early. More likely, you must know someone who enjoys such a relationship with the decision maker and who will introduce you. In short, it means networking.

"Networking" is one of the most referenced and seldom-realized activities in business. This is because so many who try to do it don't understand it. I know this because, when training people to network, I begin by asking what "networking" means to them. Typical responses include:

- Using your friends to get business
- Doing lunch
- Calling people a lot on the phone
- Asking people you know to help you get business

These views are either wrong or reflect form rather than substance.

Done correctly, networking can greatly expand your sales force and bring in business. Done poorly, it is a waste of time. I suspect that more time is wasted on so-called networking than on any other area of the professional services. This is disturbing, because the value of time spent on marketing far exceeds the value of out-of-pocket expenses in most firms. That so much is spent for so little shocks my puritan soul.

In an effort to remedy this situation I conducted a study to identify key aspects of successful networking. I interviewed and observed the most effective networkers I could find in a range of businesses, including consulting, law, engineering, accounting, architecture, construction, railroading, insurance, and office supplies, to name but a few. I avoided those who are so rich and powerful that their networking success may be attributed in part to opportunities thrown at their feet. Rather, I focused on individuals who have been successful in their chosen fields largely on the basis of their networking prowess.

One example is the late Oscar Megerdichian, the man I described in the example at the beginning of this chapter. At the peak of his career he could gain access to almost anyone he chose in the New York area through his extensive network. I have sat with him when he phoned high-level executives who dropped what they were doing to take his calls. It was transparently clear that he knew things about networking others did not.

Here, distilled and codified, are fourteen basic rules I have learned for networking:

1. Networking is helping people
This is the most basic rule and the reason selfish people fail at networking. At its simplest level, it means that if you have a choice between presenting your services to a compliant but less than enthusiastic contact or giving him a ride to the airport, you are probably better off doing the latter. Your contact will remember you better and be more inclined to help you later. You can have a nice chat while you drive.

Giving often precedes receiving in networking. In the architectural and construction industries, which rely heavily on networking for new business, the admonishment "You have to give to get" is often heard. I first heard it from Linda Lukas, perhaps the best networker in the architectural industry. If you cannot or will not help others who can live very well without you, why should they go out of their way to help you? We are not talking about charity or social responsibility here; we are talking business and even friendship. Business associates and friends help each other, though perhaps in different ways and for somewhat different reasons. This is why it can be difficult to network with those you dislike.

Exhibit 3.1 provides a checklist of kinds of help you can provide. In different businesses help is defined differently, so you must adjust your definition of "help" to your contact's point of view. A successful insurance salesman I know, a superb networker, wants to be introduced to prospective customers or people who have influence with his prospective customers. He does not consider information to be real help. In contrast, many people tied to the real estate market, be they brokers, developers, architects, consulting engineers, or construction managers, covet information. As one successful real estate broker put it to me, "I don't need an introduction. What I need is information that someone is considering a move. I trust our people to get in the door." In varying circumstances, leads, information on prospects, introductions, sales assistance, references, and ideas are but some of the kinds of help provided by networkers. If you need to verify what a contact considers helpful, simply ask. The key is to keep asking yourself, "How can I help this person?" rather than "How can this person help me?"

Exhibit 3.1
Help Checklist

Examples of help you can provide a network contact:

I. Information
    A. About a prospective client
        1. Need for service (a "lead")
            a) Description of need
                (1) Size
                (2) Timing
                (3) Reasons for need
                (4) Issues
                (5) Contact
                    (a) Name
                    (b) Title
                    (c) Address
                    (d) Phone
                (6) Decision-making process
                (7) Buyers/influencers
                    (a) Names
                    (b) Titles
                    (c) Roles in process

              (d) Concerns
         (8) Competitors
              (a) Names
              (b) Strengths and weaknesses
         (9) Changes
              (a) In need
              (b) In buyers
              (c) In decision-making process
         (10) Reasons for winning or losing sale

B. About an existing client (of contact)
    1. Changes
        a) Personnel
        b) Reorganizations
        c) Major business events
    2. Problems (client is having with contact)
        a) Existence of problem
        b) Reasons for problem
        c) Impending actions
    3. Actions of competitors to win away contact's client

C. About competitors
    1. Problems/changes
    2. New clients
    3. Successful practices
    4. Facts (number of employees or offices, etc.)
    5. Key personnel

D. About attractive new markets

II. Introductions, referrals, and references
    A. To prospective clients
    B. To network contacts who can help get business
    C. To vendor who can help improve service
    D. To prospective employees

III. Ideas and advice
    A. On how to approach a prospect
    B. On how to solve a business problem

IV. Personal support
    A. Congratulations
    B. Condolences

V. Free or discounted services

I have watched while a lot of highly paid executives talked about synergy between their firms and possible strategic alliances ("synergy" and "strategic alliance" are two more overworked and underrealized terms), but could not figure out where to begin. Often all it takes to get such a conversation off the dime is for someone to give the other side real help without setting any conditions. It is amazing what a freeing experience this can be.

Does this mean you will sometimes help someone without seeing any return? Of course. So what? When you want a favor, it will be much easier to get if you have been of real help to the person you are asking it of. The more significant the help, the greater the desire a reasonable person will feel to help you in return.

2. You must learn to recognize a lead for someone else when you hear it
Though there are many ways to help people, what you can probably provide most frequently are leads and introductions. To do this you must know enough about your contacts' businesses to recognize a lead when you hear one. Ask *them* to give a presentation to *you*. Ask what services they provide to what kinds of organizations. Ask what situations and conditions are likely indicators of a need for their services. Exhibit 3.2 provides a list of questions you can ask. When you find yourself listening to clients, prospects, and other business contacts for needs statements that apply to others' practices as well as your own, you will know that you are becoming an effective networker.

Exhibit 3.2
Questions to Ask a Prospective Network Contact

- Would you please describe your company and its services (or products)?
- Who are your clients (or customers—by industry, company size, geography, etc.)?
- Who at the client companies buys your services?
- What are some typical indicators that show there might be a need for your services?
- What are a few questions I could ask to confirm whether there is really a need, if I uncover one of these indicators?
- Who are your major competitors?
- How are you different from them?
- How do you go about finding new clients?
- How can I help you?

Leads for others can appear at any time but are particularly likely in certain situations. Every firm receives inquiries from individuals who need a service that does not quite fit with those it offers. Every time you turn away business you have a lead for someone else. I always try to make referrals in such situations.

We have all had the experience of hearing a client complain about a problem unrelated to the one we are working on. "The coffee here is lousy." "Send it to me by courier. If it comes in the regular mail, it will get delayed in our own internal mail system." Statements like these represent opportunities for someone else. Do you know anyone who could help solve these problems?

3. Networking is sincere effort rather than keeping score

Having been thoroughly indoctrinated into effective networking techniques by the pros, I am stunned by the amateurs who, upon learning rule one, help someone and then say in effect, "I've helped you, now it's your turn." Life isn't that simple, nor, I hope, that venal. Would you expect such a tit-for-tat relationship from a friend? Then why would you expect it of incipient business friendships? What does it matter if you provide five leads to an individual and he provides you his one good lead of the year? He has done his best for you. You have done your best for each other. Excellence in networking, as in anything else, requires your best effort.

Save a tactful speech entitled, "What have you done for me lately?" for those cases in which you seek to educate someone else on what networking means.

4. Networking is a sense of urgency and obligation

You do want sincere effort, and the coin of sincerity in networking is the sense of urgency and obligation to return help received. If someone helps you, you should feel an increased need to do something for her. The sense of obligation should sharpen your attention to possible leads for the contact. Leaf through your Rolodex, thinking about your contact's services as you look at each name. Is there someone there she should know? Someone who could help her even if you cannot? If you are unsure, call your contact and ask. She will then know you are thinking of her interests, and the conversation may help clarify how you can help, or perhaps spark a new idea.

Can you do a favor for a friend of the contact who has just helped you? Even if this does not help her business directly, it may do so indirectly later. Passing on invisible chits for favors goes on all the time among networkers.

5. Show how your services can add value to a contact's business

Of course, you want others to help you as you are seeking to help them. This is easiest for them if you can describe how your services enhance the value of their own. The more clearly they perceive that by helping you they help themselves, the more they will be willing to do for you. Will incorporating your services help a contact differentiate his services from that of a competitor? Let him know how. A friend of mine greatly expanded his consulting business by showing real estate brokers how they could use his services in this way. Is there a possibility that the help your services provide in solving a problem will speed progress on a project that may require the contact's services at a later date? Explain this. Whenever possible, you must position your services in a way that shows their value, not just to the ultimate prospect but also to your network contact.

6. Networking is showing gratitude

When someone helps you, you must show you appreciate it. This is particularly true if the help pays off for you. If you receive a lot of information on a prospect from a contact and then win the job, let him know you appreciate the help. Call! Write! If he provided a reference or an introduction, take him to lunch!

Networking is based on friendship, and friendships require appreciation and recognition.

7. Networking is maintaining trust

The single biggest inhibitor to networking is the fear that someone will take advantage of you or embarrass you. You can help overcome this fear in others by extending a hand when they need it, but that is not enough. Maintaining a high level of trust is essential to developing a network. All of the effective networkers included in my networking study are held in high regard by their peers and have high ethical standards.

Maintaining trust requires several things. First, it means that you will provide a high-quality service. It doesn't pay to network with hacks, because your reputation will be sullied by theirs. It also means that you will go the extra mile to clear up any problems that you might have with a client or in some other relationship. This is good practice in any event, but by itself is not enough to maintain trust in networking; you must also be forthright with your contacts. If client confidentiality or some other obligation prohibits you from providing a contact with the help that he desires in a specific instance, you must tell him so. If he understands networking, he will accept your explanation. If he does not, you will want to cut him out of your network anyway. It further means that you, yourself, will hold off pursuing an opportunity, if pursuing it might embarrass your contact. This can be very hard to do when you are under pressure to make a sale. One respondent to my survey told this story:

> I was once given a lead which I didn't pursue because I sensed that the person who had given it to me didn't want me to yet. She called me later and asked if I had gotten the business. I told her I had not and explained my reason. She was as surprised as I was embarrassed, but it was worth it in the long run. Knowing she could trust me, she became a lot more open and I've gotten a lot of business out of her over the years.

Maintaining trust also means that you do not help one business contact by placing a burden on another, unless you are in a position to request an outright favor. Rather, your objective is to help all parties involved. This means, among other things, that you shouldn't feel an obligation to introduce a member of your network to a client unless you think it will be beneficial to both and can convince both of a meeting's potential value.

Exhibit 3.3 provides a list of do's and don'ts for maintaining trust with your contacts.

Exhibit 3.3
Do's and Don'ts of Developing Trust

Do's

- **Ask a contact how confidential his information is.** If you have any doubt, it is better to ask than to violate a confidence.
- **Ask whether the contact minds if you pursue a lead he has told you about.** When in doubt, ask.
- *Always* **ask permission before mentioning a contact's name as a source of information.**
- **Call the contact who provided a lead to let him know the results of you pursuit.**
- **Show gratitude.** This applies especially when you win a job that a contact helped you win. Call. Write. Take him to lunch.
- **Help a contact who has helped you win a job by getting him a chance with the new client.** For architects and some other professionals, this means putting the contact on your team. In other fields, it means an introduction later.
- **Tell a contact when you cannot help him because of a prior commitment to a competitor.** If you take a contact's information, but plan to work with a competitor, you are using him. Users get a bad reputation in a network.

Don'ts

- **Don't share confidential information.** This is the most commonly violated networking rule. You will be strongly tempted to use any information at your disposal in the bartering of networking, but you get a reputation as untrustworthy if you violate confidences.
- **Don't ask where information comes from,** if a contact is providing it hesitatingly.
- **Don't share information provided by a contact with his competitor.**
- **Don't go around a contact to his boss when you wish to share information with his firm.** People help you, not companies. Return help to those who give it so that your contact gets credit for generating a lead.

8. Networking requires spending some of your time selling other peoples' services

From what I have said so far, you will understand why this is true. Helping some-one else sell his services is the ultimate form of assistance in business networking. If you believe in what you are selling, you are helping the buyer, too. Those who work for themselves will find this rule easy to implement. Those who work for someone else can find it harder to justify. "Jane, sales are 15 percent behind budget. What are you doing about it?" the boss asks you. If you answer, "I helped Surprise and Delight Consulting sell a $75,000 job," he may not understand. You must educate him in anticipation of such an event. The best education is showing him how such help has been returned in the past; so keep track of your successes.

At first, helping sell someone else's services may seem awkward. After all, what business is it of yours? A few successes will overcome this concern. People are often most appreciative of someone who introduces them to someone who can solve a problem. I once introduced a furniture dealer to a contact who wanted such small-scale interior design services that the firm I worked for could not help him. I told him that the dealer provided a high-quality service and would give away design in order to win furniture and carpeting business. Both the buyer and seller were de-lighted. The buyer called me two weeks after the job began to thank me for making the referral. He had not bought design services before, and had been nervous about making a mistake. He was getting first rate work and had saved his company some money. His boss was pleased. The seller received an order worth over $200,000. When you help one person in networking, you often find you are helping two.

You will also find that it is often easier to sell someone else's services than it is to sell your own. Because your perceived self-interest is low, you gain credibility. In the example just cited, I was able to tell the buyer that the furniture dealer was honest and would quote a fair price. This kind of thing is hard to say credibly about yourself, even though it is true.

The value to you of selling other peoples' services is epitomized in reverse networking. Everyone has someone he knows but from whom he feels uncomfort-able asking for business. This may be because the relationship is too personal. At some golf clubs, for example, it is considered bad form to solicit business from other members. One person I know wanted business from his son's friend's father but was reluctant to ask. Or sometimes it happens that the person in question has a strong tie to a competitor, and initial overtures have been rebuffed. In such a case you may be concerned that too much pressure will damage your relationship.

Reverse networking is one way of overcoming such obstacles. It is best ex-plained with an example: John, an accountant, wanted to do business with Ed but was uncomfortable raising the issue. He introduced Ed to a consultant, Mary, who he knew could help Ed with a problem he had mentioned. Mary made the sale, and later reversed the networking by helping position John. "Who is your account-ant?" she asked Ed later. On hearing that it wasn't John, she responded in surprise,

"You mean it isn't John? He's the best in the business. Since you know him, I thought for sure you would use him."

9. Networking is time consuming

You cannot build a network without spending time doing so. Effective networking requires long-term, consistent efforts, because trust and a track record of mutual assistance cannot be developed in a week. A major project came to me after three years of helping one trade association contact with odd bits of advice and information and a lot of listening. It was the first time he had hired a consultant in those three years, and the project took little direct selling when it came. My survey respondents have many such stories.

Your contacts must be nurtured by regular contact in the same way you must water a garden regularly to make it grow. A financial consultant who has built a successful practice in two years as a sole practitioner has said to me several times, "It's amazing how quickly the leads stop coming in if you stop calling people." No water, no harvest. You can always tell seasoned networkers, because they all complain about activities that cut into their phone time.

This means you must schedule time for networking. Oscar Megerdichian, who built a good business networking, spent the majority of his time at it. Another person I know blocks out a portion of each day to be on the phone. A third blocked out every Tuesday morning to make twenty-five calls. He would do no other business until they had been made. He didn't reach everyone he called, but the return calls would keep him in the market for the rest of the week.

When I began to network, my schedule defeated all efforts to organize in this way. The solution was to develop a list of contacts and turn to it at every period of brief inactivity. I picked up the phone when waiting for planes in airports, when a colleague was late for a meeting or when I was early, and at other loose moments. However you do it, you must find a way to structure networking calls into your schedule. The best networkers guard their telephone contacting time tenaciously and will struggle to protect it when other demands begin to distract them.

Trade associations provide a structured environment for maintaining network contacts. Most experienced networkers have one or two such organizations that they participate in heavily. Similar benefits derive from formal networking groups, which will be discussed later.

Several software programs can also help you organize yourself to network. (My favorite is ACT.) They combine the functions of your Rolodex, calendar, to-do list, tickler file, and vertical file on prospects and contacts. They will remind you to make calls, prompt you on possible follow-up to each call, keep all your records on a contact in one easy-to-access file, and otherwise help you get the job done. I recommend that anyone actively involved in networking investigate such programs.

Keeping in contact shows you are serious. It demonstrates your commitment. More practically, you will find that direct contact with people forces you to think about how you can help them and how they can help you. Over and over again networkers give and receive valuable information that would not be passed if they had not contacted each other for another reason. I once called a friend in a construction company simply because I had not spoken to him for a while. We discussed a variety of projects that we were pursuing and I learned that the decision maker for a 350,000-square-foot interior design project we were pursuing used to work at my contact's firm. My friend was able to help me with both advice and a reference, assistance that became a major factor in my firm's winning the job. Had I not made the call to touch base after a month of little contact, I wouldn't have learned of his relationship and he would have been unable to help me.

10. You must be selective about who you network with

You must spend a lot of time with your network contacts. You will be actively trying to help them. You will sometimes be laying your reputation on the line for them. You had better be careful who you network with.

First, you will want to focus on those who are good at what they do. They are the ones who have something to offer your other business contacts. They pass the first test of being worth helping. Second, you will naturally want to work with those who understand networking and are willing to develop an effective networking relationship with you. Third, you will want to focus on those who have business contacts who can help you. This means working with others who sell to the same people that you want to sell to.

In Exhibit 3.4 is a set of Network Creation forms that people I have trained to network find helpful when they are starting out and trying to figure out who to network with. Work through the exercises and see what directions they push you in.

Exhibit 3.4
Network Creation

Step One: **Brainstorming Questions**

- Whom have I received leads from in the past?
- Who sells to the same people I sell to?
- Who buys from the people I sell to?
- Who stands to benefit from the same events/circumstances that I do?
- Who do my competitors network with?
- Whom can I help?
- Who has sought my help in the past?
- Whom have I helped in the past?
- Who wants to help me?
- Who is a good networker?

List the names and ideas that come to your mind here.

_____

_____

_____

Step Two: **Category identification**

1. Review the names and ideas from the brainstorming exercise and see what categories of contacts you can identify. List them below.
2. Mark with a star (★) those categories that your instincts tell you offer the highest potential for helping you get new business.

_____

_____

_____

Step Three: **Opportunity and gap identification**

Select three high-potential categories and list three people in each who might be good network contacts. If you can't name as many as three in either category, place a star (★) in each vacant name slot. List the company and phone number for each individual, again placing stars where there are gaps in your information.

Next, rate each individual as to the level of your relationship: 1★ = Don't know, no mutual friends; 2★ = Don't know, mutual friends; 3★ = Know slightly; 4 = Know well, good relationship; 5 = Know well, other than good relationship.

Finally, rate each individual "Excellent," "Good," "Fair," "Poor," or "★" (for "Don't Know") on whether the individual is disposed to be helpful and whether you are likely to have opportunities to help each other.

Based on this analysis you can identify:

- Whom you can begin to network with immediately.

- Information you need to gather before you can start networking.

*Category:*_____

	1	2	3
Name			
Company			
Phone			
Relationship			
Disposition			
Potential			

Category:_____

	1	2	3
Name			
Company			
Phone			
Relationship			
Disposition			
Potential			

Category:_____

	1	2	3
Name			
Company			
Phone			
Relationship			
Disposition			
Potential			

There are those you will wish to avoid or weed out. They include people who only want to receive help and are not inclined to give it. You will meet many such individuals. They simply don't understand how networking works. They do not listen for leads for other people and so never hear them. Even if such a person has many valuable business contacts, the contacts are useless to you because you will never gain access to them through him. Learning to recognize those who do not have a networking mind-set will help you weed them out early. I once thought I was establishing a good networking relationship with another consultant. I helped him get a large job and he helped me get a small one. Over the next two years I helped him get four other jobs but received little help in return. When I finally raised my concern, he responded, "But I don't ever hear of leads for you." I should have seen the signs earlier. Though I had been calling him every couple of months to stay in contact, he had never called me unless he wanted something. He couldn't help me because he didn't understand networking. I dropped him.

You will also want to avoid those who view networking as tricking people. Those who constantly pass stale information in hopes of getting value in return are another recognizable group of freeloaders.

More troublesome are those you enjoy meeting with but who cannot really help you, although it seemed at first that they could. Cutting such people from the network can seem cold and personally dishonest. This can become an excuse for continuing to waste time and money on them. The solution is simple: keep them as friends, but stop fooling yourself and wasting company resources—money and your time—by treating them as valued business network contacts. If you do not really want them as friends, either, it is time to ask what you are getting out of the relationship. Is your ego involved, by any chance?

Keep this in mind: There are far more people worth networking with than you can possibly have time for. Since your own time is the most valuable resource you control, you will want to focus it on those networking relationships where there is the greatest potential for mutual benefit.

11. Networking is helping other people learn to network

Many people want to network but don't know how. The more skilled you become, the more it will benefit you to help them learn. If someone is predisposed to be helpful, especially someone you have done a favor for, make specific suggestions about how the person can help you. You will be surprised at how many generous and interested people need such suggestions before they can act. They don't yet think like networkers.

I tried to network with a consultant for many years but got nowhere and eventually gave up. One day I met someone else who could benefit greatly from knowing him, and so I introduced them. They got along famously and were able to help each other. Having made this useful introduction, I decided to try networking with the consultant again. He had always seemed to want to help, even if he had never done anything. This time I asked if he could introduce me to some specific people, instead of asking if he knew anyone who might want my services. Though he had not responded to a general request for help, he was more than willing to introduce me to the people I named. An inexperienced networker, he needed coaching on how to help me.

When providing this kind of coaching, you must avoid the appearance of too much pressure. Be sure to include caveats to your request, such as, "We must each decide what we are comfortable doing with our contacts, and I don't want you to do anything that you would find uncomfortable or think would be ineffective, but would you be willing to..." This lets your hearer know that you understand that you are not expecting the unreasonable.

12. Networking is figuring out who knows whom

There are some introductions you want badly. When cold phone calls are either ignored or passed to a lower and inappropriate level, when you don't know anyone inside, a friend of a friend can get you in the door. You must ask yourself who might know someone at an appropriate level in this company. This requires research and a good fix on who it is you want to talk with—who has the likely business and personal contacts. What schools did the person you want to talk to attend? Does he serve on any boards? Does he belong to any trade associations or clubs? Where does he live?

Mary Davis of Jannotta, Bray & Associates, an expert networker, often quotes the saying that there are never more than six people between you and the person you want to talk to. This can undoubtedly be subjected to a probabilistic proof, but at a practical level works so well that it can be accepted as true. My brother and I once made a game out of it and traced paths well within the six-person limit to such diverse individuals as Saddam Hussein, Queen Elizabeth, and Boris Yeltsin. Within the business world, the chances of being able to trace a short path are even greater.

All experienced networkers trace such paths and use them. Watching Oscar Megerdichian trace a path of contacts back to someone he wanted to meet was awe-inspiring. When you can do this yourself, you will know you have become a pro.

13. Networks age
The unavoidable consequence of this truth is best illustrated by the following story:

> When I first began networking I received immeasurable help from Oscar Megerdichian, who provided me with new business leads and several introductions that lead to the signing of important projects. More valuable still, he taught me the fundamentals of networking. He was the single most valuable network contact I had, and he died.

With Oscar's death I lost a friend I have thought of with surprising frequency, given that our relationship was basically a business one. With it he also taught me one final and important lesson. You must keep expanding your network, or it will contract. I have since noted several marketers who lost their value and sometimes their jobs because they had relied on an established network that had stopped expanding. Gradually, through retirements, deaths, job changes, and relocations, their networks had disappeared.

This never happened to Oscar. To the end he developed new contacts, many, like me, much younger than himself. His network never shrank, and, I believe, he had a richer and more personally rewarding life because of it.

14. Motivation is the most crucial ingredient in effective networking
Networking comes most naturally to extroverted individuals who make friends easily. More introverted individuals often find the concepts intimidating, and so risk discarding this approach to marketing as inappropriate for them without making a serious attempt to try it. This is a mistake. I have qualified as an introvert on every psychological test I ever took. In my experience, an individual who understands the guidelines outlined in this chapter and applies them deliberately and rigorously can outperform many more natural networkers who lack focus. More importantly, he

can successfully bring in business. He can also develop relationships of lasting personal value.

What is most important is a strong motivation to succeed and a sincere desire to help people. If you have ambition and get real pleasure from helping others, you should consider giving networking a serious try for at least a year.

Networking Ethics

I must conclude this chapter with a few comments on networking ethics. Networking is ethically neutral. There are those who use the techniques described here for legitimate business purposes. There are others who use them to fight cancer and promote world peace. Still others use them to peddle drugs, launder money, and fence stolen goods.

The most serious ethical issues for most people surround the exchange of money for introductions, references, or information. When in doubt about the propriety of any money exchange in a networking context, ask yourself these questions:

- *Is it legal?* If it's illegal, don't do it, regardless of how willing others are. Stay away from anyone who has engaged in illegal money exchanges. Just knowing about them may place you in legal jeopardy. Be particularly careful to establish what is legal if you sell to local, state, or federal governments, where you are most likely to run into laws governing exchanges of money for help.

- *Does the client know about and accept the exchange?* If it's legal and the client who is being introduced has no complaints, it is hard to see why anyone else should care.

- *Is it accepted practice?* In some industries this kind of exchange, under the name of a "finders fee," is standard practice. You can assume that most clients know about it without getting into a discussion. Be careful. This criterion becomes murky, with ample room for self-justifying activity that can cause you trouble later.

- *Is it against the rules of any organization you belong to?* Many companies and some trade associations and formal networking groups prohibit this kind of exchange.

Confidential information is another area of common concern. Such information is often more valuable than easy-to-get information. Before giving out confidential information, ask yourself:

- *Do I have a clear obligation to keep it confidential?* If you have signed a confidentiality agreement or verbally promised to keep a confidence, you should do so.

- *How strong is any implied obligation to keep it confidential?* This is a tough judgment, which you will have to make.

- *Has it become public through some other source?* If so, your obligation often ceases.

A final area of concern lies in networking with competitors. This can take two forms. First, you may want to exchange information or other help with a direct competitor of your own firm. Before doing so ask yourself:

- *Is it legal?* Some exchanges of information among competitors are against the law. This is especially likely to be true of pricing information. Avoid any such communications or any that might be interpreted as such.

- *How much do you actually compete with the other firm?* The services of many firms overlap a little. Many furniture dealers offer some design services. Real estate brokers may offer some consulting or space programming services. If there is only a small amount of overlap, you can probably go ahead and network to mutual advantage. The overlap implies a commonalty of interest. Exchanging information with direct competitors may help them win jobs and can get you fired.

When networking with two or more firms that compete with each other, you must also be careful. Sharing information received from one with another is considered unethical among experienced networkers. If you get caught doing it, you will be shunned. Once you have learned the information from another source, the restrictions are often eliminated.

Conclusion

Networking offers one of the strongest business development techniques for professionals. If you are not networking, you should consider doing so. To get started you may want to structure your efforts through a trade association or formal networking group. The next chapter will describe some of the special aspects of marketing through such organizations.

4

Special Rules for Special Networks: Trade Associations, Formal Networking Groups and Internal Networks

Case example: The Man Who Learned to Market

When the firm opened, no one at Madison Pension Services really had to market. The business poured in, and management focused its attention on handling the workload. Actuarial firms were like that in the late 1970s and early 1980s. But it didn't last.

Tax acts, especially the 1986 Tax Reform Act, eliminated many of the financial incentives that businesses had for creating pension plans, and companies began to drop their programs. Boom turned to bust.

"I never planned to be a marketer," says David Gensler, the firm's president. "I had become an actuary because I had a gift for mathematics. I didn't think of myself as a people person. I was happy just being an actuary. Still, when business began to evaporate, I had to do something. I began to call on our clients, a thing we hadn't done enough of. I also began to call on accountants and lawyers who could refer us business."

Two years after he began to market, David joined the Metropolitan Business Network, one of the oldest formal networking groups in the country. "About 10 percent of our new business each years comes from referrals from the members. That's important by itself, but the group has helped me in many other ways. There was no one in my firm who I could learn to market from. The other members of the Network were generous with their help. Participation helped me build my skills, confidence, and morale."

As the number of pension plans continues to decline, David's firm remains strong and has even grown. "I wouldn't go back to the old world in which I didn't have to market, even if I could," he says. "I feel that I'm making much more of a difference now. I'm leaving footprints at the firm."

Every networker builds his personal network over a career. It can be slow work. You can speed up the process by working through an organization, and most good networkers do. The organization may be a trade association, a formal networking group, or his own firm. This chapter describes the special characteristics of working through organizations.

Trade associations

Trade associations provide one of the few opportunities to meet large numbers of potential clients at one place. They offer a legitimate avenue for developing a relationship with prospective clients outside of a strict buyer/seller context. This helps lower the defenses a prospective client may erect when he feels he is being sold. Because others who seek to sell to the same people you do also attend the meetings, associations offer an excellent way to broaden your network of outside contacts.

So much marketing is done through trade associations that they merit a separate section of their own. My comments pertain to associations where your prospective clients constitute the primary membership—you, your competitors, and others who sell to these people constituting an auxiliary membership. Generally, professionals attend meetings of such organizations for different reasons from ones in which they and their peers make up the primary membership. At the former they market; at the latter they learn.

Working a meeting

The most common vehicle for developing contacts through a trade association is the meeting, be it an annual, national, or international gathering lasting several days or a monthly, regional gathering lasting only a few hours. It was my first attempt to work a meeting that drove me to learn more about networking. Feeling lost and intimidated, I walked into a room filled with several hundred people I didn't know. I had a drink, nibbled appetizers, and talked uncomfortably with several people. Later I listened to a dull speaker over a rubber chicken dinner. I left feeling like an outsider. I had wasted my time, and I was just telling myself "Never again," when I ran into two acquaintances on the elevator. Both praised the meeting as one of the most useful and enjoyable they had attended. Obviously I had missed something. It was then that I began my networking survey described in the preceding chapter. Most of the networking guidelines already cited apply to trade association meetings, but a few additional observations may be helpful.

In my experience the principal complaints that professionals make about marketing through trade associations are...

- ■ ...*Crowd intimidation.* For many people, attending a large event at which they know few people is torturous. After all, there are more shy people than gregarious extroverts. Learning specific techniques for working a crowd can help overcome this fear; so can recognizing that it takes two or three meetings to know enough people in an organization to begin to feel comfortable.

- *...Inability to access the in-group.* At every trade association meeting you will find people who are upset because they don't feel a part of the in-group. They complain about the stand-offishness of the regular members who make up the clientele everyone else is trying to meet, and about rules that maintain distinctions between this group and those who wish to sell to them. Don't be distracted by such nonsense. Every community of human beings has an in-group and an out-group. Your need is to become a part of the in-group or, if you cannot, to benefit from the organization while remaining part of the out-group. Complaints often come from those who know least about how to work the organization. I have attended the committee meeting of the associate members of one organization every year for five years and heard the same litany of concerns about this subject each time. While others complained, I obtained leads and contacts by working the meeting that have, on average, resulted in one new client per meeting.

- *...Cost versus return.* Trade associations absorb both time and money. Naturally you expect a return on this investment. In my experience those who complain about inadequate return usually tie it to the concerns already mentioned: Because they are intimidated by the crowds and find it hard to break into the in-group, they reason that the cost of participation does not justify the return. If you overcome the first two concerns, this one should also be resolved. On the other hand, it's possible you may be participating in the wrong organization.

Here are some guidelines for working a trade association.

Work on introductions and relationships rather than selling

The primary purpose of attending association meetings should be to meet people and develop relationships, rather than to sell your services. Once you have a relationship, you can arrange a meeting to discuss your services outside the context of the association. As at most country clubs, it is considered bad form at most association meetings to solicit business unless invited to by a prospective client. This protocol forbidding selling protects members from being inundated with sales pitches every time they go to a meeting, which they attend for another purpose. Prepare a one-minute description of your services to deliver when someone politely asks what your firm does, and reserve any direct selling for 1) those few occasions when someone asks you how you would deal with a specific situation; 2) booths, if you are willing to spend the money for one; or 3) meetings set up for this purpose after the conference is over.

Some organizations explicitly prohibit direct selling, while at others social pressure provides the primary means of communicating appropriate behavior. Everyone knows you are there to sell, but you are expected to keep within limits. Acceptable behavior includes...

- ...introducing yourself.
- ...exchanging business cards.
- ...talking about almost any subject other than your interest in doing business with the person you are talking with.
- ...asking for information about a company. The opportunity to gain information is one of the great benefits of trade association meetings.
- ...asking whether you can call in a week or two to discuss your company, if a person seems receptive.

Meet as many people as you can

Since the primary objective of attending is to meet people, you should avail yourself of every opportunity to do so, beginning as soon as possible and lasting until the bitter end. I have made several valuable contacts by sharing cabs to and from airports. Lines for food provide good opportunities for casual conversation with those waiting in front of you and behind you. So are lines for hotel registration and meeting check-in. Tours, exhibit halls, and meals provide other opportunities. When you attend a session, introduce yourself to those sitting on either side and behind you. Although it is considered odd to walk up to someone on the street and introduce yourself, this behavior is expected at an association meeting. Take advantage of this rare benefit.

Keep the conversation light. Say something nice about the other person's company or ask a few questions about it. Talk for a while and then move on to someone else.·

Breaking into a group that is conversing at a reception or other quasi-social event at a meeting is perfectly acceptable, so long as you show appropriate sensitivity. Most conversation is small talk and is open to anyone. You can enter a group holding such a conversation in several ways. The easiest is to find someone you know in the group and stand next to him or her. Otherwise, observe the group for a moment or two to see who is dominating the conversation. Enter the group and listen politely, then ask this individual a question. This shows that you are sensitive to the dynamics of the group. After you get your answer, ask another question of someone else. This shows you are sensitive to other people's desire to talk. Occasionally a group will be engaged in a serious conversation about a business or personal issue. Unless you have something significant to add, you should politely move on to another group.

Avoid getting trapped by the lost soul who doesn't know anyone and is unwilling to make the effort to meet people. He will bend your ear all night. Polite breaking-away techniques include going to get another drink or appetizer, seeing someone you have to talk to, or introducing the lost soul to a third individual (you don't have to know the third individual to do so) and shortly thereafter leaving them to talk with each other.

You should also avoid hanging around with those you know and are most comfortable with, especially other employees from your own firm. Staying with those you know is particularly tempting during the first meeting you attend, when you know few people. If you work hard at making new contacts, you will find the temptation much lower at your second or third meeting, as you find yourself with a much broader range of acquaintances.

Arrive early at local meetings held over a meal or in the evening. Most socializing occurs before the formal meeting begins, and participants usually depart promptly to get back to work or home once the event is over.

Keep track of whom you have met

As soon as possible after meeting someone, without being obvious, make a note of his or her name and company so that you can follow up later with a letter. Exchange business cards as often as possible. Effective networkers keep careful track of whom they meet. After a meeting at which you have met between a dozen and a hundred people, memory will fade quickly unless you keep a record.

Large annual meetings usually provide lists of registrants. Review these when you arrive and note whom you want to find. Each evening, review the list to monitor your progress. At local meetings, name tags are often laid out on a table at the door. Arriving early allows you to peruse the tags to see who will attend.

Make it easy for people to know you

Of course, your sole objective isn't just to get to know other people; you also want them to get to know you. Make this as easy as possible. Wear your name tag on the right so that it is turned toward a contact when you first shake hands. If you fill the tag in yourself, take pains to make your writing large and legible. When you introduce yourself, speak slowly and clearly. If possible, create some immediate link to the person you are talking with. Are you likely to know someone in common? Explore the issue. I have already noted how good Oscar Megerdichian was at this. Since meeting him I have met several others who do the same thing. They are all superb networkers. Have you or your firm worked for his company? Make note of the fact.

When you meet someone, keep up strong eye contact and devote your full attention, whether or not you perceive the person to be an important contact. This is not just polite, it is also good business. You never know who knows whom and who can help you. Some of the people who have provided me the most help over the years did not at first look as if they could. If you are at a loss for conversation, ask a question or two. Most people would rather talk than listen and will be flattered to have the opportunity. Those who do 80 percent of the talking are most likely to remember the interesting conversation they had with you, especially if the 20 percent of the talking you do is thoughtful and makes them feel good or laugh.

Be cooperative with others who are there to market

You are unlikely to be the only individual attending a meeting to market. Cooperating with others who are there for the same reason will often bring benefits.

You will also be more memorable if you play host, introducing new people into the group, drawing out those who talk least, and otherwise oiling the machinery of the conversation. This is particularly important at meals, where you may be tempted to monopolize the conversation of a prospective client on your right while ignoring the others at the table, especially the people on your prospect's right and on your left. Make a strong effort to bring them into your conversation. Others trying to make contacts are particularly appreciative of such help and will be more likely to help you later when you want an introduction. The prospect will also be impressed by your courtesy and mark you down as a reasonable person.

Find reasons to recontact prospective clients after the meeting

An important objective of attending a meeting should be to obtain a reason to follow up later with as many prospective clients as possible. The best way to do this is to find some small favor that you can do for them that obliges you to recontact them later. What the favor is doesn't matter, though it is nice if it ties into your business. The obligation may be to provide a book reference, a referral to a business contact, a clarification of some technical issue, or the name of a good restaurant in Nice. It doesn't much matter as long as it's something the prospective client wants. The obligation ensures that he will take your call later when strictures about selling are less severe. It also distinguishes you as an individual who is helpful rather than someone solely interested making a sale. It gets the relationship off on a friendly footing. That is why an effective networker will come away from a room full of people with five or six small things to do while the ineffective one will come away empty-handed.

Follow up after the meeting

Once the meeting is over, you must follow up as soon as possible, preferably within one week but at least within two. During this period your contacts' memories of you and their lingering sense of obligation to be friendly remain. These things decline with age. Break the list of contacts you have made into two groups: those requiring a phone call and those requiring a letter. I have never received business from someone I met at an association meeting whom I did not follow up with later, and I have been more effective than most. I have a friend who worked a particular association for many years and was inherently more extroverted and effective at small talk than I am. However, he never followed up after a meeting, and he produced many fewer leads and sales than I did.

To be effective a letter must sound personalized, even if several sentences are repeated in many letters. For this reason, when I note someone's name and company, I often jot down something I learned about the person or something that occurred when we met, knowing that after meeting many people over a short time I will need a memory jogger. A three- or four-word reminder can help recall an entire conversation. One of the most effective networkers I know owes a lot to his brilliance at personalizing follow-ups. His letters and phone calls always make you feel selected and specially recognized. This should be the objective of all of your follow-ups. Exhibit 4.1 provides right and wrong examples of leads to letters.

Exhibit 4.1

Personalized Follow-up Has Much Greater Impact

Right

>Dear Arnie:
>
>Ever since the ADVAC meeting I have laughed every time I recalled your comments on small-town Iowa. They took me back to my own childhood in Minnesota...
>
>Dear Jenny:
>
>I enjoyed our stimulating discussion of national health insurance at the ADVAC meeting. Until you told me, I didn't realize the cost to our country of having so many people uninsured. You have explained the issues better than anyone else I know. It is...

Wrong

>Dear Peter:
>
>It was good to meet you at the ADVAC meeting. If you ever need a...

Get to know the staff

Make a point of meeting and getting to know the staff of the trade associations you participate in. The staff often influence who participates in committees, who gets selected as speakers, and who gets offered the chance to serve as officers. They can provide information and guidance in a number of areas. Often they need help, too. They may need someone to do committee drudge work or write an article for the association's journal. Knowing and helping such people will help you participate more effectively in the organization.

Participate regularly

A trade association's strength is measured according to the support of its members. The most fundamental measure of support is member participation. Year-to-year attendance levels at national meetings are tracked with as much attention as year-to-year sales are tracked by a corporation. You will not be considered a serious player if you do not participate regularly. You will never make it into the in-group. Regular attendance is often a prerequisite to committee participation and other signs of advancement within the organization.

You will also wish to volunteer selectively to help in committee work. This will give you an opportunity to work with prospective clients in a non-selling environment, which in turn will help greatly in establishing relationships. When a committee you are serving on looks for a secretary, consider volunteering. This job provides you particularly good opportunities to work with other members.

Public speaking and writing articles for an association's publication are other ways to increase your visibility.

Pick the associations you work with carefully

It is not always easy to tell at a distance whether a particular organization is worth participating in. Often you will have to attend a meeting to find out, and sometimes you will have to attend several. Regional and national meetings of an organization can attract very different cross-sections of the membership, and participation often varies heavily from region to region. It may take several meetings to sort out who the other participants are and whether participation is likely to produce long-term value.

When I first participate in an organization, I look to see whether I can find any past clients or prospects among the attendees. If I can, this is a strong signal that other prospective clients will be there too. Early in her career an employee of mine, who was an excellent networker, attended three consecutive meetings of a trade association in hopes of turning up work. I attended the third meeting as a speaker and found one past client among the 1,200 participants. When I commented on this, she began to work a different organization with greater success. After a careful determination that a specific organization will not provide a good return on your time, it is important to cut bait and devote your scarce marketing time and money elsewhere. This can be hard if you enjoy the company of the people you have met, as my employee had. I respect her for coming to the conclusion that she should look elsewhere for prospects.

I have also known several trade association junkies during my career. Having had success with a particular organization, they seek out others to repeat the process. Since for most professional practices there are a limited number of organizations in which significant numbers of clients participate, such efforts are often frustrated.

The *Encyclopedia of Associations*[1] provides information on most trade associations in the country. You can find this reference book in most libraries.

Trade associations play an important role in the marketing of professional services. Where else can you find so many prospective clients gathered in one place, free from the corporate gatekeepers who screen their phone calls? Where else is it so acceptable to introduce yourself to total strangers? The regular pattern of meetings also provides a structure to marketing efforts that many professionals have difficulty imposing upon themselves. These last two advantages are shared by formal networking groups, which warrant a few comments of their own.

Formal networking groups

In many cities groups of business people meet regularly with the unabashed purpose of helping each other get business. Some of these are branches of national or regional chains. Others are independent organizations. Most of the participants are small business people: stationery suppliers, printers, travel agents, and the like. Almost all have a heavy representation from area professionals. Though participation by large firms is less common, a committed player from a large organization can do well. The case example at the beginning of this chapter describes the benefits that one professional has received from belonging to such a group. For the sole practitioner or member of a small firm, the structure, motivational support, and informal training these groups provide can be major attractions.

A little asking around will help you find groups in your area. Exhibit 4.2 provides a list of some of the national and regional chains. If you can't find one that is suitable, consider forming your own.

Exhibit 4.2

Formal Networking Groups

Formal networking groups exist in many cities. Most are unaffiliated with any other organization. The only way to find them is to ask area business people if they know of them. Chains of clubs are run by:

- Ali Lassen's Leads Club, P.O. Box 279-7797, Carlsbad, CA 92018. Telephone: 619/434-3761. (Roughly 300 chapters.)
- Business Network International, 268 Bucknell Avenue, Claremont, CA 91711. Telephone: 1/800/688-9394. (Over 200 chapters.)
- LeTip International Inc., 4926 Savannah Street, Suite 175, San Diego, CA 92110. Telephone: 1/800/255-3847. (Roughly 400 chapters.)

Regional chains are run by Creative Referral Networks (Kansas City area), The Business Resource Group (Northern Virginia), and Team Network Corporation (Washington, D.C., area).

These groups formalize many of the networking guidelines provided in the last chapter. Following are some of the common practices.

Helping each other

This is the avowed purpose of the organization. To ensure that it happens, most have exclusivity rules: Only one member is allowed for a specific business, in order that intragroup competition for business, which would inhibit cooperation, may be avoided. Many devote a portion of each meeting to sharing leads. Small groups of members will sit around tables and offer or ask for help at specific companies. Many organization use a form to track the number of leads provided by each member, and some require minimum quotas. At the good ones, if you don't contribute over the course of a year, the executive committee will ask you to leave. This preserves a sense of urgency and obligation.

Recognizing leads for others' services.

Formal networking groups expend a lot of effort helping the members learn about each others' services so that each will recognize leads for others when they hear them. At each meeting at least one member will describe his services, his customers, and what he sees as a good business opportunity. Members are also expected to make "house calls," one-on-one meetings between pairs of members that take place between regular meetings.

Sincere effort

Groups recognize that some individuals will be able to give more leads than others, and they accept that. They also recognize that Member A may be able to give leads to Member B, but that B will not have many opportunities to give to A. As long as B gives to someone else in the group, the one-way flow is accepted.

Gratitude

At each meeting, each member has an opportunity to publicly thank those in the group who have helped him.

Trust

A serious networking group will quickly drop anyone who violates trusts. Trust is also developed through regular contact resulting from meetings and house calls and from seeing members help each other. Because all new members are referred by existing ones, trustworthy people tend to get admitted, if a group functions well.

Time commitment

Networking is time consuming, and formal groups require a serious commitment of member time. Groups usually meet semimonthly for breakfast for about two hours. Add to that travel time, house calls, phone calls, and time devoted to helping others, and the group will easily demand 5 percent of your available time. If you cannot commit that much time or would not find doing so worthwhile, don't join a formal group. On the other hand, if you have difficulty imposing the self-discipline that networking requires, the structure of a formal group may help you.

I have participated in two such organizations in my career and found both valuable. The first ceased to work once several key members left, and the second was begun by three individuals dissatisfied with a similar organization they had participated in before. If you have a chance to join a formal networking group, ask yourself these questions before accepting:

- *Do I have anything to give to these individuals?* You have to give to get. You will want to ascertain that enough of the members sell to the same market you do for your contacts to be worthwhile.
- *What is the probability that the return I get from them is worth 5 percent of my time?*
- *Are the members serious and do they understand networking?*

Internal networks

Many professionals work for large firms offering a variety of services, which are delivered by different business units. These units are usually called "practices" in accounting, consulting, and law firms, and "studios" in architectural firms. In such cases firms grow by cross-marketing, that is, from staff members in one practice introducing their clients to staff members in another practice. Firm management can encourage cross-marketing through incentives and communications programs, but can seldom mandate them, the client/professional relationship being too sensitive to permit strong-arm tactics. A partner at a large accounting and consulting firm struggling with this problem noted that cross-marketing deteriorated markedly when several consulting assignments went sour at once. Reviving the effort, even after the consulting operation had been overhauled, proved difficult.

At large, multipractice firms the emerging marketer must make friends in other practices and induce them to help her get business. In short, she must network. While operating fundamentally on the same principles as external networks, internal networks deserve some comments of their own.

The professional who assumes that sales will be had more easily when working with an internal network than an external one will be quickly jolted out of her naiveté. The opportunity to cross-market within a firm is easier than working an outside network in some ways and harder in others. On the positive side, it results in...

- ...*clout.* Top management encourages cross-marketing through incentives, communications programs, and occasionally threats, because it is a way to increase revenues and profits.

- ...*eased access.* Most professionals will extend the courtesy of meeting with another member of their firm on request. This isn't always the case when dealing with external contacts.

- ...*exclusivity.* In external networks, exclusive relationships can be difficult to capture. The best sources of leads often want to spread their help among many contacts to earn good will from as many people as possible. They will give to your competitors as readily as they will to you. The potential for capturing an exclusive relationship is greater in an internal network.

- ...*reflected good will.* If one practice has a good relationship with a client, he will be inclined to look favorably on buying other services from the same firm.

Against these benefits must be weighed...

- ...*resentment and distrust.* A noticeable percentage of professionals are distrustful of working with others outside their practices. They are not predisposed to network with anyone. This distrust is only increased when they feel a relationship is being forced on them.

- ...*lowered perceived objectivity.* When you recommend another company, your recommendation will often be seen as objective. Proper networking means you will only refer the best. Clients will not perceive the same level of objectivity when you recommend another part of your own firm.

- ...*increased downside risk.* If an external contact you have referred lets your client down, it can hurt your own relationship with the client. If the contact is internal it will almost certainly do so. First, you and the contact share the same firm name. Second, your recommendation is likely to appear more self-serving and is therefore less likely to be seen as an honest mistake.

There are several rules to follow when dealing with internal networks.

Treat them the way you would any other network

Do not expect others in the firm to refer you business just because management wants them to. They may not know enough about your services to recognize a lead for you. They may not want to risk a valued client relationship by bringing in someone who might spoil it.

You must follow all of the guidelines for external networks. You must help your internal contacts, contact them frequently, show how your services will help them with the client, and do all the other things outlined in the first chapter on networking. That is how you will earn trust.

Leave arm twisting to the senior management, which wants cross-marketing to occur.

Recognize that the benefits of helping you are somewhat different from those received by external contacts

Internal contacts can benefit from helping you in ways that external contacts can't. They may receive a cash incentive for a referral, recognition within the firm, increased potential for promotion, and a deeper relationship with their own clients. These are the benefits you have to sell.

Of particular importance is recognition. When someone else in your company helps you make a sale, do everything you can to make sure her help is recognized. You can...

- ...*send her a thank-you letter* with a copy to her boss and her boss's boss. It will go into her personnel file.

- ...*have your boss send a letter to her boss.* Often, the higher up the recognition comes from, the more it is valued.

- ...*submit her name for an award.* Many firms have awards programs. Look into them to see whether any offers an appropriate means of showing appreciation for help received. If none exists, consider creating your own and publicizing it.

- ...*thank her in a public forum.* Don't just say thanks. Make it clear exactly what she did for you and how valuable it was to the firm and to you, personally.

- *Make sure she is mentioned for her help in the firm newsletter.*

Judge internal contacts by somewhat different standards from those you use for external ones

You will eventually drop an external contact who gives you no leads. When dealing with internal networks, you must adopt different standards. You must ask what the individual does for the firm. If the work you help her get adds significant revenues and profits to the firm, you should continue to extend help, even if you receive no direct return. You must hope that you are judged in the same way.

Expect moderately increased collections problems

In many large firms the individual responsible for a major account must approve all billing to it. This individual looks at two issues that you might not before approving a bill: the good of the firm and his own skin. This means that if the client is unhappy with your service, the account rep is less likely to take a strong collections approach than you might, because he wants to guard a larger relationship. This is a cost of the lowered perceived objectivity cited previously. Once in a while an account rep will make a freebee of your service in order to mollify a client unhappy with the rep's own work. In such cases the rep seldom pays for your service himself.

If you understand that the structure of internal networks makes such events inevitable, if infrequent, they will anger you less. Judge each case on its own merits and either drop it or appeal to a higher authority. Get on with life as quickly as you can.

Organizations provide a structure for networking. They permit you to make many new contacts in a short time and to build relationships that can be the source of new business. Any beginning networker should consider working through one.

5

Building Client Relationships
That Last

Case example: The Friend

"It has always been my belief that if you do exceptional work, business will come to you," says Bruce Pritkin, a tax accountant with Robbins Spielman Slayton & Halfon, a mid-sized Manhattan accounting firm. *His relationship with Larry, the owner of a plumbing supply company, exemplifies this approach to business development. When Larry became dissatisfied with the partner he had worked with at a small accounting firm, he transferred his business to Bruce, then a junior partner at the firm. Bruce cleaned up several problems that had been caused by his predecessor. His predecessor had recommended against Larry's setting up a pension; Bruce showed that it would not only work, it would defer Larry's taxes, giving him use of the money until retirement.*

As he learned about Larry's business and personal finances, Bruce suggested other ways to save money. Estate planning was a big issue for this family business, which was to be passed to Larry from his father. Bruce came up with a plan that greatly reduced estate taxes when Larry's father died. Larry could see that his new accountant was thinking about his interests in ways that went beyond the strict requirements of the job. He liked this, and he liked the young accountant who was taking such good care of him. They became personal friends, socializing together. He began to recommend Bruce to his friends, and Bruce's practice grew. When Bruce moved to Robbins Spielman, these accounts went with him. Larry recommended Bruce to more friends, and his practice continued to grow. Says Bruce, "I network and give speeches and do other things to find new business, but the core of my practice is based on referrals from clients who like the work I do. I have always believed that good work brings in new business."

"Everyone says that you should expend 80 percent of your marketing effort on your existing clients and 20 percent on new ones, but we don't do it any more than anyone else does," one of my first clients told me. I have heard the same message many times since.

A few firms do direct most of their marketing at existing clients and reap tremendous rewards. But most don't, even though they know they should. Why is this?

The answer lies at both organizational and individual levels. To win a new client an organization must mobilize its best marketing resources toward a specific opportunity. The period when many players must be involved usually runs a few months. For a relationship-marketing program, a firm must marshal all of its employees who have consistent client contact. If the program has a beginning, it has no end. In other words, the firm must increase the marketing capabilities of a large group of people and keep them at it for a long time. That is hard—much harder than going after a few new clients.

At the individual level, the difficulty your company has with relationship marketing should not distract you. You can run your own program. Developing a strong relationship with your clients will help ensure that your firm is considered when they have additional business. It will generate referrals. Even one client who actively boosts your services to his friends can have a major impact on your business. As one attorney who works hard at relationship building told me, "I have one client who believes in what we do. He refers me three or four new people each year. If I had a few more like him, I'd never have to make another sales call." Strong client relationships will also improve the quality of your references. If you want these benefits, first review the common obstacles individual professionals face in getting them. These are:

Lack of client contact. Relationship marketing isn't for everyone. Some people within a firm don't have much contact with clients. Some practices don't require much client contact, and some people within a firm do work that requires little. If you have little contact with your clients, you should probably invest your time on other kinds of marketing. Later, when your position within the firm changes, you can reconsider this approach.

Lack of time. This is the perennial excuse, and the answer is the same as it is for any other type of marketing: Since marketing is essential if you want your career to prosper, you must structure your effort so as to fit relationship marketing within your busy schedule.

Perception that the client doesn't want more than a project-based, business relationship. This concern arises in project-based practices. When a project ends, the relationship between professional and client changes. The professional has little business need to maintain contact, so if she calls the client, it must be for different reasons than the ones she is accustomed to. Many find it difficult to make this adjustment, especially when new projects demand their attention. The client also perceives a change and may be slower in returning phone calls. Many professionals read this as a signal that the relationship is cooling, an interpretation that may well not be valid. If a professional does not really want a deeper relationship with the client, she is likely to decide that the feeling is mutual, and so excuse herself from further effort. She may also generalize from one unsuccessful effort to all past clients.

If you recognize this pattern in your own experiences, you would do best to confront it. This chapter will provide you with some guidelines to make relationship marketing easier and more effective. If the guidelines make sense to you, give the approach another try, but if relationship marketing still seems wrong for you, perhaps you should explore some other kinds of marketing.

As the name suggests, relationship marketing requires relationship-building skills not unlike those used in networking. Indeed, relationship marketing *is* networking, only with a specific kind of contact—your clients. If you have not read chapter 3 on networking, you should do so now. Most of what you find there applies to relationship marketing as well.

Guidelines specific to relationship marketing are as follows.

Develop a relationship as early as you can
You should begin developing a relationship while you have obvious business reasons for being in contact. This can start in modest ways, such as gathering information about the prospect and establishing a rapport during the selling process. One consultant I know who has built a million-dollar practice believes this is the best way to start and maintain relationships. As he put it to me, "It takes a long time to develop business because you have to build a prospect into your network before he hires you. At a minimum that takes months."

Once you have signed a client and begun to work with him, the effort can heat up. Then you will realize that there is no such thing as small talk with a client. Instead, there is project talk and long-term marketing talk. It is during relaxed moments, when you talk about the weather, sports, a coming election, a client's children, and any other issue not related to the project, that you learn about your client as a person and begin to develop a relationship. Record this information later if you are likely to forget it.

Learn about your client
In networking you must learn about a contact's business so that you will recognize a lead for him when you hear it. In relationship marketing you must learn about your clients as individuals and as companies, so that you know how to engage them in a relationship. Exhibit 5.1 is a form for recording information on an individual. Review it, then try filling copies out for a few individuals at your best client company and see how much you really know. You should try to fill out forms for two or three different individuals at the client company, since ideally, you will have a relationship with more than one person, if the account is a large one. Review your answers and ask yourself whether you really know this client.

Information can come from many sources. *Who's Who* books provide concise descriptions of many individuals. Annual reports and 10-k forms provide a good initial source for companies. A 10-k is a form that all publicly held companies must file with the Securities Exchange Commission. It is usually available from a

Exhibit 5.1

Client Information Form: Individual

(To the categories shown here, add others specific to your practice.)

Name: _____

Title: _____

Company: _____

Address: _____

_____   Secretary's Name: _____

Phone: _____   Phone: _____

FAX: _____

Reporting relationship:

1. Boss's boss

   Name: _____

   Title: _____

2. Boss

   Name: _____

   Title: _____

3. Key Peers

   Name: _____   Name: _____

   Title: _____   Title: _____

4. Reports to:

   Name: _____   Name: _____

   Title: _____   Title: _____

Explanation (key responsibilities, probable successors, nature of relationships, etc.):

_____

_____

_____

_____

_____

Background (attach resume, if you have one):

Where raised: _____

Education: _____

_____

Previous employers: _____

_____

Career concerns (aspirations, fears, needs):

_____

_____

_____

_____

Personal Information:

Town of residence: _____

Spouse's name: _____ Occupation: _____

Employer: _____

Children's Names:	Approximate Ages	School
_____	_____	_____
_____	_____	_____
_____	_____	_____
_____	_____	_____
_____	_____	_____

Interests:

_____

_____

_____

_____

Memberships:

_____

_____

_____

_____

Other Information:

_____

_____

_____

company's public relations department upon request, no questions asked. A brief literature search in the library may also turn up articles about the company and its employees. Other vendors or a "coach" inside the company can also provide helpful insights.

When I think it is appropriate, I ask a secretary for resumes of individuals I will be meeting at a company I am selling to. Resumes provide excellent background information that might take months to gather in casual conversation.

All of these sources can be helpful, but conversation with your client will still provide the most information, especially about sensitive or personal issues. Gathering this information requires patience and tact, because appearing intrusive will damage your incipient relationship. Use your good sense. If asking a question seems appropriate, ask it. If not, hold off. Questions like, "Were you raised in this area?" are acceptable to most people after brief acquaintance. The answer may provide a variety of interesting information and grist for further conversation. If you learn that someone holds the same degree you do—you are both attorneys, say, or mechanical engineers—it is appropriate to ask where she got her degree and perhaps explore her career. If you do not share a degree, these questions may be less appropriate immediately after meeting. Like all conversations, what is right depends upon who is there and how comfortable the parties feel with each other. You must judge each situation.

The point is, if you never ask, you never learn. Most professionals err by being uninterested or too cautious. Others engage in "small talk" but make no further use of what they learn. Clients, like other people, like to talk about themselves and usually appreciate your interest. In return they provide valuable information about themselves as human beings that forms the basis for the future give-and-take of a relationship.

When someone doesn't like a question, he will send signals quickly, in the form of short answers and body language, that you have gone too far. If this happens, back off immediately. But if you exercise reasonable social judgment, it won't happen very often.

A few of my clients initially say that information gathering as I have described it here would make them feel hypocritical. I am not recommending an insincere interest in other people's affairs. I am simply suggesting that you treat a client with the same attentiveness that you would offer someone who had been brought by a friend to dinner at your house. Show the same interest in your clients that you would in such a guest by asking friendly questions.

When a client answers your questions about non-business issues, he will expect some return. That is natural. Conversations go in two directions. As appropriate, volunteer information about yourself. That, too, will further the relationship.

Different kinds of relationships are appropriate with different people

Your situation or your client's may preclude certain kinds of relationships and encourage others. All professionals must be careful not to let personal relationships interfere with their professional objectivity. Even the perception of lost objectivity can damage reputations, particularly in fields like auditing. Without rekindling the lengthy debates on how close a professional may acceptably get to a client, I suggest that you consider this issue in the context of your own practice and its standards for objectivity. In some fields the constraints are slight. Client companies also differ in the closeness they permit between their employees and outside professionals.

There can be little objection to developing a strong business relationship, one in which you are seen as a source of help and information on an array of subjects that go beyond your particular expertise, and in which you are perceived to be an enjoyable person to do business with. Achieve such a relationship and you will be far ahead of most of your competitors.

A client's personality will also determine the kind of relationship available to you. A number of authors have written about different personality types and what they imply about buyer/seller relationships. I recommend Jim Cathcart's *Relationship Selling* [1] to those who want to pursue the subject. If you are at all sensitive to others' personalities, you will adapt naturally to those who want an all-business relationship, those who like to socialize, those who want to talk, those who want to learn, those who want recognition, those who want a safe person to talk to, and so on. Relationship marketing depends on being able to figure out what kind of relationship a client wants and, so far as it is possible, giving it to him.

Needs change over time. A client who has gained confidence in your work or discretion may allow you to get closer. One who has begun to fear for his job may look for closer relationships outside his company than he has had in the past. A part of relationship marketing is monitoring the client's changing relationship needs.

Different clients want different kinds of help

Networking is helping people. This fundamental rule applies as fully to relationship marketing as it does to any kind of networking. And, as is always the case, the receiver, not the giver, defines "help." Different clients want different kinds of help, and it is your job to determine what they want. Your objective should be to become one of the circle of people the client calls on to talk over knotty problems. He will do so if he learns that you are thoughtful and provide help.

Exhibit 5.2 suggests some of the kinds of help you can provide to clients. The most crucial is good service. Unless you do well what they are paying you to do, you will have little hope of developing a relationship. That is why those few firms that do relationship marketing usually offer superior service. They have decided to build their practices on relationships with existing clients, and in making that choice, have subordinated all other marketing efforts to making their clients happy. This becomes the top concern of the CEO, with everyone else falling in line. As one mechanical engineer and superb relationship marketer put it to me, "We decided to do what everyone else talks about but never does, and really focus on our existing clients. Our strategy is to provide them with such good service that they sole-source us on most the projects we do. The way our teams are organized, the way we provide all sorts of free help, the way we hire our staff; everything we do is focused on that objective. We only seek to add two new clients a year, because that's all we can absorb. But when we get a new client, we keep it." That his company doubled in size between 1990 and 1993 during a severe recession in the construction industries testifies to the firm's effectiveness.

Exhibit 5.2

Help Checklist

I. Good service
   A. On time or early
   B. On or under budget
   C. With sensitivity to human impact
   D. With a minimum of disruption
   E. At a fair price
II. Free or discounted service
III. Business information
   A. Information about his own company
   B. Information that will help him do his job better
      1. Information on the impact of new laws/regulations
      2. Information on techniques and methods
      3. Information on information sources
   C. Ideas
   D. About customers or prospective customers
   E. About a competitor
IV. Introductions, referrals, or references
   A. To prospective customers
   B. To vendors
   C. To prospective employees
   D. To potential allies
V. Publicity
VI. Personal support
   A. Congratulations
   B. Condolences
   C. Empathy
   D. Recognition
      1. With his boss
      2. By listening
      3. With complements
      4. With awards
      5. By seeking advice
   E. Information
   F. Introductions, especially to prospective employers
   G. Friendship

This kind of marketing usually goes beyond providing good service. Professionals who build strong client relationships are eager to help in many ways. Notes a partner at a major international law firm, an astute relationship marketer, "It always frustrates me when a young attorney doesn't respond to a former client who has called up because his boss, the chairman, has asked him to look into some squirrelly idea. Some people see it as a distraction, but it's an opportunity to really help the guy. That's when you build loyalty. And you don't charge for it."

Relationship marketers don't expect their clients to pay for every minute given. All recognize that they are seeking a friendship with their clients, though in some cases it may be a friendship restricted to business. Friends help each other. Friends don't ask for money for every favor done, and they don't keep score. But friends don't take advantage, either. Relationship marketers know that when a client friend asks a favor, he will return it later if he can and when it is appropriate. Call it a marketing cost if you will, although relationship marketers tend not to see it that way. They sincerely like their clients and enjoy helping them.

For several years I had this kind of relationship with the head of personnel at a large automotive company. Because he had tact and intelligence, the CEO gave him most of the quirky assignments that didn't fit naturally in any department. He would call me from time to time to discuss his latest assignment, and I would give what help I could—free. About every fifth call, I would get a consulting project, sometimes a small one, sometimes big. He appreciated the help I gave him and gave me work when it was appropriate.

Help given freely and sincerely can generate the kind of loyalty that is the goal of relationship marketing. One accountant who had built a successful practice over twenty years put it this way: "This year some of my clients have had a hard time paying because business has been so bad. My partners are upset because I don't push them harder. But some of these companies have been with the firm for twenty years. Some are family companies, and I worked with the fathers and now I'm working with their children. They've stood by me all these years. I can afford the slow payment now. I know I'll get my money." Is it any surprise that clients show loyalty to someone who shows so much loyalty to them?

Of course, you must give this kind of help with caution. You should not give away services that are a part of the mainstream of your business, services that a client should and probably does expect to pay for. You must be careful to ensure that your view of what and how much should be given away is in sync with the management of your firm. But you cannot relationship market if your clients find that they have to pay every time they ask your advice.

NB.
DRAW
THE
LINE.

Relationships are based on trust

To a client this means:

- You will do good work
- You will not embarrass me
- You will treat me honestly and fairly
- You will look after my interests first
- You are interested in me as a person

There is an implicit understanding in business that if you do these things for the client he will do his best to give you additional business.

Many professionals deliver on these five points and then are surprised when the next project goes elsewhere. They forget two things. First, people buy on feelings and use facts to justify what they feel. If you do not have a strong relationship with your client that goes beyond the project you have just completed, he may know but not feel that you have delivered. Loyalty will be low. Relationship marketing helps you convert good work into good feelings, and trust is a feeling, not a fact

Second, sometimes a past client cannot help you regardless of his feelings. Relationships do not guarantee a specific piece of future business any more than any other marketing activity does. Marketing is a numbers game. Work at it long and hard enough and you will see the return.

Relationships require frequent contact

To have a relationship with someone you must talk with her regularly, especially while the relationship is developing. This is why it is so important to begin working on the relationship while you have an ongoing project with a client. You have good reason for frequent contact.

But what happens when the project is over and your principal reason for staying in touch goes away? You can call from time to time just to see how she is doing, but unless the relationship is already close, doing so too often will seem strange. Worse, it may mark you as a nuisance.

Alfred Hitchcock used to say that every movie needs a "MacGuffin," or a reason why the characters do what they do. It gets the action rolling but doesn't really intrude on the action itself. You need MacGuffins too, to legitimize your call. A good MacGuffin gives a call information and urgency that justify taking a client's time. It is not a trick but a valid reason for calling that also permits you to stay in contact.

All your research on your client and your analysis of ways you might help should provide you with an understanding of what a client wants and needs to hear. Some MacGuffins I have used over the past week include:

MacGuffin	*Type of Help*
Request advice on book content (4 contacts)	Recognition
Thank-you for referral (2 contacts)	Recognition
Congratulate on promotion	Personal support
Request name of vendor	Recognition
Refer possible job candidate	Introduction
Thank-you for check	Recognition
Offer free consultation	Free service
Provide help on professional association project	Free service
Provide information on potential customer	Information
Request coaching on prospect	Recognition
Provide anecdote for use in speech	Information
Provide article clipped from paper	Information
Offer lead on job search	Personal support

The frequent appearance of "Recognition" may surprise some readers. People like to be seen as authorities, and many feel good about giving advice. Their insights and ideas help me, too. Relationships go two ways. If you have helped a client often, he may be glad to do you a favor, and it will keep him from feeling so beholden to you that the relationship becomes uncomfortable.

All of the contacts I have listed were made both for the reasons expressed in the MacGuffin and because I wanted to stay in touch with these interesting people. That I received a lead for additional business during the process was a nice byproduct.

Staying in contact also means being available when the client needs you. His needs don't always occur when it is most convenient. A labor attorney who represents unions and whose practice is based on relationships notes that the marketers in his firm get calls from clients at all hours. When a client truly sees you as a friend, he feels this is appropriate. If you really are a friend, it is.

Every account should have a relationship strategy

Developing a relationship with one individual is easy; developing one with an organization requires a plan. If you are a sole practitioner, you may be able to develop and manage the plan in your head. If you are a part of a large organization with a variety of people contacting the same client, it better be spelled out. At the very least an account manager should be assigned, someone who will serve as a clearing house for all information on the client and for high-level contacts.

The plan should describe how you will get so close to a client that a competitor will have a difficult time displacing you. First it should identify the information you need about the account and how you intend to get it. Exhibit 5.1 provides a good place to start, but forms are only a tool. Think about the client. What additional questions come to mind, given what you already know about them? The client's organization, products, goals, and problems are all of interest to you. Answers to some questions usually generate further questions.

Second the plan should identify who you need to know and how you will get to know them. A valued account should not depend on a relationship with one individual. This was proven to me when I was asked to run the eastern regional office of a consulting firm. The office was losing money, and I had to turn it around. One morning a senior consultant announced that he had just picked up an assignment from a past client, a big insurance company. I was surprised. I had been totally unaware of this prospect. "Oh, he just called," the consultant told me. "There wasn't any real selling involved. Bill gave me the order over the phone. We'll do the work and send it off to him; he doesn't even want to see us. It's always that way with him." I was horrified. I did not see how we could do a high-quality job without a better understanding of the client's need than we had gotten from the brief phone order. I was also interested in relationships, not order taking.

Bill, it turned out, was a classic all-business type. He would not let us get close to him, but recognizing our need for more information, did arrange meetings with his boss and another vice president. The work we did was better for it. Within six months Bill had been fired in a downsizing, and the other relationships we had initiated preserved our position with the company after he was gone.

If possible, you or someone in your firm should know your contact's boss and his boss's boss, as well as key reports. This is delicate work, because a request to meet others in the company can be threatening to your contact. The work you are doing may offer legitimate reason for requesting an introduction. If so, use it.

Just visiting a client's office intermittently will almost ensure that you meet additional people. At other times a request for nonproject information can result in an introduction to another person in a company, because he is the one who can help you. If you are looking for opportunities to broaden your base of contacts within a company, they will come to you.

Don't overlook secretaries as relationship contacts. Often the secretary will still be around long after your contact has retired, relocated, or quit. If she likes you, she can help you establish a relationship with the new boss.

Some companies have a team strategy for working an account. A firm principal will maintain high-level contact within a client, while members of his team work the lower levels. I have seen several Big Six accounting firms do this effectively. But the process can never be rigid, because personality match must be taken into consideration. A true professional will recognize that someone else in his company is a better match with a particular client and arrange an introduction, rather than trying to develop the relationship himself.

You must develop relationships with the right clients
If you are like most professionals, you don't have enough time to do all of the marketing you want to. Relationship marketing will take a lot of the time you do have, so you had better spend it on the right clients. Among the factors to consider are the following.

- *Probable future need.* Can a company provide sufficient work for you over the next five years to warrant the investment of time you will be making? Is it large enough to offer sufficient work? Do circumstances suggest that it is likely to have needs you can help with? If not, put your time in elsewhere.

- *Work quality.* Will a company permit you to do the quality of work you need to make a profit and build your reputation as a superior firm? If not, look elsewhere.

- *Potential for a relationship.* Some clients simply don't offer much potential for a relationship. It may be culturally difficult for a client to work too closely with one firm. Most universities, for example, make a point of spreading their architectural work among several different firms. A company policy may create a distance, as can a lack of personality fit between you and the key contact. Perhaps management has too deep a relationship with someone else for you to break in. I know an attorney who serves on the board of several companies. His competitors would be ill-advised to spend much time trying to develop a relationship at those companies. In another case a board member disliked a particular architect who had once done some work there. The architect did not waste much time cultivating the account.

Most relationship-marketing programs divide clients into A, B, C, and D accounts. A accounts are those that offer the greatest future potential. They are large clients with ample future need who want and demand the highest-quality work. They warrant the closest possible attention. B accounts may be smaller but still require substantial work. Perhaps they are clients who show reluctance to enter into a relationship. Often they are assigned to emerging marketers in the firm. Typically, less effort is invested in them than on the A accounts. C accounts are still less attractive. A firm will take further assignments from them, if invited, but does not aggressively cultivate a relationship. D accounts, finally, are seen as unattractive. A firm will usually decline further assignments from them, because the work tends to be unprofitable or is unattractive in some other way.

As an exercise, break your existing accounts into these four categories. To be worthwhile, the breakdown must be based on facts, not impressions. Do you know which are your most profitable accounts? If not, make it part of the exercise to find out. Do you know who is most likely to have further work? If not, you have some research to do. Those who go through this exercise are often surprised at what they learn. They often find that marketing time has been misallocated to where the feelings are good, rather than where results are most probable.

If there is someone you like but cannot expect much work from, you don't have to stop seeing him. Recognize that you are doing it for personal reasons and focus your business efforts elsewhere.

Be sensitive to the ethical issues in relationship marketing

Developing a personal relationship with a client can plunge you into ethical situations you had better be aware of before you start. The most obvious is the concern any company might have about an employee's making business decisions on the basis of personal rather than business considerations. Merely for management to question a contact's motives for hiring you would do you and the contact serious damage. The way to avoid this is to provide such superior work that the question never arises. You must make every effort to justify the value of your work by documenting...

- *...the return on the client's investment.* This should always be your first-choice justification. If you can demonstrate that the work you did was returned twenty times over in lowered costs or added revenues, no one will ever question the relationship.

- *...quality of work.* Your responsiveness, the way you have minimized disruption within the firm during a complex project, the satisfaction of constituents within the firm with the results of your work; these should all be documented and shown to the client when you can.

■ ...*cost*. Don't get greedy. If you charge a premium over the market, you must show why you are worth it.

Companies differ in their definitions of what constitutes an appropriate relationship between a vendor, even a professional one, and an employee. Employees of the United States Postal Service have been known to return Christmas cards, because accepting them would be inappropriate. At the other extreme, some people expect to be entertained by the professionals they work with, and the companies they work for have no objections. This means you must understand the culture of each organization you seek to cultivate so that you offer neither too much nor too little. When in doubt, show you are sensitive to the issue in the way you extend an invitation. ("Every company is different in what it feels is appropriate, but if there is no company restriction I would be delighted if you would join me for...") Be careful. An employee who unwisely accepts an invitation he should not may sully your reputation as well as his own. Try to get a sense of how others in the company behave by talking to other vendors and listening to the conversations of several contacts.

At times a professional learns about things happening at a client company that a contact and friend employed there would like to know. Deciding whether to tell him something you have been told in confidence involves the professional in another area of ethical choices. If you do what is professionally correct, the contact will usually understand, but not always. When he doesn't, you can lose a client and a friend. No other alternative is feasible, because to tell him would submerse you in company politics and destroy your professional objectivity. You can, however, do the following.

■ *Warn your contact in advance that you may learn things you will not be able to share.* If you make clear in advance that your professional position must override your friendship in some situations, the problem will be less severe when it occurs. Any such statement must be low-key, or it will borrow trouble by raising concerns before anything happens. I use this approach when I take an assignment to coach emerging marketers in a firm. I make it clear up front that all communication between me and those I am coaching must be kept confidential and that I will not share it or make personnel assessments once I begin the work. To behave otherwise would make it impossible for me to do my job. Management understands this position, and I am protected if an employee tells me in confidence that he is about to quit.

■ *Limit the knowledge to those members of the professional team who do not have a personal relationship with the contact.* Sensitive information can be shared on a need-to-know basis within your firm if you are working in a large professional team. This can sometimes spare you from knowing about something that a contact would expect you to tell. Such arrangements are one of the advantages of having senior members of your firm relate to senior executives at the client firm, and junior members relate to those further down in the reporting hierarchy.

- *Help the contact deal with the information once he learns it, and give the relationship time to recover.* Once the contact learns about the information you have held in confidence, give him as much help as you can consistent with your professional position. With time he is likely to regain perspective and respect you for behaving like a professional. This is especially true if the information you learned is that the contact is about to lose his job.

- *Discourage a contact from telling you things that would place you in a difficult ethical situation.*

Helping a contact find another job is the ultimate form of help in relationship marketing. If you have introduced a contact to a future employer and provided references, he will almost always feel strong loyalty to you later. Your ability to do this can pose a third ethical problem, if your contact is employed at a client company but wants out. If a contact within a client company asks for help finding a job, you should advise him that, because of your professional obligation to his current employer, there are limits to the kind of help you can provide him as long as he is employed there.

Such ethical issues do not come up often, but you need to be prepared to deal with them if you plan a relationship marketing program.

Conclusion

If you have a strong relationship with a client, chances are that you will hear about her needs sooner than your competitors. You may even be the one who helps her clarify exactly what her needs are. When this happens, all your work has delivered you a lead, and you can shift from marketing to selling.

Relationship marketing builds customer loyalty through superior work and attentiveness to clients as people. For the right professional in the right market it can be a powerful way to get business—one that brings in a steady stream of work year after year.

6

Eliminating the Dread
of Cold Calling

Case example: The Cold Callers

Alex saw an unfilled niche in the market and went for it. A principal at the largest architectural firm in an eastern state, he noticed that most of the hospital work in the state was being done by nonresident firms. Wouldn't the administrators prefer to work with a local firm with offices close to their hospitals? Wouldn't they rather work with a firm whose employees and their families lived in the hospitals' service areas? A quick poll of a few administrators brought back the answer, a resounding yes, with the caveat that the local firm had to have hospital experience. Alex's firm had little.

He set to work with Laura, the firm's premier business developer. Unlike many people, Laura had no fear of calling people she didn't know and asking for interviews. She began to line up meetings for Alex with administrators at all of the major hospitals in the state. Through frequent calling she got to know the secretaries by name. She would send them cards when they had been ill and would call and thank them for every bit of help they provided. They worked quietly in her behalf to help set up meetings with their bosses.

At the meetings Alex learned about each hospital's needs, it's decision-making process for hiring architects, and the administrators' experiences, both good and bad, with other firms. The administrators learned about his acute interest in their problems and the high service and design quality his firm offered.

Through cold calls, Alex and Laura learned about impending projects early and established relationships with prospective clients. The administrators advised them on which projects were worth pursuing and how to pursue them. Starting with small projects, they established their reputation in the state as health care architects. Over time they built a strong health care practice based on this work.

A cold call is a visit initiated by you to a prospective client to introduce your firm and its services. While many professionals feel uncomfortable with other kinds of marketing, almost all loathe the cold call. Giving speeches at least conjures up the idea of recognition, respect, and a listening audiences. Networking implies camaraderie and mutual exchange. Cold calling conjures up a vacuum cleaner salesman, an image that few professionals embrace.

Your reaction to cold calling depends, in part, on your profession. In the built-environment industry (architecture, interior design, and consulting engineering) most professionals would acknowledge its usefulness, whether or not they make any cold calls themselves. Accountants, actuaries, lawyers, and management consultants are far more likely to dismiss this approach. Many protest too much, however, when they claim that cold calls simply don't work in the professions. There is ample evidence to show that they do for many practices.

Between 1987 and 1990, a consulting firm specializing in strategy implementation grew its revenues fivefold to well over $100 million a year. An active cold-calling program was the source of most of its new clients. Through cold calling a friend of mine at a large compensation consulting firm developed a profitable practice from a base of zero in spite of protestations from others in the firm that it could not be done. A large law firm succeeded in a major geographic expansion, largely through the cold-calling efforts of a small team. An outplacement firm did the same thing. Such examples prove that cold calling can work for both individual professionals and for firms.

When in doubt, give it a chance. No other technique will get you face to face with so many prospective customers to learn about their specific concerns and to talk directly about what you can do for them.

There are three basic parts to a cold call:

1. Getting a meeting
2. The meeting
3. The follow-up

Getting a meeting

The cold-calling process tends to follow an iterative pattern shown in exhibit 6.1. You initiate contact through a referral from a mutual acquaintance or through a letter. You then phone the target to request a meeting. Once you have met, the process begins again. You follow up with a thank-you letter and request a second meeting either with the same target or with some one he refers you to. The pattern continues until you make a sale or reach a dead end. At each stage in the process your objective is to build relationships and obtain increasing commitments that will ultimately lead to a sale.

Establishing contact

In your initial letter, you may request a meeting, but your true objective is to induce the target to take your phone call. This is a more limited commitment than agreeing to a meeting and so is easier to get. To get it, word the letter in a way that

Exhibit 6.1
Cold Calling Follows an Iterative Pattern

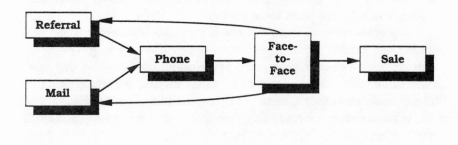

makes a no-answer difficult without the benefit of a phone conversation. This means the letter should be short; the more information you give, the easier it will be for the target to decide not to meet. It should begin with a clear request to talk or meet briefly. It should mention a subject or choice of subjects likely to be seen as important to the target and about which you have specialized knowledge. Subjects might include trends affecting his industry, impending legal or regulatory issues, or opportunities he is likely to be pursuing. This part of the letter should include a one-sentence description of why you would be worth talking with on this subject, if the target is likely to be unfamiliar with your firm. It should close with a vague offer to induce the target to take your call for clarification before deciding whether to meet with you. Exhibit 6.2 provides an example of such a letter.

Exhibit 6.2
Sample Letters

Dear Mr. Hansen:

I will be in Boise several times over the next two months and would like to meet with you. My firm specializes in cost reduction and has recently completed a study of overhead cost structures in the frozen food industry. It covers thirty-two firms and looks at twenty-eight different variables, correlating each with profitability and market share. I thought a discussion of trends in the industry might be of mutual interest.

I will call in the near future to see if we can arrange a meeting.

Sincerely yours,

Dear Ms. Perez:

I would like an opportunity to meet with you. My firm specializes in retail design, and our recent work for Rachel's, Mr. Harper's, and Clothing Bazaar has increased floor space by an average of 7 percent at their downtown stores. All report increased sales since renovations were completed. I thought a discussion of trends in floor layout and design might be of mutual interest.

I will call you in the near future to see if we can arrange a meeting.

Sincerely yours,

When writing the letter avoid being presumptuous. Don't say, for example, "Executives in your position need to know..." Instead, base your claims on your experience: "Many of the natural-gas suppliers I work with have wanted to know..." Don't be arrogant or egotistical. Don't say, "My knowledge of this issue would be valuable..." Once again, build off your experience. It is better to sound tentative than to sound as if you know the target's mind: "I thought the experiences of others in your industry might be of interest to you." Avoid making the target feel he will become obligated by meeting with you. Don't say, "I would be happy to fly to Boise to meet with you." He won't want to incur the burden of asking you to incur such an expense. Say, "I will be in Boise on other business over the next month and would like to take advantage of the opportunity to meet with you." As stated, keep the offer vague: "I hope an exchange of ideas on this issue might be mutually beneficial." He will have to talk with you to figure out what that means. After writing the letter, reread it and see whether there are places where you can replace "I" with "you" by rewording it. This will make it sound more prospect-focused.

Following up by phone

Once you send such a letter, be sure to follow up. Most people don't.

Your next goal is to get the target on the phone. Has this ever happened to you? You call to ask for an appointment with a prospective client. "Is Mr. Arbuthnot in?"

"No," the secretary responds. "He's out until tomorrow. May I take a message?" You hesitate, decline to leave a message, and say you will call back later. Hanging up, you feel disappointed, but also relieved that you did not meet with clear rejection.

What about this? You call a prospective client and are answered by a voice mail system. You leave a concise message that receives no response. A week later you do the same thing with the same result. After that you make no further contact.

Getting a meeting requires working with secretaries and voice mail systems. When you call, more often than not your contact will be out or busy. If you expect to get nothing from these situations, you will get just that. Alternatively, you can use them to your advantage.

I prefer to deal with secretaries than with voice mail systems. I can have a dialogue with a secretary. If I treat her properly, she can provide me with information and help. One of her principal jobs is to serve as gatekeeper, a role that many professionals perceive negatively. What they forget is that gatekeepers are responsible for letting people in as well as keeping them out.

Rose Begnal, a former executive secretary who now works for the outplacement firm Jannotta, Bray & Associates, Inc., once put it this way: "To get past the secretary you have to empower her to become your friend. Her impression of you may also be the first impression her boss gets when she talks with him, so remember: Your first interview is usually with the secretary."

So how do you get a secretary on your side? As one former secretary put it too me, "Give her the respect and the information she'll need to talk with her boss about you, and don't ever let her get the impression that you're trying to deceive her." Secretaries are often faced with what she calls the "fool-you factor," epitomized by the person who calls up using the boss' first name and pretending to be a friend. Such ploys aren't appreciated, since it is the secretary's job to help the boss manage time wisely.

Instead, demonstrate an understanding of the boss's problems ("I know he must be very busy..."), then ask the secretary to help you, letting her know concisely what you want—presumably you want a brief meeting—and why the boss might benefit from taking the time to meet with you. The reason for your call must be carefully selected to provide value to the prospective client.

You must work with two criteria when establishing a reason for making a visit, information and urgency. If you offer information of value to the prospective client and there is some urgency about the visit, you can often get a meeting. If you simply want to describe your services, your chances of getting face to face are lower. With some reflection, most professionals can come up with an array of information of value to prospective clients, including the following.

- *Industry information.* As a professional, your knowledge of what is going on in an industry or particular field of activity (product liability, salesperson compensation, etc.) give you information that many targets would like to have.

- *Techniques or practices.* Is there some aspect of your service that differs from that of your competitors? Does it solve problems your target faces? Are they the kind of thing that a well-informed person in your target's position would want to know about?

- *Project information.* Is there a project you have recently completed that the prospective client would like to hear about? Some professionals are precluded from discussing past projects by confidentiality agreements. Others can use recent projects as a subject for discussion even with direct competitors of the past client, so long as they show reasonable discretion.

■ *Study results.* The results of a study can provide a sound basis for a meeting. Some firms conduct surveys as a part of the projects they do for clients and then offer to discuss survey results with participants as a benefit for participating. These follow-up visits are thinly disguised cold calls.

A prospective client is most likely to agree to a meeting if he perceives some urgency associated with it. I am not recommending panicky insistence that he must meet now before it's too late, but rather a statement that there is strong reason to meet sooner rather than later. Urgency can result from…

■ *…an opportunity that will be lost.* As suggested earlier, you can state that you will be visiting the prospect's city in two weeks and are not sure when you will be back again. There can also be opportunities specific to some professional practices that will be lost if too much time passes.

■ *…a problem that will be avoided.* Changing tax and other laws are examples of factors that can create a need for a client to get information quickly. Several environmental consulting firms in New Jersey were able to use regulations dealing with underground storage tanks to create reasons for meetings.

■ *…a need to stay current.* Your prospect may benefit from being the first to know about the information you are providing or from knowing about it when his boss asks.

Obviously there can be other reasons for urgency, and you should reflect upon the specific nature of your practice in order to identify them.

I frequently receive calls from salespeople who want to introduce their companies and services but offer no special information or claim to urgency. I seldom meet with them, being too busy for casual meetings. When I do, it is because they have called me at a time when I feel at least a modestly urgent need for information they might have. In other words, I am supplying the rationale for the meeting, and they have simply gotten lucky and reached me on the right day. When making cold calls, you yourself should identify the value of a meeting for the prospect and reduce to a minimum your dependence on luck.

Getting the most from the gatekeeper

When you call to ask for a meeting, your manner must communicate that it will be worthwhile. You must sound confident and well organized. Even so, the chance that you will be able to speak to the boss immediately is small. When this is the case, you should make the most out of the opportunity to talk with the gatekeeper. From her you can learn the following.

Are you, in fact, speaking to the prospective client's secretary?

Good networkers and salespeople always establish who they are talking to at the beginning of the conversation. The secretary can provide a lot more help than others who answer the phone. If you aren't speaking to the secretary, you may have accidentally determined when she breaks for lunch or coffee. This can be useful information, as you will see.

93

What is her name?

A helpful secretary can make your job a lot easier if she wants to. Showing a personal interest by asking and remembering her name is always worthwhile.

"For most people," Rose Begnal says, "there's no music sweeter than the sound of their own name." As you get to know the secretary during the follow-up calls and visits, she is likely to prove increasingly helpful if you make the effort to establish a relationship. The same, of course, applies to receptionists and people who back up the secretary when she's away from her desk.

Is she disposed to be helpful?

Some secretaries are more willing to help than others, depending on their personalities and their bosses' instructions. Those few who feel it's their obligation to bar anyone trying to sell anything—often with instructions from the boss—pose a serious obstacle. By testing a secretary's attitude with a few easy questions about the boss's availability, you can determine whether your future calls should be planned to coincide with her lunch break.

Breakthrough sometimes comes when you circumvent an unhelpful secretary. After repeated efforts to reach one prospective client, I decided to call on Christmas Eve, a time when his secretary might be out, while he, being Japanese, would almost certainly be in. It worked.

When is the boss expected back?

Professionals who sell successfully make efficient use of scarce marketing time. Knowing when the boss will return saves precious minutes that can be used productively elsewhere. By calling when you know the boss is in, you increase your chances of reaching him and diminish the probability of getting caught in a game of telephone tag so frustrating to both of you.

Asking when you might call back has another benefit. It's often answered with information on the boss's activities. "He's in Europe this week," "She's in budget meetings all day," "We're in the midst of an acquisition, and I'm afraid she's not around much," or "He's in the hospital" are tidbits that give you a sense of the boss's activities and provide subjects of conversation to help you develop rapport when you do speak.

When is the best time to call?

A good secretary is likely to know at what time of day her boss is most receptive to answering calls. Knowing this gets you through at a time when the boss can focus on your concerns. If you have been playing telephone tag, setting an exact time to call is particularly important to end any frustration for your contact.

Has the letter you sent been received, and if so what has been done with it?

If you have written in advance of calling, the secretary probably knows how the boss wants you treated. If he wants to see you, the secretary will take aggressive steps to arrange it. If you have been passed on to someone else, she can connect you immediately. If the boss has decided not to meet with you, she can let you know before the boss has to say so directly. With this information, you can back off and plan another way of gaining access.

94

Can the secretary schedule a meeting for you in the boss's absence?

Many secretaries have the authority to schedule meetings for their bosses. If you have a sense that the boss may have a strong reason for meeting with you but you are having difficulty reaching each other by phone, ask the secretary whether she can set up a meeting for you. Failing that, she can probably schedule a time for a telephone conversation as a first step.

Is there information about the company or her boss that she can provide you?

Most secretaries can send annual reports or brochures on their company, and sometimes even a bio of the boss. In one case a secretary told me that her boss had formerly worked at a chemical company. I was able to incorporate several chemical company examples in the description of my services, to good effect.

At times the secretary can also help ascertain which aspects of your services might be of most interest. "I want to make the best use of his time," you might say. "My firm assists in both acquisition and divestiture of real estate. Is your boss more focused on one of these areas than the other?" The answer to a question like this can improve the value of the meeting you have with the boss for both of you.

Secretaries are also natural sources of information on the correct spelling of a boss's name, title, and address, as well as the person's direct phone line, directions to the building, and similar details.

Can she ask the boss a question for you?

If this isn't your first call and you are simply seeking a bit of additional information from the boss, the secretary can probably get it for you if he is unavailable. The boss will appreciate this efficient use of his time, and the secretary will appreciate the opportunity to help you both, since that is her job.

Can you help me?

When efforts to approach the boss fail and the secretary seems disposed to be helpful, a direct appeal for guidance can produce surprising results. The work you have devoted to develop a relationship pays off at such times. Once I was frustrated in my efforts to recontact a prospective client after an initial show of interest. I finally told the secretary that I feared the project I was pursuing would slip between my fingers if I didn't reach the boss soon. Could she help me? She suggested I call another individual who was also working on the project. I did, I was given a meeting, and we were eventually awarded the job.

Voice mail

Voice mail systems have proved the bane of cold callers who have developed a knack for working with secretaries. How can you develop a relationship with a machine? You can't, but you can begin an admittedly one-sided relationship with the person who listens to your messages. You develop this relationship with your tone of voice and the words you choose. This means you should be upbeat, businesslike, and direct in stating the reason for your call. Ask for a return call, promising that you will keep the conversation short. You must keep this promise later. When you leave your phone number, say it slowly.

People who use voice mail instead of a secretary often answer their own phones when they are in the office. By calling at different times of day, especially early or late, you can sometimes catch them in. Finally, many voice mail systems provide the option of reaching a secretary. If you have found an urgent reason for calling, as discussed previously, you have good reason to try this approach. When the system offers no way of reaching a secretary, try hitting the pound (#) key or pound followed by zero or just zero. You will often be connected with a human being. If this doesn't work, try calling the main number of the organization and asking for your target's secretary.

Once you're connected

Whether working through secretaries or voice mail systems, you will eventually be connected with most of the prospects you target. Keep the conversation short and to the point. State who you are, what you want, why a meeting might benefit your prospect, and, if you have one, your reason for urgency. Then wait for a response. If the prospect cannot meet with you in the near future and puts you off, ask whether you can schedule a visit for three months from now. If he declines, acknowledge that he must be busy and ask whether you can call back in three months. He will have a hard time saying no to this request, and by granting permission creates an obligation to take your call.

Your objective should be to keep the phone conversation to less than five minutes. Longer than that and you risk holding the meeting over the phone, which you must avoid. A friend of mine once did this on a project he felt well positioned to win. The prospect began to question him, and he responded as helpfully as he could. After the phone call the prospect could see no reason for a face to face meeting. My friend had answered all his questions. When the prospect finally awarded the job, it went to a competitor who had met face to face and built a rapport.

Once a prospect agrees to a meeting, you have achieved an important goal. You will usually get in to see him, even if the visit is postponed several times.

Be persistent

An electrical engineer-turned-business developer at his Rochester, New York, firm once commented to me how difficult his associates found working with him on cold calls. The large number of telephone calls required to arrange a meeting discouraged them. That many prospects don't return calls hurts many professionals' pride, and they do not want to appear a nuisance by calling repeatedly. I now this because I ask many professionals how many calls they would make to a target before giving up. Most say either three or five. In doing so they grossly underestimate what it takes to get a meeting.

Such reticence results from transferring standards developed when dealing with clients to cold-call prospects. When working with clients you enjoy a certain importance in their eyes; when working with a cold call prospect you don't. When a prospect doesn't return a call, it should not be seen as a reflection on you, personally, but on the absence of a relationship. That is what you are working to change. Repeated calls are not usually a nuisance. The prospect can always continue to ignore you, just as you may ignore calls from someone you don't know who is trying to sell you something. Do these calls make you angry or contemptuous? I doubt it.

Persistence differentiates the casual caller from the serious. Many is the time I have finally reached a prospect after weeks of leaving messages, only to be greeted with an apology for the lack of response. An agreement to meet almost always follows. It has taken me up to a year to get meetings with some prospects. The wait has often been worth it.

To give you a sense of what persistence means, I have included two diagrams of efforts I have made to get meetings with potentially large accounts. (See exhibit 6.3.) In both cases I tried to reduce the coldness of the initial calls by finding contacts either inside or outside the company who would provide me with a referral. The diagrams show the multiple paths I explored to find a route in, some of which were abandoned because I succeeded in getting a meeting with a key player. Had that effort failed, I would have pursued the alternatives further. Note that in both cases it required thirty calls to get a meeting, while the target contacts required ten calls each over a period of about two months before I reached them and lined up meetings.

The professional unaccustomed to cold calling also has to learn that the total time required for such an effort is not great; in the examples used for exhibit 6.3 I spent perhaps an hour and a half at most on the phone for all the calls made to each prospect. This investment was well worth it, given the potential for business both offered. Besides, neither target was upset with the frequency of my calls. Rather, both were apologetic about being so difficult to reach, and both readily gave me a meeting, in part to make up for not responding. Rather than hurt me, my persistence distinguished me. You need the call discipline to be persistent, an untiringly courteous phone voice, and a little ingenuity. I finally reached Prospect 2 by calling her at 8:00 a.m., when she answered her own phone.

I have discussed call discipline in the chapter on networking. To succeed at any marketing activity requiring relationship building, whether it be networking, cold calling, relationship marketing, or publicity, you have to have call discipline. You have to find a way to make dialing the phone an important part of your schedule. Whether you set aside an hour each day or a morning each week or commit yourself to making a specific number of calls each day does not matter, so long as you make the calls. Most experienced cold callers sitting down at the phone will make a couple of easy calls first, calls they know will be taken. This warms them up for the hard ones.

Many firms employ professional business developers to relieve professionals from the burden of setting up meetings. These individuals are generally college-educated and trained in the firm's services, markets, past projects, and staff. They develop relationships with gatekeepers and prospects and get the professionals they work with in the door. It can be highly successful approach, if you can afford it.

Exhibit 6.3
The Importance of Call Persistence

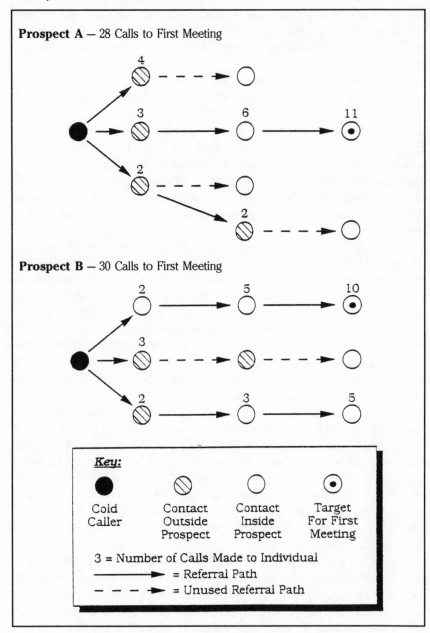

Prospect A — 28 Calls to First Meeting

Prospect B — 30 Calls to First Meeting

Key:

| Cold Caller | Contact Outside Prospect | Contact Inside Prospect | Target For First Meeting |

3 = Number of Calls Made to Individual
———————► = Referral Path
— — — ► = Unused Referral Path

The meeting

A partner at a Big Six accounting firm described his problem this way:

> Our people are good at getting leads, but they don't know what to do with them. They attend an event and collect business cards, but they don't know how to follow up. They sometimes set up a meeting, but they don't know what to say when they get there.

A partner at a large consulting firm expressed the same concern after we discussed the need for call discipline. "I've thought of setting up meetings, but I don't know what we should do when we get one." Confusion over what should happen at a cold-call meeting inhibits many professionals from arranging them. Whether through experience or intuition, they sense, correctly, that simply making a presentation will not produce results. So what else can they do?

Cold-call meetings are in many ways indistinguishable from sales meetings. Detailed information on how to handle such meetings is provided in part II of this book. If you plan to make cold calls, you should read the first three chapters of part II with special care. However, a few comments specific to cold calls are warranted here.

The objectives of a cold call should be...

- ...to learn enough about the prospect to determine whether she might have a need for your services, what value these services would return to her, and what should be done next to establish whether there is a match between you and the prospect.

- ...to provide the prospect with enough information about your firm to give a preliminary sense of the value you can provide her, if any, and commit to another meeting, if appropriate.

This sequence—learn first and provide information second—is important, because until you learn, you don't know what information to give. It is also problematic, because having requested the meeting, you have created the expectation that you have something to say. Successful cold calling requires that you flip this expectation so that the prospect sees the meeting as hers.

In order to obtain the meeting, you have promised to provide information of value—the results of a study, a review of a project you have completed, or information on your services. You must deliver it. Begin with a *short* introduction of yourself, your firm, and your subject. Rehearse it so that it takes no more than five minutes. Then turn the meeting over to the prospect by saying something like this:

> There are many things we could go into about (the issue of concern to your industry, our new service, the project we completed for the XYZ Company, our study of firms in your industry), and I want to make this time as useful for you as possi-

99

ble. Would you tell me a little about your company and its situation and why you were interested in taking time for a meeting on (our services, the project, the study)? That way I can focus on the aspects most important to you.

In other words, you can provide more value if you understand the prospect's situation first, a truth that gets her to talk. It also shows you are focused on her needs instead of selling your services.

Once she begins talking, your objective is to keep her going using the questions described in chapter 10. Specifically, you want to find out what value solving a particular problem would have to her company and to her personally. Questions like, "Why hasn't action been taken on this situation before?" and "What difference would it make to you (your company) if it were fixed?" help establish the value that your service would provide.

As she describes her situation, you must ask yourself, "What parts of my knowledge of (the issue, my services, past project, study) relate to these needs?" If no parts do but you feel your firm could help the prospect with her concerns, make her an offer: "We had planned to talk about (our new service, past project, study), but it doesn't really pertain to the issues you have raised. There are other ways we could help you. Would you like to talk about that or stick to the original agenda?" Most will accede to the suggestion and change agenda.

If you see no match between your services and her needs, say, "I'm not sure how (our new services, past project, study) relates to the situation you have just described. Let me give you an overview, and you may understand better than I do. Feel free to interrupt me at any time." In such cases keep the presentation short, unless the prospect demonstrates strong interest. You don't want to waste her time by going over material of little interest.

By the end of the meeting you should know whether there is an opportunity to pursue. If so, either suggest a specific follow-up or ask the prospect how you think the two of you should proceed. Make it clear that you would be delighted to visit again at no obligation. Kind prospects often hesitate to take advantage of you when you wish they would.

If there is potential for a sale, always try to advance in a way that requires some commitment from the prospect, be it more time, arranging a meeting with others, or sending you material to review. Her willingness to take action is a sign that she is working to make something happen and not just taking your time. If she is unwilling to commit to one action, suggest another that requires less commitment. If possible, leave the meeting with an obligation to get back to her with some piece of information she wants.

If you see no fit between your services and the prospect's current needs, acknowledge that you don't, thank her for her time, and ask whether it would be acceptable for you to call back in six months to see whether her circumstances have changed.

Plan your meeting so that you don't exceed the time allotted to you. When you leave, you should have talked no more than 30 percent of the time.

Just as you need call persistence, you will need meeting persistence. Scheduled meetings with prospects will get canceled or postponed. Occasionally you will be stood up. A large percentage of your meetings will lead nowhere immediately. If cold calling is to work for you, you must have the resilience to keep at it. Marketing is a numbers game.

Follow-up

Always follow up a cold-call meeting with a letter. By the second or third meeting you should have moved from cold calling into either relationship marketing (chapter 5) or selling (part II).

Conclusion

Cold calling requires a long-term commitment, time, technique, and a tolerance for rejection. No other marketing technique will put you one-on-one with so many prospects talking about issues of concern to them. That is why cold calling is among the most powerful marketing techniques available to you.

7

Marketing by Mail

Case example: The Source

By chance Dennis developed expertise in an emerging area of insurance law. He received one case as an outgrowth of claims work his firm was doing for a major insurer, and a couple of others followed. Dennis had seen a manual produced annually by a competitor on another area of insurance law and distributed free of charge to clients and potential clients. Seeing a void, he developed a manual on his new specialty, crafting it to meet the needs of middle managers at insurance companies. The first issue was only ten pages.

Over the next ten years he revised it annually or semiannually, and it is now almost three hundred pages long. Each time he updated it, he sent it out with a personalized letter. Over the years he has developed a proprietary mailing list of people interested in this particular area of insurance law by gathering cards at conferences, adding names of clients and prospects and responding to requests from those who have learned about the manual from others. Today his name is synonymous with this particular practice, partly because of the work he does in the field but also because everyone with an interest in the field knows the manual. He has become the source for information in this specialized area. The manual confirms his expertise to new acquaintances, opens doors to people he doesn't know (if they work in this area, they will usually accept a visit from its author), and provides a regular reminder in the form of a useful tool for those he has worked with in the past.

Maurice Fulton, who gave me my first job in consulting, once said that in the early days of his career, shortly after World War II, he could send out one big mailing and "make our nut for the year." The world has changed. Professionals compete intensely, and almost all employ some kind of direct mail in their marketing mix. Few see the kinds of results my former boss saw, yet they persist, for several reasons.

First, direct mail seems easy in comparison to many other kinds of marketing. It lacks the potential for direct rejection inherent in a cold call. A mailing can be sent out quickly with a minimum of fuss, compared to writing an article or networking. Much of the work can be delegated to the administrative staff. Second, it may seem cheap. After all, we all send out letters every day and seldom think of the cost. Certainly it is a low cost way to deliver a message to a large number of people. It is an accepted way for professionals to sell their services.

Professionals who have little marketing experience will almost always think about developing a brochure first and suggest a mailing second. That most mailings are grossly ineffective seems to deter no one.

Direct mail can be a productive way to market your services, but when done right, it is neither easy nor cheap. To make it effective you must work with a limited number of variables, which include:

- Objective
- List
- Frequency
- Message
- Offers

Many professionals miss one or more variable.

What are you trying to accomplish?

There are several legitimate objectives for a mailing, the most obvious being...

- *...to remind past clients, prospects and market contacts of your existence.* The typical newsletter serves this function. Direct mail shows your continued interest in a past client the way a Christmas card shows interest in a relative you see less often than you should. Clients are more likely to think of you when they have a need or when they talk to someone else who has a need, if you jog their memories this way from time to time.

- *...to build name recognition.* Name recognition makes it easier for you to get in the door when you make a cold call. It increases the likelihood of a prospect's calling you if he is given your name by a friend. Even our best clients may not know about the full range of our services, which, after all, change with time. Direct mail ties your name to a specific array of services.

- *...to generate leads.* Few professionals can sell their services by mail the way L.L. Bean sells clothing, but they can generate qualified leads. This allows them to focus marketing efforts on prospects with the greatest potential of hiring.

- *...to position a phone call.* Professionals often send letters advising a prospect that they will call to request a meeting. I have discussed this use of mail in the chapter on cold calling (chapter 6).

You can seldom meet all these objectives with the same mailing. You must decide on the primary objective of every mailing so that the remaining variables can be adapted accordingly.

Who are you mailing to?

Many of the direct-mail pieces you send will be tossed without being read. These pieces are useless to you. The quality of the list you use influences the percentage of waste. A mailing sent to a well-targeted list of prospective clients will have a far smaller waste factor than one for which the list has been chosen carelessly.

Most professionals use two kinds of list: those they create and those they buy. Created lists are made up of the names of past clients and prospects, vendors, employees and past employees, and other business contacts and friends. In my experience most of these lists are in disarray. They are created casually to meet a specific need, grow haphazardly, and are maintained poorly. The first list, compiled for a specific mailing, say a change of address when a firm is small, may have two thousand names. Ten years and twenty mailings later, it may contain twelve thousand names, with no indication of when each record was added or last updated or who submitted the name, no way to tell who these people are (past clients, vendors, etc.), and little checking for accuracy or duplication.

Few firms have the attention span to fix the resulting mess. Busy professionals, who, after all, are the ones who know something about the people listed, can seldom find time for so tedious a task. The formats for the entries often complicate correction. Title and department, for example, may have been allocated to one field in the original data base. Practical use later may require sorting your list by one or the other of these, which will be impossible without splitting them into separate fields. Parsing a field, as any data base specialist can tell you, requires a visual review and manual correction for each record.

If you are creating a mailing list, you can avoid many of these problems and significantly increase the effectiveness of your mailings if you create a separate field for each element of a record. Elements that should constitute separate fields are shown in exhibit 7.1.

If you already have a list that is in disrepair, you should fix it as soon as possible, since the problems can only get worse as it grows and ages. The appropriate repair sequences is:

1. *Purge*. Conduct a detailed review of the list to eliminate as many records as possible and identify those you know to be inaccurate. This will reduce the number of records to be repaired.
2. *Repair*. Modify the data base to fit the format shown in Exhibit 7.1.

A list should be purged periodically, and your new data base format will make this much easier. Alternative purging methods include: 1) a visual review of all records that have not been updated within the past five years; 2) a review by each professional of the names he or she has placed on the list; 3) an annual first class/return-requested mailing (this can simply be one issue of your newsletter or

Exhibit 7.1
Mailing List Fields

Field	Comment
1. Form of address	Mr., Ms., Dr., etc.
2. First name	Full first name as it appears on business card
3. Middle initial	
4. Last name	
5. Salutation	Bob, Liz, Dr. Smith, etc. for personal letters
6. Title	
7. Department	
8. Company	
9. Parent company	
10. Street address	
11. Post office box	
12. City	
13. State	
14. Zip Code	
15. Date	Date entered or last updated
16. Source	Initials of professional contributing name, other list it came from, etc.
17. Industry code	Specific codes for banking, manufacturing, etc., and for vendors and other nonclient contacts
18. Job class code	Adjustment for diversity of titles: Include codes for key categories of contact, such as Personnel, Purchasing, Facilities, etc.
19. Interest group	Classification of interests for targeted mailings

other regular mailing); or 4) an annual reader response questionnaire of the kind used by controlled-circulation magazines.

Lists can be purchased from one of several sources:

- List merchants.
- Directories. (You can either buy preprinted labels from the publisher or extract names from the directory by hand. Before doing the latter, you should carefully read restrictions placed on the use of names by the publisher. Most publishers deliberately include false names and addresses to catch those who use listings without authorization.)
- Magazines.
- Trade Associations.

Many lists can be presorted for you, so that you purchase only those names most likely to be valid prospects. Names can be sorted according to geography, size of company, industry, and job title.

When preparing a list, you may wonder how many people to include from one company. I once heard a consultant claim that he had informed all of the Fortune 500 companies about his services through direct mail, only to find out that he had sent material to one person in each. Companies neither know about your services nor buy them; people do. The number of people in a company who should receive a mailing depends on the company's size—the bigger the company, the larger the number of people who should receive the mailing—and on the nature of the mailing. (The topic may have broad or narrow appeal.)

When planning a direct mailing, you must choose what list or lists you intend to use, since that decision will influence both quantities and content. For example, an environmental consultant mailing a white paper featuring a case study on underground tanks at a service station might want to purchase a list of service station operators to complement his own past client list.

How often should you mail?

Like advertising, direct mail depends upon frequency of exposure for impact. You will have to make frequency decisions early. If you don't, you may find yourself short of time or money to complete an effective campaign. A one-time mailing may not be worth the effort, depending on your purpose and content.

Frequency decisions should be closely tied to purpose. A newsletter to remind past clients of continued interest should be sent two or three times a year, every year, especially if it is your primary vehicle for doing so. A direct-mail campaign to increase your reputation and name recognition within a specific industry will require three or four mailings closely sequenced. If you mail less frequently, a high proportion of your audience will forget about the first mailing by the time the second one arrives. When the Clean Air Act was passed and major employers had to reduce the number of employees commuting by car, a traffic engineering firm sent out a succession of three mailings, notifying major employers about what they would have to do to comply. The firm quickly emerged as the expert on this subject in its region.

A campaign to find prospects might require only one mailing if it includes an attractive-enough offer. "Offers" will be described on the following page.

What should you mail?

The success of a direct-mail effort depends heavily on the message you send and the form you send it in. Your objectives help you determine both. Here are some possible formats.

Letters

Letters, especially personalized letters, are more likely to be read than anything else you can send and can be used alone or in combination with other materials.

Brochures

Brochures make poor mailers because they tend to be bulky and expensive to mail, they lack the news value required to induce a recipient to read them, and they are usually not sufficiently targeted to a specific need or issue. This does not stop many professionals from wasting money by sending them.

Newsletters

Commonly used and usually boring, most are expensive and ineffective. A high-quality newsletter requires a major, consistent effort. Don't bother unless you are willing to make the commitment. Since the advent of desktop publishing, the marketing newsletter has been so overworked that some firms avoid the term and appearance. They depend on memos, reports, manuals, and other materials to serve the same purpose.

Reprints

The time spent writing an article can be leveraged by mailing reprints with a cover letter. The fact that a journal published your article implies you are an expert.

White Papers

More proprietary than reprints, white papers let your targets feel they are receiving special information not generally available. Sometimes they take the form of a memo on an important topic.

Gifts

The gift must be worth having; otherwise it is trash. Gifts are best if tied to a message about your services. For example, an architecture firm I worked for once mailed bookmarks with pictures of libraries it had designed to librarians.

In developing a mailer, consider the following guidelines.

The message must be tailored to your audience and your objective

A white paper on maximizing the value of local area networks might be suitable for chief information officers, but don't send it to CEOs. A CEO might pass a short letter, stating that your firm has helped other companies lower client/server costs by over 20 percent, to his information officer, but he will almost certainly trash the white paper. Materials sent to senior executives should stress high-level benefits, such as increased sales or market share or lowered costs. Those sent to lower-level managers require a higher level of proof of your technical competence.

Mailings to current and past clients will also have greater impact if tailored to interest. This is clearly the trend among sophisticated relationship marketers. Charles O'Neill, a Boston-area lawyer who has built a substantial estate planning practice, classifies his clients by interest. He tries to send each interest group a mailing on a relevant topic or service a couple of times a year. Says O'Neill, "They know I am thinking about them and their interests, and that helps build client loyalty."

[handwritten margin note: DO AS FOLLOW UP TO RELATN SHIP MKTG.]

Insist on excellent layout and graphics

Desktop publishing has raised the standards for all direct mailings. Most people make an almost instantaneous decision about each piece of mail they receive, categorizing it as wanted or unwanted. The latter is thrown out within seconds. Because the decision is so quick, it is influenced by visual appeal more than by content. Here are some simple guidelines to increase visual appeal.

- *Retain a lot of white space on the page.* Pages that are crammed with information look time consuming and hard to read. Instead of putting a lot of information on a page, shorten your content and make sure that every word counts. Alternatively, if you really must, you can lengthen your document.

- *Make sure the print is easy to read.* The type size should be no smaller than 12-point. It is better to use serifed than unserifed fonts.

- *Keep paragraphs short.*

- *Use graphics.* Photos, graphs, tables, charts, and lists are all more accessible than large blocks of text.

Be sure that those portions of the text most likely to be read are especially compelling

Titles, headings, first sentences, and first paragraphs require special attention. They must stimulate curiosity or create a sense of urgency to read further. After completing your content, revise these portions of it, as needed, to make it grab the reader's attention.

Personalize your mailing whenever possible

Anyone is more likely to read a personalized letter than one that is obviously a mass mailing. There will be cases where the size of the mailing prohibits personalization, but today's data base and word processing technologies are constantly increasing the size of mailings that can be effectively personalized.

The rewards of personalizing can be substantial. A group of accountants, all on the faculty of a university, decided to establish a firm to cater to the accounting needs of the affluent. They sent a series of personalized letters to high-income individuals in the market area they had picked, announcing the opening of the firm and playing on the cachet of their university affiliation. Initial responses to these mailings put them in business.

How can you generate leads from a mailing?

Many products are sold directly through the mail, including clothes, camping equipment, food, furniture, tools, and bric-a-brac. Companies selling these goods can rely on direct mail for three reasons: Goods are moderately priced, they are returnable, and they are convenient to purchase. Professional services don't meet these criteria and so cannot be sold directly through the mail.

Nevertheless, you can use direct mail to induce a prospect to call or otherwise tip his hand that he is in the market for your services. This is a great benefit, because it allows you to focus your most expensive marketing on a prequalified list of prospects. To get this information you must make an offer.

An "offer" is anything of value that the reader can obtain by contacting you. To be effective in lead generation, it should require readers to reveal that they have a need that somehow relates to your services. Here are some examples of offers.

- **A checklist of issues to consider** when undertaking a _____ (fill in the blank) project. Checklists have the advantage of being relatively easy for most experts to create. They are also perceived as reader-friendly and useful. An architecture firm generated sixty qualified leads from colleges and universities considering building or renovating libraries from an offer for a checklist.

- **A booklet of information** on an appropriate subject. Large accounting firms make effective use of this kind of offer with booklets on doing business in specific countries or on specific tax issues.

- **An audit or review** of a particular aspect of a company's business. Real estate brokerage firms will often offer to review a company's leases free of charge. Among consulting firms, this kind of service is known as a "fishing license" because it provides such a good opportunity to identify sales opportunities. Often provided free, professionals sometimes charge a modest fee for this service to further prequalify the buyer before making a significant time investment.

- **A white paper** entitled "Do You Need a _____ (fill in the blank with marketing, environmental, cost reduction, etc.) Consultant?" People debating whether to hire a consultant or anxious to convince their bosses to do so will often request such a document.

Offers must be clearly identified and easy to obtain. Prominently display your phone number and provide a response card when making an offer. Remember that offers must require a low level of commitment, and that in your mailing you are selling your offer, not your full range of services.

Conclusion

Direct mail permits you to reach a large audience at a relatively low cost with a specific message. It provides a means of generating qualified leads worth approaching with more costly marketing efforts. Some firms market by mail. If you do, take the time to do it right.

Once you have identified a prospect through direct mail, you must convert him into a client using cold calling and selling techniques described in other chapters.

8

Organizing Seminars and Conferences

Case example: The Intrapreneur

In the early 1980s, Jim, an associate at a large consulting firm, recognized that American manufacturers would have to modernize their manufacturing practices thoroughly in order to regain their competitiveness in world markets. An industrial engineer, he saw an opportunity to develop a practice of his own in advanced manufacturing methods.

With the firm's support he put together a half-day seminar on the subject and took it on the road to six cities. He invited representatives from mid-sized manufacturing companies unlikely to have in-house staff able to revitalize manufacturing processes alone, and limited attendance to roughly twenty people per session to ensure intense interaction. He followed up personally with each attendee who had shown interest in his approach.

Today Jim heads a substantial practice. "The seminars were the foundation of this business," he says. "The work they generated kept us so busy for the next two years that we almost didn't have time for any other marketing. They established us in this business."

The popularity of conferences and seminars results from the distinct benefits they offer. Attendees prequalify themselves as prospects; if they weren't interested in the issue being discussed, they wouldn't come. You get to talk with them face to face, both formally during presentations and informally during breaks, meals, and receptions. As a speaker, you are automatically classified as an expert.

Because seminars can run from a few hours to several days, they can be adapted to a wide array of subject matter and contexts. The flexibility of seminars and conferences can be seen in the variety of some I have been involved in, which include...

- ...*a series of late afternoon seminars* for past and prospective clients spread over two years, each using a panel to address an issue of current interest from different perspectives. Each was followed by a cocktail party. Objectives included maintaining the hosting firm's reputation as a leading-edge professional in its field and strengthening relationships with past clients and prospects.

- ...*a half-day seminar* arranged and paid for by a specific client about to undertake a major corporate change. Speakers briefed the management on personnel, facilities, and other aspects of the change. The objectives were to provide the client's management team with background it would need to oversee the change process and to demonstrate that the firm organizing the seminar could assist throughout the project.

- ...*a two-day conference* run by a professional conference organizer on a highly technical business issue, attracting participants from across the country. The fundamental objective for the organizer of the conference was to make a profit.

- ...*a series of two-day training conferences* offered at several locations across the country to teach the fundamentals of a specific business activity to those just beginning their careers. Though run at profit, the primary objective of these conferences was to develop long-term relationships with prospective clients.

Each of these programs resulted in new business for some of the speakers.

Unlike most forms of marketing, you can sometimes charge for seminars, covering your marketing costs and even making a profit.

With these benefits come associated risks and costs, especially if you plan a large conference for which you will charge a fee. If it is a one-time event, a conference is a high-fixed-cost, low-variable-cost enterprise. The time speakers must invest to prepare remains constant regardless of audience size. Marketing costs are also usually fixed, consisting of a large mailing. This leaves the duplication of handouts as the major variable cost. A two-day conference can cost you a bundle if too few participants attend to defray the hotel charges. By forecasting your costs, you can easily run a break-even analysis to calculate how many participants you need at a given price to recoup your costs. The fee from every additional attendee is almost all profit.

A large conference requires many hours of preparation from many people. This differs from many of the other marketing techniques described previously, which can be done by a single individual. A small seminar, over a breakfast or at the end of the day, can be set up and run by one person if time is available over an extended period, but it is a method that lends itself more to an organization.

Exhibit 8.1 provides a checklist of the specific tasks you must complete to run a conference. Variables for setting one up include subject, length, timing, location/accommodations, mailing list, invitations/flyers, speakers, supporting materials, informal interaction time, and fee.

Exhibit 8.1
Conference & Seminar Organizer's Checklist

(Note: List is not strictly sequential, because some of the steps are iterative.)

I. Select subject
    A. Brainstorm alternatives
    B. Review for conferenceability
        1. Is it educational?
        2. Is it urgent?
        3. Does it lend itself to solutions?
        4. Do we have the resources/knowledge to handle it?
    C. Select subject
II. Determine length (One hour, half day, one day, two days)
III. Establish schedule
    A. Set date(s)
    B. Set completion dates for key tasks
    C. Monitor and revise periodically
IV. Select speakers
    A. Brainstorm alternatives
        1. Internal
        2. External
            a) Past clients
            b) Other experts
    B. Review for suitability
        1. Knowledge
        2. Drawing power of name
        3. Speaking ability
    C. Invite speakers
        1. Invite and confirm availability
        2. Invite fallback speakers, as needed
V. Select site
    A. Review alternatives
        1. Internal
        2. Hotel
        3. Conference center
    B. Inspect site alternatives
        1. Meeting space
        2. Break-out space
        3. Socializing space
        4. Sleeping accommodations
        5. Food service
        6. Logistical support
            a) Photocopying

       b) Audio-visual equipment

       c) Telephones

       d) Message service

       e) Rest rooms

    7. Financial terms

  C. Negotiate terms and reserve space

VI. Mail invitations

  A. Create invitation list

    1. Brainstorm alternatives with planning team

       a) Internal

       b) Purchased

          (1) Determine fit

          (2) Determine cost

       c) Provided by speakers

    2. Select and assemble list

    3. Produce invitations

       a) Draft copy

          (1) Describe theme

          (2) Describe benefits

          (3) Note who should attend

          (4) Describe schedule and content

          (5) Describe speakers

          (6) Describe logistics

            (a) Time

            (b) Place

            (c) Fee and payment

            (d) Registration/response form

            (e) Accommodations

            (f) Directions

       b) Design, print and mail invitations

       c) Create list of confirmed attendees

VII. Order refreshments/meals

  A. Select caterer/provider

  B. Select menu

  C. Place order

VIII. Rehearse speakers

  A. Schedule rehearsal

  B. Coach speakers (see Coach's Checklist on page 159)

  C. Determine need and arrange for audio-visual equipment

IX. Prepare materials

  A. Collect copies of speakers' exhibits

  B. Collect speakers' bios

  C. Collect white papers/article reprints

  D. Prepare title page and table of contents

E. Duplicate and bind

F. Prepare speaker evaluation form

X. Arrange and check seminar logistics

    A. Reception

    B. Registration

    C. Name tags

    D. Coat room

    E. Speaker introductions

    F. Writing materials for attendees

    G. Materials delivery

    H. Seating arrangement

    I. Water for speakers

    J. Podium and lighting for speakers

    K. Audio-visual equipment

    L. Heating and air conditioning

    M. Hosts and helpers from firm

XI. Run event

XII. Follow-up

    A. Thank-you letters to attendees

    B. Thank-you letters to speakers

    C. Phone calls, as appropriate

Is It Conferenceable?

I once suggested a conference theme to a professional conference organizer. She thought about it for a moment and then responded, "It's an interesting idea, but is it conferenceable?" Conferenceability was a new concept to me. It means that the subject for a business conference must...

- *...be educational.* People come to conferences to learn. Entertainment is a plus, but promotion of your business is acceptable only if it is heavily disguised. There has to be something worth learning.

- *...be urgent.* There must be a need to know now. A conference on "The Population Explosion of 2090" is not likely to draw many people. AIDS conferences draw thousands many times a year. I use the term "urgent" here loosely to mean that there is value to learning something now rather than later.

- *...lend itself to solutions.* The conference must offer attendees solutions or progress toward solutions, because people attend business conferences in order to solve problems better.

You should test any subject against these criteria. If it does not meet them, try something else. Hit a winner and you can draw a large crowd. One law firm offering a seminar on the North American Free Trade Agreement in Mexico City attracted over two hundred representatives from Mexican companies.

Good subjects for conferences or seminars often begin with the following phrases:

- *How to...* ...Plan, Design and Build a Data Center. ...Protect Your Assets in the Event of... ...Negotiate a New Lease. ...Build Effective Teams. ...Get Better Results from Your Advertising Dollar.
- *What You Need to Know About...* ...The New (fill in the blank) Law. ...Drugs in the Workplace. ...Terminating an Employee. ...Outsourcing. ...Doing Business in Europe.

A brainstorming session of half an hour can usually provide you with a good assortment of subjects to pick from.

A matter of hours or days

Next you must decide on the conference's length. You can determine length by asking yourself the following questions.

- *How much time and support do I have to set it up?* A two-day conference requires much more work than an evening seminar. You must adjust the length to the level of effort you can put into setting it up.
- *How much content do I have to offer?* There is simply not enough material for a lengthy conference on some subjects. When the Americans with Disabilities Act first passed, many people needed to learn about it quickly, because there were potentially stiff legal penalties for noncompliance. However, the legislation was so new that many of its implications were still uncertain. It constituted an ideal subject for a half-day or evening seminar, but few people had the knowledge to run a longer one.
- *Is my audience willing to pay?* A two-day conference gets expensive, and most firms expect to be paid for them. The audience, in turn, is faced with not just a fee but a substantial opportunity cost in time invested away from other duties. A longer conference must therefore deal with a particularly weighty, urgent, or complicated subject. Generally you must also have a longer mailing list to find people with budgets and schedules that will allow them to attend.
- *How many speakers can I attract?* Plenty of multiday conference use only one speaker, but if you try to hold the audience all by yourself, you had better be good. Using three or four speakers a day diversifies your risk. Some of the time the audience will be listening to some exceptional speakers, even if not all are of equal quality.
- *How geographically scattered is my market?* Few people will drive more than an hour to attend a breakfast or evening seminar. Assuming a 10-percent response rate to your invitations (an optimistic target), you will need to invite two hundred prospective buyers of your services to attract

a twenty-person audience. Identifying so many prospects within a one-hour travel time is easy in some businesses but impossible in others, even when more than one person is invited from the same organization. The wider the geographic area you need to draw people from, the longer your conference will have to be to justify longer travel times.

Timing will also affect attendance. Most are scheduled to avoid summer vacations and end-of-the-year holidays. Longer conferences tend to be scheduled for either the beginning or end of the week, allowing participants to travel on the weekend and perhaps enjoy a short vacation at the city where the conference is being held. In the suburbs, short seminars tend to run in the late afternoon, allowing attendees to leave work a little early and avoid rush-hour traffic. Center-city seminars often fare better over breakfast or lunch. By the end of the day city commuters want to get home.

Location

Possible locations for your seminar or conference include your own offices, a hotel, a corporate or privately operated conference center, or space borrowed or leased from another organization. If your office has adequate meeting space and is close to the market you are trying to reach, holding the conference there provides you the opportunity to show the place off and introduce other members of the firm. The location serves as a subtle advertisement for your firm. At one seminar I ran, an attendee noticed material on work the firm had done in the Czech Republic. He was about to start a project there himself. This kind of serendipity is more likely if a seminar takes place in your office.

Hotels and conference centers offer logistical support unavailable at many offices for conferences of a day or more, including full audio-visual support, eating space separate from meeting space, and almost enough telephones for everyone to use during breaks. Most hotels will provide meeting space free if you guarantee a minimum number of room rentals. Room rates are negotiable if you expect a large number of participants. More importantly, you will want to negotiate the cost of meals and break-time refreshments. This is because participants pay for rooms themselves, while you pay for meals and refreshments either out of conference fees or out of your own pocket. Talk to several hotels, see the space they plan to give you, look at rooms, taste the food, check out logistical support such as photocopying and audiovisual equipment, request rates, and ask for references from others who have held meetings there. You will then be in a position to negotiate with several hotels to get the mix of service and cost that suits your needs.

Pulling them in

Most seminars are marketed by direct mail. The longer the seminar and the more you plan to charge for it, the longer the list will have to be to identify an adequate number of candidates. A breakfast or evening seminar can get by with a much shorter list. When I ran a series of after-work seminars followed by a cocktail party, the first one had an invitation list of three hundred, which grew to about five hundred a year later. The acceptance rate for each seminar was about 10 percent, and almost exactly half the people who accepted showed up each time. Review the section on lists in chapter 7 when preparing a mailing.

Because the quality of your invitation or flyer greatly influences attendance, it deserves special attention. For a one- or two-day conference, the flyer should include seven things.

- *The conference theme.* The reader should be able to determine almost instantaneously what the conference is about. The wording should be as compelling as possible. The title *What is the Competition Doing?* will entice more people to read the flyer than will *Competitive Intelligence.*

- *A concise description stressing benefits.* Don't leave it to the readers to figure out what they will get out of attending. Tell them up front:

  A two-day conference on the latest developments in competitive intelligence. You will learn:

  □ *New methods for determining competitors' pricing.*

  □ *Little-known sources of information on competitor profitability.*

  □ *Ways to check the reliability of industry "gossip."*

  This example may seem a hard sell to some. Professional conference operators usually employ a hard sell and make a profit by doing so. If you tone down your flyer, be sure you don't obscure the benefits in the process.

- *A description of who should attend.* This inclusive list indicates who the conference is designed for and allows the reader to say, "This is meant for me!"

  Who Should Attend:

  □ *Strategic Planners*

  □ *Marketers*

  □ *Competitor Analysts*

  □ *Business Unit Managers*

  □ *Strategy Consultants*

- *A review of the schedule and content.* In this portion, list what will occur from the morning through the afternoon of each day, noting speakers and subjects followed by two or three bullets stressing the benefits of each:

  Day One:

  9:00 - 10:15 a.m.
  Determining What You Really Need to Know:
  Dr. Roger Skulk

  □ *Setting Priorities in Information Gathering*

  □ *Avoiding Information Gaps*

□ *How to Respond to "It Might Be Nice to Know..."*

...and so on.

■ *A concise speaker description.*

■ *Logistics of time, place, fee, payment, registration, and accommodations.* This should include directions to the site.

■ *A sign-up sheet.* This can be a tear sheet or a response card.

A famous speaker, of course, deserves top billing. If you have one, resequence your material accordingly. Invitations to short seminars will be less elaborate but should include most of the same information.

The speakers

People who organize seminars for the first time often see themselves or others in their firm as primary speakers. You can often do better by including outsiders and sometimes by using them exclusively. Doing this will make the seminar seem less self-serving, which frequently results in higher attendance. Prospective clients will shun a seminar if they sense they may be submitted to an hour-long advertisement. A.T. Kearney periodically hosts one-day seminars for key business leaders. These seminars almost always feature a big-name, outside speaker who draws in the crowd. Kearney consultants sit with the audience where they can discuss the seminar and develop relationships.

Among the outside speakers you can choose are past clients, representatives of companies in businesses that sell to the same clientele that you do, and experts. Experts include academics and a wide array of other specialists who don't compete with you. When selecting a speaker or speakers for a seminar, you will want to consider...

■ ...*drawing power.* Some names attract more attendees than others. A client with stature in his industry will often attract his competitors, who are probably good prospective clients for you.

■ ...*availability.* One of the most onerous tasks in organizing a conference or seminar is lining up speakers. This needs to be done early in the process, because everything else hinges on it.

■ ...*knowledge.* The speaker must know the subject matter. Firms that use only their own employees as speakers often can do so because they are presenting highly technical material that is little understood by outsiders.

■ ...*speaking ability.* The quality of the speaking will determine the success of the seminar. Don't subject your audience to the expert bore. Rehearse the speakers.

■ ...*balance.* If you have several speakers, make sure they present different points of view. Otherwise you will get a me-too presentation.

■ ...*price.* Most firms want to avoid paying speakers.

If you do decide to speak yourself or to use others in your firm as speakers, you can do two things to make sure that you will be perceived as an expert rather than a salesman. First, seek out someone else to sponsor the event. Firms that run conferences for a profit will often accept good ideas, especially if the firm suggesting a subject is willing to help pay for it. Alternatively, you may be able to interest a trade association or other group in sponsoring the program by stressing its benefits to members. Be careful. Outside sponsors will sometimes invite a competitor to speak with you, and will seldom bar a competitor from sitting in the audience. If you have strong reason for using an outside sponsor, I would not let this risk deter you. The benefits of getting face to face with a large number of prospects usually outweighs the risk of competition.

If you plan both to host an event and to speak at it, you *must* stress the content and benefits in your flyer. The more people understand about what they will learn, the less they are likely to fear an advertisement. Remember, people attend a seminar to learn, not to be sold!

A chance to talk

People attend seminars and conferences not only to hear the speakers but to talk to their peers at other companies. They want to compare notes, commiserate, look for jobs, and relax with others who understand their problems. These periods of informal interaction also offer you the best opportunities for building relationships and generating leads. Arrangements for this activity deserves careful attention. You need to block appropriate time for it—before a breakfast or dinner seminar, after an afternoon seminar, and at several convenient times during a conference.

You will need space that encourages interaction. That means open space out of traffic flow where people can stand and talk to each other without interruption. Comfortable sitting space in small clusters helps too.

During this time you and others from your firm should play host, circulating to make sure you meet everyone, making introductions, and absorbing those at the fringes of the conversations into the center. Above all, you should get others to talk. They have had a chance to hear you during the presentation. Now it is your turn to listen and learn. Learn names, learn personal interests, learn business responsibilities and concerns. This information will allow you to follow up later with a personal note to each individual.

Have a few stock questions to get others talking, like, "What is your specific interest in coming to this conference?" or "What do you think of the seminar so far?" Also, have questions that will draw out the silent individuals in a group. If one individual dominates the discussion with his reason for attending, wait for a pause and say, "That's interesting." Turn to someone else and say, "Did you come for the same reasons or different ones?"

Using your networking skills, you should be listening for ways you can help those you talk with. An obligation to call a participant with information he is looking for creates a means of keeping the relationship alive later. Create a list of these obligations for use after the conference.

The opportunity to establish a relationship with your audience is one of the primary benefits of running a seminar or conference. The chance to do so is largely restricted to informal interaction periods. Work hard during these periods and you greatly increase your chances of obtaining business later.

Money

Few firms charge for seminars running less than a full day. A one- or two-day conference, however, can cost thousands of dollars to put on. Because of the substantial educational benefits they provide, attendees are willing to pay for them, and most, though not all, firms charge a fee. You should consider doing so.

The more your conference looks like one run by a trade association or other third-party conference operator, the more you can charge attendees. This usually means several presenters from a variety of organizations, high-quality audio-visual materials, a binder full of training materials, and good-quality conferencing space. Individuals with unusually strong credentials as experts and trainers do present alone for two days and charge, but they are in the minority. For prevailing fee structures, review fliers for conferences that you receive by mail. As of this writing they run between $600 and $1,200 dollars per attendee for most two-day programs. Charging a fee can enhance the credibility of your seminar. It shows that people will pay to hear what you say and is an indicator that you intend to educate, not advertise.

Something to take home

For-profit conferences universally provide participants with printed material summarizing what they have learned. If your event is free, you must decide whether to do so. Materials you can use for this purpose include copies of exhibits used by speakers, white papers or reprints of articles on the subject, and speaker bios.

A high-quality package of materials adds to the professional appearance of a seminar and gives those who attend something they can save with your name on it.

Following up

Within a week of a conference's completion you should follow up with letters to everyone you have met, thanking them for attending. If you have promised someone information, you can put it in the letter, or, if appropriate, call. As in all forms of marketing, follow-up has a major impact on lead generation and separates the serious marketer from the casual one.

Conclusion

Conferences and seminars demand more of those who sponsor them than many other forms of marketing. They are expensive, complex, and deadline-oriented. Hundreds of tasks must be completed on time. You can postpone a cold call or a mailing, but once a date is established, you cannot postpone a conference.

These concerns must be weighed against the power of the conference. It is a marketing activity that can pay its own way in fees. You establish yourself as an expert. You do so, in most cases, without having to compete for attention and you have a strong opportunity to develop personal relationships you can build upon later. Seminars and conferences will remain one of the most powerful tools for marketing professional services.

9

Getting Publicity

Case example: The Publicist

Glenda, a litigator in a Midwestern city, had a way with words. Part of her success resulted from using concise, colorful phrases that juries remembered. One morning when she came into the office, the senior partner complimented her on the good quote she had received in the city's largest newspaper. She looked at a copy and found that two phrases she had used with a reporter the day before had been quoted. The conversation had been casual and almost accidental. A friend had suggested the reporter call her because she had experience in product liability law, which might be pertinent to a story he was writing. The afternoon the story appeared, she received a call from a small corporation with a product liability problem. It became the first client she sold entirely on her own.

She called the reporter to thank him for the quote, and he asked her about another story he was working on. She couldn't help him, herself, but referred him to two people who could, explaining exactly why it might be useful to talk with each of them. From then on she and the reporter spoke every month or so, and once in a while she would end up with a quote. Occasionally another reporter would get her name from one of these stories and call her too. She would incorporate him into her network of press contacts. When she learned that a local radio talk show was going to do a story on dangerous Christmas toys, she sent a letter along with some press clippings to the host, who invited her to speak on the program. This time she received two calls from prospective clients. Glenda had become a minor media star, and honing her public relations skills, built much of her practice around the leads her publicity generated.

When the *Wall Street Journal* twice quoted a competitor on a subject I knew a lot about, I became so irritated that I began a campaign to obtain a similar quote for my firm. Three months later a reporter from the *Journal* referred to a study I had done in a small article that appeared well back in the paper. My study received but a sentence or two. I was not mentioned at all, and the name of my company only once, but the following week three prospects called as a direct result. Had I had any doubts, this would have convinced me of the power of media relations.

Media exposure will help build your reputation and generate leads. What is more, according to a study by D.F. Blumberg Associates, companies that call you because they have heard about you in the media are substantially more likely to hire you than those whom you call first.[1] All experienced professionals know this, at least intuitively. There are at least four reasons why it is true. First, such prospects have prequalified themselves on the basis both of need and of an interest in hiring you. As will be explained in chapter 18, this is especially helpful for those practices where client need is infrequent. In such cases proactive selling approaches tend to be ineffective, because looking for a client who has the need today is like looking for a needle in a haystack. This problem is compounded if the client's need is also confidential. Second, the publicity has reassured the prospect that you are a credible source of help, reducing the selling you have to do. Third, the majority of professionals are far better reactive than proactive sales people, and responding to the prospect's call requires reactive selling only.

Prospects want to hire a firm that has relevant, successful experience, and publicity spreads news of your successes across the market. As one attorney said, "You have to let other people know you have done a transaction. That's what builds your reputation in this business. You do that by getting the right reporters to write about it."

If a prospect has read about you in the papers or heard you quoted on the radio or TV, his willingness to give you a meeting or include you among the firms being considered for a project increases. Press clippings can also prove your expertise and reputation to prospects you have reached by other means. Public relations, then, can be a valuable part of your marketing effort.

Many professional firms want good media exposure, but few get it. Many do not understand the process for getting good coverage. The lack of knowledge keeps many from trying. Others try ineptly, fail, and give up. Some firms find it difficult to attract media attention because the businesses they are in don't offer much good material. An engineering firm that designs mechanical, electrical, and plumbing systems for grade school renovations will have less opportunities for exposure than a consulting firm that specializes in disaster recovery, simply because disasters attract more publicity than school renovations. In spite of these deterrents, almost any professional who is willing to learn the process, can think creatively, and makes the effort can get media coverage.

Most neophytes to public relations hold a number of mistaken beliefs that diminish the effectiveness of their efforts. These are so common they warrant comment before I proceed any further.

Mistaken belief #1: *My primary objective is to promote my firm.*
Promoting your firm may be an underlying reason for making the effort, but when you sit down to talk with a reporter or write a press release, your primary objective

should be to help the reporter prepare a good story. If you are not helping, he will quickly lose interest in you, not just for this story, but for others as well. You should ask yourself what you have that might help the reporter. Do you, yourself, have direct experiences that might be interesting? Can you refer the reporter to someone else he should talk to? Are there reports or studies the reporter should know about because they address the issue he is investigating? Use the reporter's time well and you have a good chance of becoming a source now and in the future. Abuse it by treating him as nothing more than a vehicle to promote your firm, and he will soon catch on and talk to you only if he absolutely has too.

A surprising number of people must learn that the media do not exist to promote their companies and services. Rather they exist to educate and entertain their audiences. If they fail, circulation or audiences decline, they lose advertising revenues, and eventually cease to exist.

Mistaken belief #2: *The process starts with a press release.*
Press releases may be the logical starting place if you are reporting on promotions of firm personnel or other routine matters. They are not the best place to start on any major story. There are many things you need to do before deciding whether to write a release; these will be described below. In spite of this caution, releases remain a valuable tool. A detailed description of their use and format is included in appendix C.

Mistaken belief #3: *Reporters are primarily interested in facts.*
Of course reporters are interested in facts and information. That goes with the job. But in my experience facts and information are relatively easy to come by. If you talk to enough people you will usually get plenty for a story. Having information is a prerequisite to getting interviewed, but by itself will not get you mentioned. I will give guidance on how to get mentioned elsewhere in this chapter.

Mistaken belief #4: *If I help a reporter, I'm entitled to coverage.*
When I first began to work with the media, I spent several days helping a reporter from *Inc.* magazine with a story. She needed a case study of a company move to fit a relocation theme issue. I identified a past client interested in the publicity, gathered background information, and spent a day driving her to the client for the interview. In total I invested several days, and time is money.

Shortly before publication she called to inform me that her editor had decided not to run the story. I was speechless. Would my client be upset? What would my boss think about the waste of time? I leaned on her and leaned hard, but of course she held her ground.

I look back on this incident with embarrassment. Up to the point I started leaning, I had done a professional PR job, earning the reporter's respect and gratitude. Had I accepted the decision to drop the story graciously, she probably would have wanted to help me in the future either by using me as a source or by passing my name on to other reporters. As it was, I lost not only the story but also a valuable contact, and marked myself as a rank amateur into the bargain.

Reporters have no obligation to use any source they talk to, even if that source has been extremely helpful. Especially at high-end publications such as *The Wall Street Journal, Business Week, Fortune,* and *Inc.*, evidence that a reporter included quotes in direct exchange for getting information could get him fired. The ethics of journalism dictate that accurate reporting and a good story must be the only criteria for deciding what gets included. This standard protects reporters from political and economic influence that might undermine the media and endanger both our freedoms and our wallets. (Some readers will recall an incident in which an influential reporter was caught using publicity in his column to manipulate stock values.) The more influential the media, the more carefully it will hold to this standard.

This means that sometimes you will work hard to help a reporter on a story, but you won't get mentioned. Or you will be named but not your company, so that no one reading the story can find you. It happens. When it does, accept the reporter's explanation graciously and supportively, thank him for his attention, and offer your help at any time he needs it in the future. Ethical standards aside, reporters are human and they do have a sense of obligation. When someone has helped them, they will try to give that person coverage if they can find an appropriate opportunity to do so. Keep at it and you will get the press you want.

This high standard does not apply everywhere. Trade publications unashamedly boost a particular industry, profession, or trade, and no one expects them to do otherwise. In this context, the risk that your help will not result in publicity is greatly reduced.

Unabashed boosterism is far preferable to what you find at some less meticulous media. Smaller and more desperate for revenue, some regional and local organizations will inform you directly or by inference that advertising dollars can be swapped for publicity. Editorial staffs sometimes stand up to such policies, but during a recession when advertising dollars decline and everyone fears for his job, they are less likely to do so. You must decide whether the resulting publicity warrants the advertising expense and the sick feeling in your stomach that come with such a deal.

Having cleared up the most common misconceptions about media relations, we can now look at what the professional should do to get good publicity.

You must know your market
You must "sell" your story to the media by convincing them that it has value to their audiences. The first step in this process is to determine which media organizations serve audiences who might have an interest. You must know your market, and that means knowing what audiences are targeted by what publications and programs and also what approach they take with those audiences. You must know the kinds of stories they typically run and the kinds of content such stories require. How much data are they likely to want? How much reporting is done through interviews? Will they only interview one company in an industry, or will they always talk to several? This research is quite similar to the research you would do before writing an article.

Sources of information include:

- *Bacon's Publicity Checker.* Published annually, this source provides background information on the media. Unfortunately, only large libraries carry it. Try an advertising or public relations firm or your company's public relations department.[2]

- *Personal inspection.* You should familiarize yourself with any publication or program you seek to place a story with. If it is a newspaper or magazine, review back issues. If it is a radio or TV program, listen to it several times. Does what you see and hear tell you something about what they are looking for? It should.

- *Advertisers' kits.* Many media companies produce kits of materials for advertisers that provide data on audiences, information on upcoming themes to be covered, and other information useful to you. These kits are usually free for the asking.

- *Interviews with reporters or editors.* Take a reporter or editor to lunch and ask him to tell how his particular program or publication selects stories and who its primary audience is. Ask how you can be helpful to them. These people can tell you things that are not easy to find out in other ways. For example, some of the national business media are far more likely to publish stories on publicly held companies than privately held ones, because investors make up an important part of the audience. I only found this out by talking with their reporters.

Second, you must know something about individual people within a specific media organization, because people make decisions about what stories to pick up. Rather than blindly submit your story, whether by press release or phone call, you will succeed more frequently if you direct it to that individual who is most likely to be interested. Reporters work beats, or subject territories. In an ideal world, if you misdirect a call or press release, the receiver will pass it along to the right individual. In reality people make mistakes, get distracted, and get lazy about doing things that are not personal priorities. Getting the story to the right person first not only avoids these problems but also demonstrates your professionalism.

Finding the right individual is not always easy, especially at large organizations. While reviewing back issues or listening to programs, try to identify reporters covering related stories and start with them. During your lunches with editors or reporters, ask who covers the beats you are interested in.

A little time invested in research before you begin to promote your firm will greatly improve your results.

You must create a network of media contacts

Networking is helping people, networking is recognizing a lead for someone else when you hear it...All of these guidelines delineated in the chapter on networking apply to media networks as much as they do to any other. Work your media contacts in the same way and you will see amazing results.

This means, of course, that you must understand what "help" means to a reporter. Help can be:

- A lead on a hot story, before others hear about it
- An approach to a story the reporter may not have thought about
- Names of people she can contact to help her with a story
- Good quotes (see below)
- Good use of her time, such as not wasting it with useless stories

In return you increase your chances of learning about a reporter's story idea, since reporters will often discuss a concept with someone they trust, whom they think can be helpful. This will give you the chance to help her frame it in a way that may get you mentioned. Every year Moran, Stahl and Boyer, a consulting firm, helps one of the national business magazines rank American cities. The opportunity for such blockbuster publicity came from such a conversation.

If you choose media relations as an adjunct effort, you can still see results from a more modest investment of your time than a full networking program requires.

You must recognize a good story when you see one

Every project you do, with the insights you gain from completing it, generates possible material for a story. The hard job is determining what approach to a story would have the most interest to a particular publication or program and its audience. In short, you need an angle.

Reporters always use an angle to work a story. This is the same concept of an angle that I used in chapter 1 on article writing, and they use it for the same reasons you or I would: An angle focuses material on the interests of a particular audience. By doing so it helps the reporter decide what portions of the mass of information collected on a subject belong in the article. It provides a purpose to the piece that pushes the writer beyond a simple recitation of facts.

The closer you can come to suggesting a good angle to a specific reporter, the greater the chances that he will see potential in the story. This means you must develop a nose for a good story.

When you evaluate something about your business as a potential story, ask yourself these questions.

- *What makes it news?* Most of the media are interested in subjects that can be classified as news. That means they must be current, informative, and, whenever possible, urgent. The tenth anniversary of your firm may be current, but it fails to meet the second two criteria for most media. A law or accounting firm might be able to report on how different kinds of clients are responding to a change in the tax laws; this meets all three criteria.

- *Can you tie it to a national or regional issue or trend?* One way to make something newsworthy is to tie it to broader trends. The prohibition against the use of Freon and halon in refrigeration, air conditioning, and fire suppressant equipment provides an opportunity for a number of architects, consulting engineers, consultants, and lawyers to get publicity for their projects or views. One large architectural firm received coverage in *Fortune* by tying its work to the corporate trend toward suburban campuses.

- *Can you tie it to someone who is newsworthy?* Your clients are often more newsworthy than you are. When a real estate broker fills a building with a nationally known firm, he may be able to build a story around the event, which becomes newsworthy in part because of the client's name. A transaction for a large client may provide its attorneys with an opportunity for publicity.

Completing the exercise in exhibit 9.1 will increase your understanding of these three criteria.

Exhibit 9.1
Is It Newsworthy?

Make three copies of this form and fill it out for three projects or events you have worked on.

Project or event: _____

1. Is it news? (Is it current, informative, urgent? Who would it be news to? Why?)	
2. Can you tie it to a bigger issue or trend? (How does it relate to something in your region or the nation?)	
3. Can you tie it to someone newsworthy? (Is some person, company, or organization affected who appears in the news for other reasons?)	

You can sometimes find ways to create news

Do you have or can you create information that would be news to others? Many firms have done this and reaped publicity rewards.

There are four typical vehicles for creating news. The first is an *event*. Ground breaking, topping-off, and opening ceremonies for new buildings have become events staged for the media. A seminar can also provide grist for a press release.

The second vehicle for making news is *a report* or white paper. New tax, environmental, labor, and other laws often provide an opportunity for a firm to prepare a paper on their implications. Reports on opinions also get coverage; some firms have conducted face-to-face interviews with past and prospective clients in order to collect them. Though expensive, the personal contact is seen as a worthwhile marketing cost. Still other firms have been able to extract portions of work done for a client, expand upon them and issue the results as a report.

The third vehicle is a *survey*. Reports on surveys appear in the press almost every day. The contents need not be earthshaking to be newsworthy. At the peak of two recoveries, surveys I conducted showed that labor shortages resulted in increased turnover, rising compensation costs, and reduced hiring standards. Both times these less-than-surprising findings were reported on the front page of *The Wall Street Journal* and on radio, because they filled a void. Reporters could use unemployment statistics to show that labor was scarce, and they had plenty of anecdotal information on the impact of the shortages, but my study provided the only statistical evidence that linked the shortage to problems.

Of course, the cost of conducting a survey can be high unless you have an artful way of capturing the data. Much of the data for my labor shortage survey was collected from personnel officers I made speeches to. By leaving a brief survey form on every seat, I was able to collect many responses at little cost. I have seen a major consulting firm collecting survey information at a trade show booth. Other organizations have been able to convince a publisher to incorporate a brief survey in a magazine with responses recorded on the response card that allows readers to request information from advertisers. Data can also be a byproduct of normal business operations, such as the space availability studies prepared by many real estate brokerage firms.

A final category of "made news" is the *statistic*. These data may appear annually, quarterly, or on some other regular basis and provide indicators of business or other conditions. Runtzheimer International's reports on regional variations in living costs, for example, have become an accepted source for a specific statistic. The firm has received tremendous publicity as a result.

Usually such statistics are a byproduct of a firm's normal operations, but some companies have been able to take publicly available data and manipulate it in a way that provides something newsworthy. To develop a statistic that can be identified with your firm, you must identify how data that you have access to and to which you can provide a special interpretation can be related to nationally or regionally important trends.

You must speak quotably

I noted previously that having information may get you interviewed by a reporter, but will not, by itself, get you mentioned. To get mentioned you must be worth quoting. As investigative reporter Carl Hiaasen put it in his comic thriller, *Tourist Season*, "...in my business, the coin of the realm is a good quote—it's the only thing that brings a newspaper story to life. One decent quote is the difference between dog food and caviar..."[3] A good quote helps the writer and gets you mentioned. As a derivative benefit it gets your name into the publication's files, increasing the odds that you will be called the next time someone writes on a related subject. This means that you must learn not just to help reporters but to speak quotably while doing so.

Look at the front page of any issue of *The Wall Street Journal.* You will see that an article has three kinds of sources. First there are those who are central to a story and must be quoted, if possible: the president of the company being discussed, a whistle-blower, or other key parties to an issue. Second there are people with inside information, like customers, vendors, and trade association heads. Finally there are outside experts, usually professionals like consultants, attorneys, and accountants. The best quotes are taken from each group. For most professionals, the biggest opportunity to get quoted is as an expert. Because there are usually so many experts to choose from and because their comments are not essential to the story, experts must make a particular effort to speak quotably, if they want to get mentioned.

Some people have a knack for speaking quotably. For most of us it requires practice. I must concentrate hard on speaking quotably when I talk to a reporter, and I still fall far short of several people I know. I have progressed to the point that I can predict with near-perfect accuracy which statements I make will get printed. Read some well-written newspapers and study the quotes carefully, especially those made by outside experts. See whether you can get a flavor of what makes them attractive to the writer. Some of these characteristics are...

- ...*brevity and decisiveness.* Most quotes are short. They must capture an opinion or fact in few words. There is little room for the balanced, on-the-one-hand-and-on-the-other statements that, as professionals, we may feel compelled to make. A reporter is more likely to quote two different experts with opposing opinions to create balance in a story than to quote one who is able to express both points of view. It makes better copy.

- ...*color.* The more colorful the statement, the more quotable it becomes. Similes and metaphors often appear in the press, some ("...like Bambi caught in the headlights") becoming clichés. Colorful words also help. For a while referring to someone as a "wannabe" almost assured a quote. Even a standard opinion can get quoted if it is worded originally.

- ...*controversiality.* Anyone who struggles to appear reasonable sacrifices quotes unless he can make reason sound controversial (by making a curse-on-both-your-houses statement, for example). Controversy is generally more exciting than reason, and reporters strive to add spice to their pieces. Think of some people you know who get quoted frequently in the media and you will realize that they often say things that the rest of us would cringe to utter.

- ...*cynicism or hope.* Reporters can often use cynical or hopeful statements to balance public relations hype or group despondency. By using such statements, the reporter proves that he is not accepting at face value what others say. They prove the reporter is not naive, a thing reporters must never seem.

If you have a knack for the epigram or the bon mot, you should consider incorporating a media relations effort into your marketing program. Note that quotable statements should go into your press releases as well as into your conversations with reporters.

My clients sometimes feel self-conscious practicing speaking quotably, but it is essential to learn how. The importance of a good quote was brought home to me by another experience with *The Wall Street Journal*. A reporter called, and several people in the firm I worked for provided him with real help, including background information and, with the client's permission, a perfect case example. When the story appeared, our background information was used and our client was quoted extensively. Compelling quotes from two of our competitors, speaking as experts, also appeared. We were not mentioned at all.

The standards of the *Journal* required that the reporter interview our competitors, and I realized later that their statements had been much more quotable than the bland ones we had made. We had done all the work and they had gotten the benefit.

Exhibit 9.2 lists some questions that a reporter might ask you. See whether you can come up with some colorful quotes in response to them.

Exhibit 9.2
Say It Quotably

Here are four statements to a reporter. Reword them to make them more quotable.

1. The people laid off by (name an industry or company) will find it difficult to find another job.
2. Most companies shouldn't spend time on that issue anymore.
3. Depending on how you interpret the facts, he might have done it because he was dishonest or because he was naive.
4. We haven't given up yet.

There is no right answer, but examples of more quotable alternatives include:

1. Many will never work again.
   - A few might find jobs in the industry, but most will have to find some other way to make a living.
2. That issue is as dead as the flat earth theory.
3. He may have been naive rather than dishonest, but...
   - Alternative A) ...naive people shouldn't be in this business.
   - Alternative B) ...that won't bring back the widows' and orphans' money.
4. This is only round one.

A call from a reporter may be blind luck or may result from hard work to attract his interest. In either case you must make the most of the opportunity, for it may not come soon again. Stop. Think about what you are going to say. Speak quotably.

Try to involve your clients in your public relations effort

Your clients may be bigger, better known, and so more newsworthy than you are. Moreover, your expertise, knowledge, and accomplishments all derive from the work you do for your clients. To a large degree your stories are their stories. Much of your ability to get good press depends upon your ability to use your clients' names.

Yet your clients have no obligation to help you publicize yourself. They have paid you for your services and have publicity needs of their own. They may not want any publicity. Under these circumstances your ability to get your clients to work with you can determine the success of your publicity campaign. To get as much help as possible from your clients follow these rules.

- *When in doubt, ask.* If you have any doubt about whether a client would mind your using its name, ask. It is hard to imagine publicity so good that it is worth alienating a good client.

- *Learn the client's predisposition for publicity early.* If they are against it, this will save you the time you might devote to planning a publicity effort they will not accept. An architectural firm hoped to get a lot of publicity about a new headquarters it had designed for a not-for-profit organization, only to find that the organization's management was afraid such publicity would call attention to the cost of the new building. Publicity plans had to be adjusted accordingly.

- *Offer the client good publicity whenever you can.* If you know that a reporter is writing a positive story that a client might be able to contribute to, find out whether they would like to be quoted. Helping them get good publicity may make them more willing to help you in the same way later. Clients that are not large enough to have a public relations staff are likely to appreciate your offer to serve as their publicist.

- *Work with your clients' public relations staff.* By knowing what kinds of publicity they plan around the project you are working on, you may be able to find ways both to help them and to get some publicity yourself.

- *Warn them about impending bad publicity.* By doing so, you show you are on their side.

- *Get a commitment for help from as high up in the organization as possible.* Corporate public relations staffs will cooperate with you more fully if they have been asked to do so by the boss.

- *Show them what you plan to distribute, if you plan to use their name.* By showing them the portion of any release that pertains to them, you avoid misunderstanding. Also, they may object to something that seems positive or innocuous to you. You can usually get a twenty four-hour turnaround or less by using faxes. Public relations departments understand deadlines.

Recognize that reporters have different obligations and ethical standards from yours

You must exercise caution when speaking to the media. You may know this, but understanding why will help you talk with reporters more effectively.

Everyone has obligations that supersede even close friendships. If, for example, you knew about a major financial problem at your company, you would probably feel obliged to withhold it from a reporter who was also a friend. Similarly, because of his obligations as a journalist, a reporter friend might feel obliged to publish a story or quote that you would rather not see appear.

Good stories aren't easy to write, yet truth, circulation, and the reporter's job depend on them. This creates pressures to do things that are not easy for an outsider to understand. Take the case of the Chicago reporter who called me about a large city agency long ago. The agency, at the time, was doing a lousy job, but I didn't want to go on record as saying that. I had to work with the people there. Still, his question seemed fair enough: "What were five good and five bad things that I could say about (the agency)?" I answered and went happily back to work.

The next day a friend commented that the agency must have really done something to make me mad. With a sick feeling I looked at the paper. There, accurately quoted, were the five bad things I had said about the agency...and nothing else. After smashing my coffee cup, I calmed down and analyzed what had happened. Obviously, no one had wanted to offend the staff of the agency. The story was filled with quotes that would have made a flack grin. Other sources had been smarter—or more experienced—than I was. They had stuck to the good stuff, leaving the reporter with a badly lopsided set of quotes. The reporter knew what was happening and that he was onto something. He needed balance to keep his readers' and editor's interest in the subject. He needed someone naive enough to speak his mind. He found me.

I did not make this mistake again. When asked for an opinion, I answered much more carefully thereafter. Sometimes I have even told a reporter that I have had both good and bad experiences with the press, most of the bad ones involving being quoted out of context. I then offer to give him my opinion, if he will exercise caution not to do what the reporter in the preceding anecdote did. This has saved me similar embarrassment, but has also gotten me cut out of some stories altogether.

Always ask yourself how a reporter might use any quotes you give him before you answer, and then choose your words accordingly. Don't say anything, even off the record, that you would be unwilling to see in print with your name attached unless you know the reporter extremely well. Even off the record, the quote had better not be too tempting. Not all reporters are ethical; some will use anything you say, regardless of whether it is on the record or not.

If you understand the media and know how to work with them, you can enjoy publicity that will build your reputation and bring in leads.

Part II

Sales Tactics: How Professionals Advance and Close Sales

This section of the book tells how to turn leads into sales. It covers basic selling, proposal writing, presenting, and fee construction. The level of skill required to sell professional services has increased in recent years, for several reasons. First, the long recession and slow recovery of the early 1990s severely hurt many professionals' practices. To get new business they have had to sell harder and smarter than in the past. The recession has also helped overcome the lingering effects of former prohibitions against many kinds of marketing and sales, prohibitions that were formally eliminated in the professions in the late 1970s. Lifting these bans freed professionals to market and sell more directly than they did in the past. As this has occurred, selling techniques have improved in all industries, and literature on the subject has reached more professionals. Meanwhile, the competition is stiffer than ever before. As in other businesses, the nationalization and internationalization of markets has increased the number of competitors most professionals are likely to face. Troubled economies and weak sales have pushed professionals to expand their services into areas previously left to others.

You cannot afford to be one of the dying breed of professionals who repudiates selling and salesmanship as unprofessional. History is full of generals who lost wars because they ignored the latest weapons as unsportsmanlike. You must develop the skills learned by the best in your business to win new clients. Selling is becoming so important to the professions that over the next five years most firms of any size will implement sales training programs. Some of the largest ones already have.

Selling, like lead generation, requires learnable skills, which include listening, questioning, persuading, presenting, closing, and negotiating. You have already seen in exhibit 0.1 how much selling skills overlap with some lead generation skills. That is why, when you become better at one area of marketing and selling, you also become better at others.

133

A lot of good material exists on selling skills. In addition to reading this section, you may wish to read some of the other literature. I have included a list of the best books in appendix E. Almost all break the sales process down into parts, and all have at least four in common. They are:

- Establishing rapport
- Getting Information
- Giving Information
- Responding to concerns

Chapters 10, 11, and 12 deal with the last three of these parts. I will deal with the first here.

Establishing rapport

This is the brief period at the beginning of a sales meeting before you start to talk about the prospect's needs and your services. It is a time for small talk. Though you will not want to waste the prospect's time by letting it run too long, it does serve an important purpose; it is a time when you can talk more as individuals than as business people.

During this time you can accomplish several things.

- *Make introductions.* If you don't know everyone in the room, introduce yourself and tactfully try to determine who they are. Of course, this will be easier if you have established who is going to attend before the meeting. You can also introduce anyone who accompanies you.

- *Make a personal contact with each person present.* Unless you are meeting with a very large group, you should bring each person present into the small talk, however, briefly.

- *Determine whether there are any outside factors that will affect the meeting.* Often you will be aware of factors not directly related to your meeting but of importance to your prospect. Perhaps the company has recently been in the news. It may be appropriate to ask about such issues during the small talk. Sometimes you learn something of value to the rest of the meeting. Once in a while you will learn that the prospect is so distracted that it would be best to reschedule for another day. If this seems to be the case, make the offer. He will appreciate your considerateness and feel an obligation to be more attentive the next time. If he declines, reconfirm the time he has available for you. It may be less than you expected, meaning you will have to readjust your plans for the meeting. The act of committing to a specific period of time will help the prospect refocus on the meeting's agenda.

- *Establish or reaffirm a personal link to the prospect.* This is the time when you can learn about or remind the prospect of common interests or other personal links. Doing so will often get the meeting off on a better footing. It helps build a personal relationship, and professional sales is founded on building relationships.

10

Questioning and Listening

Questioning and listening comprise a crucial first stage in your sale. This stage should be discrete from presenting and responding to the prospect's questions. In many cases it will take up the first part of your meeting with a prospect. If the prospect expects a formal presentation, questioning and listing may have to take place at a separate meeting or meetings before the presentation. By questioning and listening you learn about a prospect's needs. Only when you understand his needs can you know what aspects of your services to present.

The two most common mistakes in selling professional services, mistakes that make all experienced rain makers shudder, are

- Talking too much
- Describing how the professional will help before adequate information is gathered on the prospect's needs

Untrained salespeople have an irrepressible urge to strut their knowledge. They often create a wrong paradigm: Selling = Talking. They seem to say to themselves, "Well, I'm here to sell, aren't I? I only have an hour. I better get talking." Ask untrained professionals how much time during a sales meeting they should be talking and most will say 50 percent, recognizing that they exceed that amount. But selling is more listening than talking. The most skilled rain maker will talk only 20 to 30 percent of the time. They listen well, then make a few words tell.

At times the untrained salesperson's compulsion to talk verges on rudeness. I could cite many cases, including some from my own early years in consulting, before I received professional sales training. One will suffice.

After months of work I arranged a meeting for the firm where I was working with the representatives of a Fortune 50 company. Prior to the meeting we all agreed that it would be best to ask the prospects about their needs before describing our services. After introductions I set the stage by saying that although I had had an opportunity to talk with our guests, the others on our team had not. Since it is always best to hear things from the source, would they mind describing their situation again?

The prospects were delighted for this chance—most people would rather talk than listen. The senior representative began, "As you are probably aware from the press, our company is shrinking its work force, including our department. At the same time we are under increasing pressure to deliver new projects quickly..."

While the prospect's mouth was still open to complete his sentence, the senior member of our team, a principal of the firm with over twenty years of experience, jumped in with an anecdote demonstrating our ability to deliver fast-track projects like no other firm. A short way into this story the prospect closed his mouth, hardly to open again during the entire meeting. The principal was totally oblivious to what he had done.

This man is not unusual. In my experience many professionals interrupt their prospects to score points and are unaware that they do so. Never interrupt a prospect. *Never* interrupt a prospect! Watch yourself to see whether you are doing it. Ask others to catch you if you do. During this stage of the sales meeting, listen; if you must talk, talk with a question that will keep the prospect talking. Take good notes. You can tell your story and make your points later, when you know more.

Think of selling as fishing. Lures are the questions you choose to engage the prospect and develop his interest. Casting is your skill at asking them. Fishing requires patience. You have to cast many times before you get a nibble. Once you get the prospect on the line, you must play him with more questions or he will snap the line and get away. Only when he is tired of talking can you reel him in with your presentation.

Don't think of selling as a game of basketball in which you score points. Too much aggressiveness and you will find you are scoring points against your prospect.

Eliciting information on a prospect's needs requires good questioning and listening technique, because prospects don't talk freely. They are inhibited from giving you a full understanding of their situation by...

- ...*time constraints.* The prospect is busy and probably doesn't have time to tell you everything you would like to know.

- ...*self esteem.* Giving you a full story might embarrass the prospect. He may be reluctant to admit how little influence he has on the buying decision or that he is ignorant of certain facts. He will almost certainly not admit that he finds hiring a professional threatening. Yet any of these things may be true.

- ...*self-interest.* The prospect may feel that telling you too much could hurt him. He may be afraid of word getting back to others in the company if he shares negative opinions. He may fear that your price will go up if he shows how much he needs you or that you will decline to bid on the project if he tells you that he favors a competitor. Prospects often feel that sensitive information should be kept from you until you are actually hired.

- ...*etiquette*. All buyers will view it as bad manners to pass on certain kinds of information. This sometimes applies to information that would seem too self-laudatory. A story of a feud between departments heads is another example. He will never tell you he doesn't like you.

- ...*confusion*. The buyer may not understand his own needs. This is extremely common in some professions. In such cases the buyer simply draws the wrong conclusions from the facts at his disposal.

- ...*unconscious behavior*. Everyone who has sold knows that some buyers sound optimistic and others pessimistic. Two people reporting the same situation can give it quite different spins depending upon their personalities.[1]

A commonly heard phrase among professional sales people is that buyers are liars. I detest this view because it suggests that buyers should meet a standard no one else does. Buyers, like other human beings, are incapable of being completely open and forthright. They need encouragement to talk more freely. This is also true of your boss, your peer, and your employee. Depending on how you work with the buyer, you can either raise or lower his inhibitions. When you lower them, the quality of the information you get improves.

You can encourage the buyer to give you information with the following.

- *Recognition.* People respond to positive feedback, such as "Your comments are very helpful." You must use recognition carefully, however, so that you neither sound like a toady nor unduly bias the information you get.

- *Empathy.* Showing interest in and sympathy for the buyer will generally improve the information you get. A comment like "That can't be easy for you," does this.

- *Rewards.* The buyer will give you more information if he understands how it will help him. This can include helping him hire the best professional, do his job better, avoid specific problems, etc.

- *Personal satisfaction.* The buyer may feel good about helping you if he likes you or feels an obligation to you. He may enjoy the mental stimulation or fun of talking with you.

- *Catharsis.* Occasionally a buyer may benefit from the opportunity to vent pent up feelings to an outsider.[2]

Different buyers will respond to different kinds of encouragement.

As the seller, you must lower the buyer's inhibitions about talking with you by effective encouragement. You have several tools to do this.

How to ask a question
The most obvious tool is the question. You will get more information from answers to your questions than from any other source. The quality of that information will depend in part on how good your questions are.

Start by knowing what you want to learn before you talk with the client, whether face to face or by phone. Exhibit 10.1 provides a list of some of the things you might want to know. Review it before you go to a meeting and set your information objectives according to the specifics of the situation. The first two columns list information you will want to know about the buyer's need and his process for hiring a professional. Borrowing from linguistics, I refer to the questions in the second column as "deep questions" because they are universal to all professions.

Exhibit 10.1
Question Planning Form

What the seller wants to know		What buyer can answer
Seller's Objective	Deep Question	Surface Questions
I. Questions about the prospect's needs		
A. To establish issues	What do you need?	Please give me the background on your situation. Please tell me about your reason for asking me to meet with you.
B. To establish cause	What created the need?	How did it start? How did it happen?
C. To establish urgency/ complication	Why do you need me? Why do you want help now?	This has been going on for some time. Why hasn't it been resolved? Why is this on your mind now?
D. To establish scope	What issues do you want me to address?	What needs to be dealt with now?
E. To validate buyer's diagnosis	How do you know you have this need?	What indications do you have that this is happening?

F. To establish company value/ implication	What difference would having this need met make to your company?	What will happen if the problem persists? What difference would it make to have it fixed?
G. To establish person value	What difference would having this need met make to you?	What is your personal interest in this problem?
H. To establish personal values	What difference would having this need met make to other participants in the buying decision?	Please tell me a little about their interest in the project.
I. To establish desired outcome	What results do you want?	What would you like to see happen? A year from now, if this problem were fixed, what would be different?
J. To establish performance measures	How will you know your need has been met?	How much do you expect to save? When do you need this completed? If we gave you a (plan, methodology, etc.), would that help you?
K. To establish project size	What are the basic parameters of the need?	How many employees do you have? How many square feet will it be? How many...

II. Questions about the hiring process		
A. To establish process	What are the steps in the process for hiring a professional?	Please tell me a little about how you plan to go about choosing a (consultant, lawyer, architect, accountant)? _____ _____ _____
B. To identify participants	Who else will participate in the selection process?	Who else is on your committee? What is the (affected departments CEO's) role in this? _____ _____ _____
C. To establish timing	When do you expect to make a decision?	When do you expect to make a decision? When do we start? _____ _____ _____
D. To understand your relationship to the buyer	How likely are you to hire me?	How did you hear about my firm? Why did you call me? What issues will your selection of a professional hinge on? Are you considering other firms? How would you compare us to the competition? _____ _____ _____
E. To uncover impediments	What is delaying hiring me?	Please give me an update on the project. _____ _____ _____

F. To determine readiness to close	Are you ready to hire me?	When do we start?
		Where do we go from here?
		Would you like a proposal?
		_____
		_____
		_____

Because you must place questions in context and couch them in words that will lower the buyer's inhibitions, you can seldom ask these questions directly. This results in "surface questions," those the buyer will understand and feel comfortable answering. Because the form of surface questions depends heavily on your specific profession and practice and the specific context in which you ask them, I cannot give you precise words to use. The best I or anyone else can do is give you a general idea of the kinds of surface questions that will elicit answers to your deep questions, and leave it to you to come up with words that are suitable. Space is left in column three for you to practice devising surface questions. As an exercise, do so with a particular prospect in mind.

Note that to make a sale you will want an answer to every deep question listed. When answering one question, a buyer will sometimes volunteer an answer to a second. But if he doesn't, you must have a surface question ready to bring it out. Develop a question plan before you meet with the buyer.

There is no substitute for a clear knowledge of what you want to know. Some professionals take great pride in their ability to wing a sales meeting. The ability to do this can certainly be an advantage at times, given that the unpredictable often happens in sales. But to use this ability as a justification for ill-preparedness is as foolhardy as ignoring safety precautions with a gun because you happen to be a good marksman. Real professionals neither respect nor indulge in such vanities.

In constructing your surface questions, make use of the two basic question structures.

- *Open questions* encourage the buyer to talk at length by putting only the broadest parameters on what information you want. Such questions often begin with "why," "what," or "how," as in, "Why are you considering hiring a (specific type of professional)?" or "What gives you an interest in my firm?" Though technically not questions, polite demands can also be open: "Please describe (your problem)."

    Open questions are particularly good for eliciting needs, opinions, values, priorities, and sensitivities. They permit you to explore a subject without presuming to know where the answer might lead. They give the prospect freedom to decide what it is important for you to learn.

- *Closed questions* require a narrow answer, such as a date, fact, or number. Questions that can be answered yes or no fall into this category. They usually begin with such words as "when," "how many," or "will."

   Closed questions serve two purposes. They help you elicit specific facts you need on the client's need, such as its size and schedule. They also help you confirm what you have learned from open questions or by other means. ("Am I correct in understanding that you...?")

You must decide when to ask specific questions. The sequencing and timing of your questions will help determine the quality of the information you get back. Often a closed question confirming your prior knowledge is a good place to start. (I understand you have a patent problem. Is that correct?) Next, ask several open questions to establish the prospect's concerns as fully as possible. (Please tell me about your reason for asking me to meet with you. How did this problem arise? What responses have you considered? What help would you want to get from me?) Open questions are usually followed by a series of closed questions to gather facts and confirm what you have learned. (How much is this problem costing you? When did it start? Would you consider a settlement that would allow him to license the patent?)

Once you have collected information in one area, you should move on to the next with a second set of open questions, followed by more closed questions. (Where would you like to go from here? What is your process for hiring counsel? When do you plan to make a decision?)

Beyond this general framework for sequencing questions, you will want to save sensitive questions, if they must be asked, until you have talked with the prospect long enough to establish a rapport.

How to listen to an answer

How you listen affects both you and the buyer. You learn more if you listen well, and the buyer will judge your interest in him and his problem by how well she perceives you to be listening. To listen well you must use your body, voice, ears, and eyes.

Body techniques include sitting with pen poised to take notes, looking at the seller with interest, and waiting for a response to your question. Note taking implies interest in what you are hearing and helps your memory later. It will also inhibit your own tendency to talk.

At times you should listen without taking notes. If you are waiting for the answer to a sensitive question, you might wish to gaze at the seller with your pen conspicuously laid on your pad, showing you understand that the topic is a sensitive one.

The most potent listening technique is simply not talking. Don't talk about yourself or your firm during this portion of the meeting. Don't relate interesting stories of your own, even if they are relevant. Don't interrupt with another question. Don't talk! When you don't, the buyer will usually fill the void. When the buyer seems to have finished answering a question, especially an open one, wait for several seconds before asking another and continue to look at him intently. The silence and encouragement your posture gives will often stimulate him to talk more.

Some verbal encouragement is necessary, of course. But you must keep clear the distinction between verbal encouragement and all other kinds of talk. Verbal encouragement does not sell; it helps overcome the buyer's inhibitions about talking. It is brief. It is focused on the buyer. When you say, "This is extremely helpful" or "How interesting!" you encourage the *buyer* to keep talking. If he gives insufficient information on a subject, you can encourage him by saying, "Tell me more about that."

In different situations, a buyer will be more comfortable talking with either an insider or outsider. If you sense this, a few words of encouragement can keep him talking. If for example, he briefly volunteers some sensitive information, you may choose to take the role of an insider by saying, "Yes. I'm aware. What do you think about it?" Understanding that you are in the know will probably encourage him to give more information. Sometimes an insider is one who has seen such a situation before. You might say, "Yes, that often happens in situations like this. This is helpful. Tell me more." You might say "We found the same thing at XYZ Company. Tell me more." At this point you should avoid relating an elaborate story of a past project that shows your inside knowledge. There will be time for that later.

At other times you will sense that the role of an outsider will get you better information. A comment like, "Obviously, I won't get that deeply involved in your personnel issues, but I can do my job better if I understand the sensitivities. What role do you think he will have in the project?" may keep a buyer talking.

When you are not talking, use your ears. Your understanding of what you hear depends on three things.

- *What is said.* The words the buyer uses when answering your questions are your principal source of information. You can learn about his concerns and opinions. You can learn his view of the facts. All of this is valuable, though it must be treated with caution. If you ask about the decision process for hiring a professional, and the buyer tells you that she will make the choice, that is valuable information. She may be the decision maker. She certainly either thinks she is or wants you to think so.

- *How it is said.* The buyer's specific choice of words also informs you. Small contradictions or qualifiers and the use of vague or evasive language ("That will be decided some time in the fall." By whom?) are all indicators that the buyer may feel inhibited about telling you something. If, after telling you that she will make the hiring choice, she says that she will just want to run her decision by a couple of people to keep everyone in the loop, she is telling you that the decision may not really be hers to make after all.

- *What is not said.* The absence of information also informs you. In our example the sudden appearance of "a couple of people" who are involved in the choice of a professional and about whom you know nothing is a sign that the buyer feels inhibited about telling you something. It also informs you of a potentially serious gap in your information. A few open probes may overcome inhibitions and fill this gap. ("That's great. If there are other people interested in the process, we want them to be happy with the choice as much as you do. Could you tell me a little about them?")

Finally, observe the buyer carefully. This is listening with your eyes. The buyer's level of eye contact, his gestures, and his posture all provide information about the buyer and what he is telling you. You want to watch for signals that he is uncomfortable with what he is saying: Hesitation, avoidance of eye contact, shifting posture, and running a hand through his hair may all be signals. This is especially true if such body language is combined with verbal signals.

When this occurs, you have a choice. You may want to try to open up the issue with an open probe. ("You just said...Tell me a little more about that.") You may choose to encourage the response by a) providing recognition ("That's very perceptive. Tell me more."); b) showing empathy ("That could put you in a tough spot." Pause and wait for a response.); or c) offering a reward before you probe ("I know what kind of difficulties that can create. I think we can help there. Tell me more."). You may feel that the issue is so sensitive that pursuing it would antagonize or embarrass the buyer. If so, make a note of it, so that you can try to find out about it later by other means.

Visible changes in the buyer's intensity and emotions also provide clues about personal concerns and priorities, which may be distinct from those of the company.

Asking the right person

Long ago I was pursuing a project at a division of a large conglomerate. I had worked for other divisions and the parent and I knew the COO; I was pretty sure I would win the job. When it went to a competitor, I called the COO. "I would have liked to see you get the job," he told me, "but the people in the division wanted the other guy. They showed me your credentials and his and he didn't look bad, so I let them hire him. They're the ones who have to live with the result. Between you and me, they may have liked the fact that he didn't know me." In fact, I had relied too much on my relationship with the COO and not devoted enough attention to learning about the people who ran the division.

Often, several people are involved in hiring a professional, and they are involved in different ways. Governments and universities often use committees to make hiring decisions, and some committees have no dominating member. But for most sales there is a single individual who will ultimately decide who is hired. This individual works with others to arrive at a decision. Responsibilities she may give to others include...

- ...*screening*. The decision maker may want to avoid the time required to evaluate every possible contender for the work. She may ask someone to select the best candidates, then choose from among this smaller group.

- ...*advising.* She will want experts to advise her about the candidates. Experts can come from inside or outside the company and are often attorneys, engineers, purchasing agents, or other specialists. She may also seek advice from those within the company who will have to work closely with the professional and live with the results of his work. By seeking their advice, she often hopes to increase their acceptance of the professional's work later. These people will then have input on needs and selection criteria.

- ...*recommending.* She may ask these same people whom she should hire. She may not be obliged to accept their recommendations, but she will pay a price if she ignores recommendations too often.

- ...*deciding.* She may delegate the decision to someone else. This may occur if she is satisfied that all of the professionals under consideration can do the work, or when she is particularly anxious for the individual to whom she delegates the decision to support it, once it is made.

Your chances of making a sale will be greatly enhanced if you can talk directly with all those involved in hiring, ask questions, listen, and develop a relationship. Sometimes you will be introduced to them without having to ask. When you aren't, you must proceed carefully; a buyer will sometimes feel threatened by a request to meet others in the organization. If you ask to see others in the firm, always tie it to one or both of the following:

- *Need for specific information.* The more you can legitimize your need to talk with additional people by a real need for information that they can best provide, the less resistance you will get from the initial contact.

- *Need to develop buy-in.* If group buy-in on the results of your work is crucial to project success, you can request to meet key participants in order to develop rapport prior to being hired.

Some professionals insist on meeting all participants in the buying decision as a precondition to submitting a proposal. You must decide whether the risks of such a demand outweigh the potential benefits.

Once you have gathered information on your prospect, you are in a position to present how you can help meet his needs.

11

Presenting

To do interesting work you must first convince the prospect that you should be the one to do it. All the effort to generate a lead and the hours spent developing a relationship and collecting information on a prospect will only produce work for your firm if you can persuade the prospect to hire you. Often this happens during a presentation.

For most professionals the presentation is the climax of a sale, the single most visible point of success or failure. Present well, and negotiations on fee are a manageable finale; present poorly and the music ends abruptly. Professionals who say, "We won (or lost) it in the presentation" seldom use such language for the proposal or information-gathering portions of the sale.

Prospects also see presentations as the culminating event in their selection of a professional. From debriefings on lost projects, I learned long ago that when proposals are submitted simultaneously with presentations, prospects place overwhelming weight on the presentation. When asked about both, they could barely recall the proposals but cited many details about presentations.

You may present formally, using slides or transparencies before a committee, or informally, chatting across a table with one buyer. Whatever the format, your presentation will be better if you do the following.

Remember that a presentation is only a small, though important, part of a sale

Your presentation will be better if you recognize that it is only a small part of a sale. If you have gathered good information on the prospect, her needs, and the competition, and developed a relationship with some or all of the buyers, the presentation itself will go better.

I would like to suggest that those who have turned to this book for guidance shortly before they must present review the preceding chapter on questioning and listening now. It may not be too late to gather information that will make the difference between a good presentation and one that is off-target. A year ago I coached a group of interior designers on a presentation they were preparing for one of the largest banks in the country. Early in our planning it became apparent that the team lacked knowledge about the prospect's needs. I recommended postponing the rehearsal until the afternoon to give the team a chance to call the buyer with questions. When we reconvened, the presentation was completely overhauled on the basis of the information that had been collected in a single phone call. The designers won the project.

Planning for every presentation should begin with a review of:

- Background on the prospect company
- Background on the people you will be presenting to
- Background in the situation the company faces
- Background on company needs
- Background on special needs of the people you will present to
- A review of any formal requirements for the presentation requested by the buyer (length, content, etc.)
- Background on the competition and its strengths and weaknesses

This is all information you should try to collect prior to the presentation.

Plan your presentation from the buyer's perspective

With this background information you can plan your presentation from the buyer's perspective. This means that you must consider what it is like to sit and listen to several presentations in a row. You can be reasonably assured that it will be...

- *...confusing.* Unless the presentation is very clear, the buyer will have to make inferences about the importance of what is being said. Sometimes those inferences will differ from the ones the presenter wants him to make.
- *...repetitious.* All of the presenters will claim to be the best. They will all claim to be good listeners, to be responsive, to be the oldest and the biggest. They will all claim that their top people will work on the engagement. This will make it hard to differentiate among them.
- *...boring.* Because it is repetitious and because many who present will do so poorly, the process won't be much fun.
- *...hard to remember.* Because the presentations will be boring and repetitious and because everyone's mind wanders during presentations, the content will be hard to remember. It may also be hard to remember which competitor said what.
- *...cold.* One-way communications predominate in many presentations. Most one-way communications are cold, and it is distasteful to hire someone you feel cold about.

The more competitors are asked to present, the more formal the presentation format, the more compact the schedule for the presentations, the more confusing, repetitious, boring, hard to remember, and cold the process will be. Though one-on-one, informal presentations are easier on the buyer, you are safest assuming that the same concerns apply.

To overcome these obstacles, your presentation must...

- ...*be persuasive*. It must clearly and logically explain why you are the right one to get the job.
- ...*be memorable*. A day or a week after the presentation, the buyer must be able to remember you and your message.
- ...*create an emotional link with the prospect*. It must show that you care about the prospect and will be good to work with.

Focus on benefits

As a young consultant I presented to Vernon Loucks, the president and later chairman of Baxter International. During the presentation he interrupted me three times to ask, "Why is this important to my company?" He taught me a lesson I have never forgotten: At all times the presenter owes it to his audience to make it clear why he should be listening. In a sales presentation, this means focusing on benefits.

You persuade by showing benefits. During your presentation you can stress the attributes of your firm and how you will provide your services. These are called "features." Or you can stress the results you can provide, results that the prospect has said he needs. These are called "benefits." You are far more likely to make a sale if you stress benefits.

To do so requires a sharp ear for what a benefit is. Each of us has a tendency to define benefits in terms of the most obvious outcomes of our work and to overlook benefits that the prospect may desperately want and that we can provide. An example is issue resolution. A benefit derived from the work of many professionals is getting an issue resolved so that a client can get on with his business. Clients will pay good money for help of this kind, especially if conflicting views have obstructed progress. Some professionals fail to recognize this need when they hear it and so fail to stress the issue-resolving benefits of their services.

Exhibit 11.1 provides a list of benefits that professionals provide. It is not definitive, nor are the categories discrete, but it has stimulated the thinking of many professionals about the broad range of benefits they actually provide. Review it and see whether you can cite a case in which you provided each benefit to a client. It will be good practice.

Avoid the temptation to present newly discovered benefits to every client. Remember that "benefit" is defined by the buyer, just as "need" is. Stressing something that the buyer sees no need for at best wastes valuable presentation time and at worst shows you weren't listening.

Does this mean that you should ignore the features of your firm? No. Use them as proof of your ability to provide benefits. If they don't support a benefit mentioned by the prospect, however, you should probably leave them out. Exhibit 11.2 lists several benefits of a professional service firm. As an exercise in relating features to benefits, list one or more features or other proofs that support them in the space provided.

Exhibit 11.1
Benefits Checklist

(For idea generation only. This is not a definitive list, nor are categories discrete.)

- Better decisions
  - ☐ Issue clarification/diagnosis
  - ☐ Better information
  - ☐ Better process
  - ☐ Reduced uncertainty/risk
  - ☐ Faster information
  - ☐ Better analysis
  - ☐ Objectivity
  - ☐ Lack of fear
- Increased revenues
  - ☐ Increased market share
  - ☐ More sales
    More loyal customers
    Better product availability
    Better product selection
    Better pricing
    Better service
  - ☐ Cash awards
- Issue resolution/change
  - ☐ Information
  - ☐ Validation
  - ☐ Issue clarification/diagnosis
  - ☐ Consensus development
  - ☐ Generating commitment
  - ☐ Awareness building
  - ☐ Perceived objectivity
- Cost reduction
  - ☐ Staff
  - ☐ Equipment
  - ☐ Facilities
  - ☐ Inventory
  - ☐ Utilities
  - ☐ Raw materials/parts/product for resale
- Cost avoidance
  - ☐ Financial stewardship
  - ☐ Better vendor selection

- ☐ Lower prices
- ☐ Negotiating skill
- ☐ Lower fines or fees
- Increased productivity
  - ☐ Better organization
  - ☐ Better employees
  - ☐ More efficient systems
  - ☐ Better work flows
  - ☐ Better equipment
  - ☐ Fewer errors
- Management support
  - ☐ Manpower/adjunct staff
  - ☐ Specialized expertise
  - ☐ Sleep insurance
  - ☐ Financial stewardship
  - ☐ Objectivity
- Speed
  - ☐ Faster decisions
  - ☐ Faster inventory turns
  - ☐ Faster production
  - ☐ Faster product development
  - ☐ Faster product delivery
- Problem avoidance
  - ☐ Experience/knowledge
  - ☐ Due diligence
  - ☐ Risk identification
  - ☐ Avoided litigation
  - ☐ Confidentiality
  - ☐ Favorable rulings
- Personal satisfaction
  - ☐ Prestige of working with you
  - ☐ Mental stimulation
  - ☐ Increased job security
  - ☐ Safe place to talk
  - ☐ Avoidance of pain/suffering
  - ☐ Sleep insurance
  - ☐ Friendship

Exhibit 11.2

Supporting Benefits with Features

> *Identify at least one feature that helps create each benefit.*

Benefit	Feature
A. Diagnostic ability *We can identify the crux of your problem.*	
B. *Issue resolution* *We will help your management achieve consensus.*	
C. Cost avoidance *We will save you money.*	
D. Increased productivity *We will increase your employee's effectiveness.*	

Answers:

There is no single right answer. Sample right answers might include:

- A. Specialized industry or functional experience of firm and team members. Methodology used for diagnosing.
- B. Facilitative techniques.
  Experience of team members in developing consensus.
- C. Cost reduction methodology.
- D. Methodology used to increase productivity.
  Relevant degrees or certifications of staff members working on assignment.

Link your firm's services to the core objectives of the prospect

By showing how your services will help a client achieve his core objectives, you provide the most fundamental demonstration of benefits. A close link to the prospect's highest-level objectives is not only persuasive but memorable. It is a good way to begin your presentation. It shows that you are focused on the prospect, rather than on yourself, that you understand what he is trying to accomplish, and that you will help him accomplish it.

It also implies that during the course of your work, when you must make judgments, you will make them with the client's highest interests in mind.

Review your background information on the prospect to identify these core objectives. Annual reports and articles in the press are one good place to find them, though you should confirm with the prospect the continued importance of objectives gleaned from these sources. Look and listen for the key messages. Is the company focused on quality, on becoming a world-class competitor, or on becoming a price leader? Such statements express core objectives. Next ask yourself how the issue you are being asked to address ties into these objectives. If it is not obvious, ask. Write a simple sentence that expresses this relationship. Finally, write a sentence that expresses the relationship between your services and the core objectives by addressing the issues in question.

Exhibit 11.3 provides an example of this process.

Exhibit 11.3
Linking Benefits to Prospect's Core Objectives

Client:	Large U.S. pharmaceutical company
Core objective:	Become a world-class competitor in the pharmaceutical industry
Project: A. State need B. Link to core objective	Build new research campus to: ■ provide state-of-the-art research facilities, and ■ attract top-caliber research talent needed to compete on a global scale
Architect's benefit Link to core objective	Design a world-class campus that will: ■ attract the best research talent because of the quality and attractiveness of the facilities, and ■ be built within budget to preserve funds for the research needed to earn world-class status.

Differentiate your firm through the consistent use of a theme

Every presentation should have a theme. Akin to the angle you use when planning an article, the theme ensures the focus and clarity of your message. Develop it around the most compelling reason that yours is the right firm to do the job. Very possibly this can be derived from the exercise you have completed to tie your services to the prospect company's core objectives.

The theme should differentiate your firm in one of two ways:

■ *More-Is-Better.* This approach assumes that others offer fundamentally the same services you do, but that you offer a higher quality or quantity. Unless you dominate a market, this approach is risky. Prospects seek a floor level for most attributes and discount the benefits of levels above that floor. Thus, having done twenty projects similar to the one you are being considered for when a competitor has done only three may give you specialized knowledge that translates into shorter learning curves, better diagnostic ability and better solutions. But having done seventy similar projects when a competitor has done forty 1) may not be perceived as a great advantage, and 2) is difficult to verify. You probably don't know what claims your competitors are making. Proving the value of having more of an attribute is often difficult and sometimes impossible.

■ *Different-Bundle-of-Benefits.* You can also suggest that you offer a different set of benefits. Yes, you offer *a, b,* and *c,* as other firms do, but you also offer *d,* which no one else does. If *d* is something valued by the prospect, this is a powerful argument. Examples of this kind of differentiation include the following.

□ *People:* A consulting firm hired the top quality expert from a company with an internationally acclaimed quality program to head up its total quality management practice.

□ *Methodology:* A university professor developed a methodology to assist lawyers in jury selection and developed a large consulting practice around it.

□ *Range of services:* A consulting firm gained significant advantage by offering one-stop shopping for a full range of services associated with a particular kind of project, when competitors dealt only with pieces.

□ *Relationships:* A civil engineering firm stressed its special relationship with planning and zoning boards in its state when competing for work from developers seeking to do business there.

□ *Knowledge:* Attorneys at a large law firm wrote a book on U.S. securities law for European companies and used it to demonstrate knowledge specialized to the needs of that market. This became its sales theme.

□ *Responsiveness:* An executive search firm located offices in intermediate-sized metropolitan areas to provide it with an advantage when competing against large firms with offices based in major metropolitan areas. It sold its services to firms located near to its offices by promising responsiveness based on proximity.

□ *Reputation:* In each field there are firms that have developed strong reputations that have helped them sell business, because buying from them seems low-risk. McKinsey is the best example in consulting.

If you can choose among several differentiators in developing a theme, remember to select the one of most importance to the prospect you are selling to. Do not expect to pick one differentiator and use it forever; if it works, others will soon imitate you.

You should be able to express your theme in one sentence, just as you do an angle. Try completing the following sentence with a specific prospect in mind: "We are the firm best able to help you because..." Try different endings until you find one that you think the prospect will find compelling. Examples of alternative endings include...

- ...we have specialized methods and data bases that will ensure rapid project completion and reduce your costs without damaging product quality.
- ...we have an unequaled track record of defending corporations in employee-initiated suits in this court system.
- ...we have specialized knowledge of the accounting practices in your industry and so can help you defer and reduce taxes.
- ...we are the one firm that combines high-quality medical facility design with internationally acclaimed aesthetic design.

Once you have a theme, you can build your presentation around it.

Outline the case you want to make
Next, create a clear, logical, and concise outline of the case that will demonstrate that yours is the best firm for the job. Note any statistics or other proofs that you may want to use to support your argument. Make sure that each point supports your main theme.

If it helps you to write a draft of the presentation, do so, but do not use it to rehearse from. You write only to ensure that your reasoning is sound. Memorizing opening and closing lines can help you to get started and to end. The rest of your presentation should not be memorized.

Use examples to make your services more tangible
In a weak economy, my firm hungry for work, I flew to Cincinnati to call on a small metal fabricator thinking of building a branch plant. At first the prospect seemed promising; the president was determined to lower his labor costs by establishing a branch plant and wanted help deciding where in the South to locate it. That was my specialty.

Then he told me the size of the plant, twenty people. Because it was my business I knew instantaneously that the additional overhead of the branch plant would eat up any labor savings. There would never be a payoff on the initial investment.

When the time came for me to present, I began with a story. I told him of a well-known metal fabricator I had worked with that also wanted to lower labor costs. Instead of moving to the sunbelt, the company located its twenty-person plant in a small town in Wisconsin within a three-hour drive of its Chicago-area headquarters. Labor costs were as low as anywhere in the South, and overhead was limited to one foreman-cum-plant manager. Whenever human resource, engineering, or other help was needed, someone from headquarters got in a car and drove up to the plant. This would have been impossible at a distant location.

Largely on the basis of this story, the client hired me. It had showed him that...

- ...I understood his core objective to become a low-cost producer.
- ...my experience had value to him.

- ...I would be creative in addressing his problem.
- ...I would save him money.

Better still, it did so in a way that was more persuasive and memorable than if I had spoken in abstractions. That's a lot to get from one short anecdote.

The value of a good anecdote was summarized to me by another prospect who had hired a competitor. He said, "We saw our problem in the story they told." He saw his problem in the story my competitor told. Now that must have been a good story! It had made a service, which the buyer could not experience until after a professional was hired, seem tangible. Ever since I have sought to make my stories meet this standard.

Professionals rely on anecdotes to sell their services. In fact, the heavy use of anecdotes is one of the primary differences between selling professional services and selling products. In part this is because professional services are so abstract; in part it is because professionals must sell themselves. This is a very different proposition from selling a widget. The statements "This is a great widget!" and "I am a great accountant (or actuary or architect or consultant or lawyer)!" have quite distinct impacts on the listener.

Exhibit 11.4 lists some of the characteristics that buyers typically like to find in the professionals they hire. How do you claim such attributes without seeming immodest? Through the artful use of anecdotes.

A good anecdote is...

- ...*relevant.* The prospect must be able to identify with the protagonist in the story. Build relevance by describing those characteristics of the past client that most resemble the prospect, be it industry, location, size of company, or similarity of need. It is hard to use a story about a casino operator with a publisher of Bibles. If the prospect doesn't see the relevance, he will discount the message, however apt.

- ...*benefits-oriented.* A good anecdote highlights the benefits of working with you by showing either the good things accruing to someone who did or the bad things besetting someone who didn't.

- ...*brief.* An anecdote that gets too long ceases to be one. If a story gets too long it becomes a distraction from the main theme of your presentation instead of a reenforcement. The anecdote should run five sentences at most. Three are better.

- ...*made up of four key elements.* It must have a plot (need to lower labor costs, for example), a character (a metal fabricator), action (driving to Wisconsin) and an outcome (bigger success than a sunbelt plant would have made possible).

If it also has humor, so much the better.

Some professionals become so proficient at telling anecdotes that they overuse them. Often this results from a shortage of other selling skills. Do not fall into this trap. Professionals who have an anecdote showing how great they are for every

Exhibit 11.4

Adjectives Used to Describe A Good Professional

- Experienced
- Smart
- Insightful
- Empathetic
- Objective
- Trustworthy
- Client-focused
- Professional
- Wise
- Savvy
- Interesting
- Conscientious
- Self-controlled

- Knowledgeable
- Expensive but worth it
- Attentive
- Analytical
- Creative
- Innovative
- Sensitive
- Persuasive
- Ethical
- Practical
- Tactful
- Energetic
- Concerned

sentence spoken by a prospect are annoying and lose jobs. Use this tool sparingly when it counts the most. Just one story closed my sale to the metal fabricator.

Remember that what people *see* is as important as what you say
I once lost several sales in a row to a competitor. In debriefings with the prospects, two said that he had a better data base than I did and so could complete the project more quickly and accurately. I knew this was not true from an employee who had formerly worked for the competitor. A few weeks later I sat in on a presentation he gave at a trade association meeting. He put up a slide that struck me like a rock. This single image is what had convinced my prospects of his superiority. With beautiful simplicity it created the impression of a wealth of useful data. I developed a knock-off exhibit and stopped losing jobs to him.

I have always remembered this lesson in the value of superior presentation graphics and have striven ever since for the same combination of simplicity and substance that my competitor had found in that one exhibit. What your prospects see is as important as what you say.

For guidelines on preparing presentation visuals by one of the leading experts in the field, see appendix B.

Remember that what you do is as important as what you say
I once monitored a presentation in which the three team members each stated what good listeners they were. They also talked so long that there was no time at the end of the presentation for the committee making the selection to ask a single question, even though it had requested twenty minutes for this purpose. Which

message do you think was strongest? The repeated statements about listening well or the evidence that this team felt that it was more valuable to use its time talking than listening?

I listen well. I'm enthusiastic about your project. I care about you. I know what I am talking about. We are a team. These and many other messages are delivered more by how you act than by what you say. This means that your presentation must be structured to demonstrate key attributes that cannot be communicated with words.

For example, a joint-venture team of architects and engineers lost a project because the architects and the engineers unwittingly sat at opposite ends of the table during the presentation, destroying the image of unity. All three members of the selection committee commented on this split in debriefings.

The next time this team presented, not only did they sit together, they all wore maroon suspenders. It was done subtly (not everyone removed his jacket, for example), but the client got the message. After sitting through five back-to-back presentations, the selection committee could still recall the words of the "red suspenders *team*" (emphasis added). The team got the job.

Like this team, you must decide what aspects of your presentation require reinforcement from your behavior and then plan to act accordingly. Here are some things you can emphasize.

- *Enthusiasm.* Physical animation communicates enthusiasm. Smiling, holding your hands open in front of you while making a point, and moving deliberately closer to your audience as you speak all create the sense of enthusiasm.

- *Interest and caring.* Strong eye contact communicates interest and caring. Many presenters let their eyes wander aimlessly during a presentation, or, worse, look frequently at their boss. Maintain eye contact with your audience.

- *Listening ability.* Ask a question during the presentation and then listen carefully to the response, looking intently at the speaker. Make a *short* comment at the end that shows you understand what he has said. Be careful to ask a question that is thoughtful but unthreatening.

- *Confidence and knowledge.* Standing with your feet set slightly apart and arms at your sides communicates confidence in what you are saying. Avoid rocking from foot to foot, holding your hands in the fig leaf position (hands clasped at groin), or putting hands in your pockets or behind your back.

Some people find standing with their arms at their sides unnatural. It does not appear so to the observer, and his opinion is the one that counts. If the discomfort is acute, try holding a pointer or a pen in your hand, but don't fiddle with it.

Remember that how you say it is as important as what you say

Take the three words, "Oh, it's you." Depending upon tone, volume, rate, pitch and accent you can communicate many different messages with them, including, I love you, I hate you, I expected someone else, it's good to see you, and I'm bored. You can do this naturally without any training in theater or communications. Try it. I mean it. Close the door to your room and try it out loud.

Your voice will communicate underlying messages, called "subtexts," during your presentation, and you can control these underlying messages as naturally as you did when saying "Oh, it's you." Before speaking, repeat to yourself the underlying message that you would like to give. It will come out in your voice when you begin to present. Examples include:

- *Interest, caring, emotional linkage.* "I care about you."
- *Enthusiasm.* "It's great to be here!"
- *Confidence.* "I know."

Practice the statement that communicates your subtext aloud to a friendly critic until you can say it convincingly, then go right into a rehearsal of your presentation. Ask the critic if the message is coming through. You may feel awkward doing this at first, but it works.

The words you choose for your message are also important. Don't talk about "I" and "we" and "our clients"; it sounds self-absorbed. Talk about the prospect, using "you." Instead of talking about "our methodology" talk about "how we will help you." Always ask yourself, "Is what I am saying focused on this prospect, or could I be saying the same words to any prospect?" If the latter, fix it.

Rehearse!

I have known many professionals who claim that they do better without rehearsing, that they are more natural and that the words are more fluid. This claim is preposterous. Politicians rehearse, actors and musicians rehearse, professional athletes practice. They do it because it makes them better, even though it takes time and can be painful. Professionals don't wing it.

The real reason most avoid rehearsing is to avoid the embarrassment. People who take this position don't realize that they will embarrass themselves anyway if they don't, although the prospect will be too polite to say so. That they feel better in a presentation than in a rehearsal doesn't make them better. It just means they have more adrenaline in their bloodstream.

Embarrassment at rehearsals often derives from ineffective critiquing, which destroys confidence in how a professional presents but doesn't show a better way. If this is your problem, be sure to rehearse with a sympathetic critic of your choosing who has read the critiquing guidelines that follow.

If you are presenting as a team, you must rehearse as a team. Each team member needs to hear what the others will say so that content can be coordinated. For group rehearsals I recommend the following set of rules.

- *There is only one coach.* Ideally this will be someone who will not attend the presentation. No one else is allowed to make comments, except on technical issues the coach doesn't understand. Having more than one critic is destructive.

- *The coach represents the prospect.* The presentation is made to her.

- *Everyone must rehearse.* No one is excused. You can't build a fluid presentation if some team members don't participate, and you can't build team morale. Each must try speaking as if this were the real presentation.

- *Everyone must actually rehearse.* General discussion of roles and subjects is planning, not rehearsing.

- *No one is allowed to rehearse or present from a written script.* If you do, you will look at it often. This breaks eye contact with the listener and creates the impression of lack of confidence. Write a script to get your thoughts in order, if it helps you. Then list the four or five major points, plus a statistic or two you might forget on a 5" x 7" card. That is all you should use when you speak.

- *If someone is having special difficulty, the coach should work with him alone* later to avoid taking the entire team's time.

- *Only criticism that can be acted on is allowed.* Saying that I am confusing or boring or cold does not help me because I cannot act on it. I certainly am not being any of those things intentionally. Tell me what to do with my voice, my body, my hands. Tell me how to change the graphics I am using or how to shorten my anecdote. Tell me to increase my eye contact. Tell me to talk directly to you, using the word "you." Tell me to use simple language, avoiding professional argot. If you can't do these things, don't coach. If I can't act on what you say, it isn't coaching, it's complaining. Many people can coach, but it takes concentration.

- *The coach will not correct specific words unless they are objectionable to the prospect.* The goal is to obtain fluency with subject matter, not to memorize a speech. Presenters will use somewhat different words when they actually present. Now they are working on ideas, sequence, and delivery.

- *If the coach cannot answer the question, "Why is what the presenter saying important to me and my company?" she will stop the presenter* and help him reformulate his words to make this clear. The audience always needs to know why it should be listening.

- *The coach will observe herself as a listener.* If her attention wanders, it is a sign that something is wrong with the presentation, not with her listening. The coach must figure out what is wrong and recommend a fix.

Unless she is experienced, the coach should read this chapter before the rehearsal so she will understand the larger issues of what constitutes a good presentation. Exhibit 11.5 provides a checklist the coach can use while rehearsing a presenter.

Exhibit 11.5
Coach's Checklist

Content

- Is it clear?
  (*Solutions:* Reword, reorder, state reason for listening, shorten, delete tangential content, avoid technical language and argot)
- Is it concise?
  (*Solutions:* Fewer words, fewer subjects, fewer or shorter examples)
- Is it persuasive?
  (*Solutions:* Stress benefits, work on delivery, use anecdote, provide proof)
- Does it engage me?
  (*Solutions:* Stress benefits, use "you" instead of "I," customize it to prospect's situation, use anecdote)

Delivery

- Posture
  (*Solutions:* Stand straight, don't rock, hands at sides, shoulders back, feet slightly parted)
- Gestures
  (*Solutions:* Sufficient movement at key points, clear and decisive)
- Eye contact
  (*Solutions:* Look at coach; don't look at notes or visuals or boss; if you must refer to notes or visuals, pause while you do so and begin to speak again when eye contact is reestablished)
- Volume
  (*Solution:* Use more resonance)
- Emotional impact
  (*Solution:* Work on subtexts)

During your presentation or after it, the prospect will want to talk. Actually, I prefer to seed the presentation with a few questions of my own to create a dialogue. These are often confirming questions or questions offering simple choices, which we can then follow up on. Dealing with the prospect's questions is the subject of the following chapter.

12

Handling Prospect Questions and Concerns

Throughout the sales process your prospect will ask questions. How you deal with them will have great influence on whether you get his business. He will use your answers not just to judge your capabilities and approach, but also to decide what you would be like to work with.

Often the most satisfactory answer is given before a question is asked. Telling your mother that you won't be able to call her on Mother's Day because you will be traveling in Indonesia is better than answering, "Why didn't you call me?" You should try to preempt as many questions as you can.

Michael Graves, the famous architect, beautifully preempted a critical question when he presented his credentials to design a college library. The selection committee had announced that it was most concerned about meeting schedules and budgets. Because famous designers are perceived as unconcerned with both, it was easy to predict that the committee would want to grill him in this area.

His opening words to the committee were, "During this presentation, I'm not going to say a word about schedules or budgets!" This stunned the committee and grabbed its attention. He went on to describe a similar project he had designed. As he completed his description his project manager jumped up and quoted the words on a sign she held: "Delivered on budget and two months ahead of schedule." Graves went on to describe another project, and another. Each time the project manager interjected the same kind of commentary. He won the job. The committee never asked about his ability to meet schedules and budgets.

Before any meeting with a client, and especially before a presentation, review your knowledge of the company, its issues, and the people you will be meeting with. What concerns about you are they most likely to have? Answer their questions before they come up and your answers will be more persuasive. The more sensitive the issue, the more important it is for you to be the one to bring it up.

160

Chapter 10 on questioning and listening tells you how to elicit a prospect's concerns. The foundation you have built by questioning and listening helps you preempt a prospect's questions later. Use this information before the questions start and you will have less need for the rest of the guidance in this chapter.

When a prospect does ask a question, do the following.

Determine why he is asking it

Prospects ask questions for several reasons. Knowing the reasons will influence the way you answer. When your spouse asks what you are doing on Saturday, it helps to know why he or she is asking before you respond. It's the same with client questions.

A question can be inspired by one or more of the following desires.

- *To gather information.* This is the most obvious reason, and sometimes it is the only one. If a prospect is confused or needs information you have not provided, he will ask a question.

- *To gain recognition.* A prospect can show how smart he is or regain attention from a speaker by asking a question. He may be seeking recognition from you or, more likely, from others in his company who are present.

- *To advance the conversation.* The prospect may have accepted or rejected what you have said to this point and want to move the conversation ahead.

- *To express skepticism about what you are saying.* A question can be a polite way of saying, "I don't believe you."

- *To test you.* A question may be asked simply to see how you handle it.

Use some standard techniques for all questions

There are three common techniques in responding to all of these five kinds of questions. First, if you don't understand a question or are uncertain about why it is being asked, ask the questioner to clarify it or to elaborate. At best answering a question you don't understand wastes time. At worst it can cost you a sale.

Second, encourage the questioner by acknowledging that his question is welcome. This can be done with a smile and a nod or with a brief statement that summarizes or amplifies it. Avoid the sophomoric habit of responding, "That's a good question," every time you are asked one. The objective is to make the prospect feel good about asking the questions and show that you welcome the dialogue. This will ensure that your response doesn't sound defensive. Defensiveness or the appearance of defensiveness can hurt you. Prospects prefer not to work with someone who will react defensively every time they ask a question. The appearance of defensiveness now will lower your prospect's opinion of you. It may also deter him from asking further questions, and it is through his questions that you learn about concerns that could keep you from getting the job. You want him to ask questions.

During a presentation you can encourage questions by asking one yourself. Say, "We are about to change subjects. Do you have any questions up to this point?"

Third, keep answers short. I have seen many professionals get themselves into trouble by giving long answers when short ones would have served. Long answers risk creating new concerns or boring the prospect. A prospect seldom wants a long answer. You will sound more confident and businesslike if you give a short one. Professionals violate this rule so often, it bears repeating: Keep answers short!

If your firm has several people at a meeting, avoid letting every person respond to every question. Prospects find this irritating. Let the senior person on your team direct each question to the single appropriate respondent.

Answer questions seeking information directly and concisely and at the right time

These questions seek information that the prospect clearly needs but that you haven't yet provided. "Can you meet with my boss next Monday?" "What kind of documentation do you provide?" "How many of our people will you interview?" All these questions probably express a sincere desire for information and can be answered directly in a few words.

Sometimes a prospect will seek information prematurely. The most obvious example of this is asking about your fee before a project's scope has been determined. Usually it is best to postpone answering such questions by saying, "I can't answer that quite yet. Let's talk a little more about your situation, and then I can tell you." If you do this, make a note of the unanswered question and answer it at the appropriate time. You will appear attentive to the prospect if you remember to deal with his postponed concern without being prompted.

Often it will be important to learn a prospect's reaction to your answer to an information question. After answering, ask the open question, "How does that seem to you?"

Answer recognition questions by giving an appropriate level of recognition

When someone seeks recognition, she often does so by disguising a statement as a question. Questions beginning with, "Don't you think that..." or "Isn't it true that..." are usually of this type. So are very smart questions asked in a way that calls attention to their smartness. The way the question is posed seems to beg the response, "Gee, that's a good question." Recognition questions are sometimes deliberately oblique, requiring you to ask the questioner what she means. That gives her the chance she seeks to speak. If someone asks, "Are you taking into account the Ishtabibbel factor?" count on it's being a recognition question.

In a one-on-one meeting you may want to explore the questioner's opinions for a time until you sense she is satisfied with your recognition of her knowledge. In a larger meeting, unless the senior representative of the prospect team is seeking recognition, keep the response short and move on. A simple "Yes. I can see you've dealt with this kind of issue before" is probably sufficient.

It becomes more awkward when you disagree with the statement disguised as a question. When this occurs, the questioner has unintentionally asked a test question, because others present will judge your tact, honesty, and ability to deal with difficult situations by how you answer. Before answering, ask yourself whether you really understand the question. If not, ask for clarification. When you respond, use nonargumentative language. Rather than disagreeing yourself, provide evidence based on the experience of others. "That may be true, but many companies have found that..." takes the onus of disagreeing off you and allows the questioner to back down gracefully.

When a prospect seeks to advance the conversation with a question, establish why he wants to advance before doing so

When a prospect asks an advancing question, he is deliberately shifting the conversation to the next subject. Information questions can have the same effect, but do not have the same intent. The two types can be distinguished by timing. Prospects usually ask advancing questions after a subject has been discussed. These questions could logically be preceded by, "Now that I understand that subject, let's move on to the next one." An information question that could advance a conversation comes earlier in a discussion and is, in effect, an aside, which could be introduced with, "By the way..."

An advancing question signals that the prospect is ready to move on. Sometimes this is favorable ("How soon can you start?" and other words we like to hear), but don't assume so unless it is obvious. Questions that change the subject may mean that the prospect has decided he doesn't want to hire you and wants to get the conversation over with. If the advancing question is other than an obvious buying signal, establish where the sale is at before answering it. Use an open question like, "Yes, we need to talk about timing next, but before we leave this subject, what is your sense of how our service responds to your situation?" If he raises a concern, explore it fully with follow-up questions before responding. A hasty, inappropriate response will simply increase his resistance.

If the reaction is favorable, move on to the next subject.

When a question expresses skepticism, you must respond with proof

No salesperson, even if he is a professional, is totally disinterested; when it comes right down to it, he wants to get hired. Prospects know this and will sometimes use questions to show their skepticism about what you are saying. When a prospect asks a senior professional, "How much will you, yourself, actually work on this project?" she may be seeking information. More likely she suspects a bait-and-switch, with the senior professional being replaced by a junior once the firm is hired.

You can best answer skeptical questions by offering proof. You might ask, "If the president of the firm sent you a letter committing 30 percent of my time to your account, would that make you feel more comfortable?" You might acknowledge her reason to feel skeptical ("Yes, I know everyone promises you he'll give you his personal attention. I can understand why you ask.") and then offer to provide her with references who can testify to the level of attention you give. Each time you are asked such a question, ask yourself what evidence you could provide that would prove the claim being questioned. Here are your choices.

- *Statistics.* These are useful when past performance is quantifiable.

- *Testimony.* A good reference from a past client can reassure a prospect on subjective issues. Sometimes you can use a testimonial letter, but a direct conversation between the prospect and the past client is more convincing.

- *Documents.* Examples of deliverables and documentation of methodologies can help dispel concerns about what a client is going to get and how it is going to be provided.

- *Assurances and certifications.* These help address skepticism about commitment or credentials. To say, "If you are concerned about that, I would be happy to include a commitment to it in our contract," is usually compelling. The strongest assurance is some form of guarantee.

- *An anecdote.* Sometimes an anecdote that shows how you handled a previous client's concern can reduce skepticism. This is especially true of the prospect is expressing skepticism about you or a member of your team, that is, if she is concerned about one of the attributes listed in exhibit 11.4.

To answer a test question, you must first figure out what you are being tested on

Many years ago I made a presentation to the senior management of a defense supplier. I had had five previous meetings at the company and had been told bluntly that I had to be vetted before I would be allowed to present to the president, whom everyone feared. Now I had the chance to present to him while all his understrappers watched.

Three-quarters of the way through my presentation he said, "What you're suggesting is going to cost a lot of money. Why should we spend so much? I think we should..." He then suggested a childish solution that would have eliminated the need for my services. I had the flu, I had had four hours' sleep the night before and driven three hours to get to the meeting. All my work to sell the engagement was about to go down the drain. I reflected for a moment and realized his words were a challenge. As kindly as I could I said, "Frankly, I think you're being naive, if you think that will work." No one spoke. All the understrappers looked up at the ceiling or down at their notes. I waited for a reaction. The boss smiled at me and said, "I think we should get started" and left the room. I had been approved, and I never had a moment's difficulty with this man again. He had wanted to know if I would stand up to him and give him honest advice, and I had proved I would.

Any professional who has sold for years has stories analogous to this one. Prospects often ask professionals test questions, though the context is usually less dramatic than in the preceding story. If you buy a copier, you test it for resolution, speed, and ease of use. When you test-drive a car, you floor it to see how it accelerates, take a few turns, and try the brakes. You test a professional with questions.

You can recognize a test question because...

- ...*it challenges you personally.* This is a test of your personal honesty, tact, courage, objectivity, creativity, or other personal characteristic listed in exhibit 11.4. It has nothing to do with your firm or features of your services, although it may be disguised to appear as if it does.

- ...*it feels more like a test than other questions.* You will sense that there are right and wrong answers already framed in the questioner's mind.

- ...*it comes as a surprise* and does not fit with the favorable tone of preceding conversations. This occurs when the prospect decides to test a favorable opinion of you. He has suddenly become concerned that you may be just a good salesperson.

A prospect will seldom tell you what you are being tested on, so figuring it out is part of the test. Exhibit 12.1 presents several test questions prospects have asked me. Suggest reasons why a prospect might ask them and then, with a specific prospect in mind, try to answer them.

Exhibit 12.1

Sample Test Questions

These are all questions prospects have asked. Why did they ask them? How would you respond?

A. Why is this engagement important to you personally?
B. What can you tell me about yourself that is personal and that no one else knows?
C. What is the quickest way to get this sheet of paper out the door?
D. Why not just do it this way?
E. Why should I believe you?

Reasons for test questions:

A. To determine motivation and, therefore, commitment to engagement. To determine whether it would get personal attention.
B. To determine willingness to work closely with prospect and be open with him. Willingness to commit to him, personally, and not just his company.
C. To test creativity. (The fastest way was to wad up the sheet and throw it.)
D. To determine savvy and tact.
E. To test courage, tact, and honesty.

Test questions require that you provide a proof. The proof may be in the way you answer, as in the preceding example. It may be an anecdote that reveals something about you. It may be a reference who will testify to your personal attributes.

Position any reference you give.

References testify that you are as good as you say you are. Because they are perceived as more objective than you are, what they say will weigh heavily. Of course, you want to select your references carefully, but you want to do more than that.

Call each reference and ask permission to use his name. First, this is common courtesy and warns the reference that a call is coming. Second, most people will feel a stronger obligation to take the call and respond favorably, if they have agreed with you directly to provide one. Third, it gives you a chance to prime the reference for probable questions. If you say, "I think they are likely to be concerned about our ability to work in a fragmented organization and achieve consensus. I'd like to give your name as a reference because there were aspects of that in our work for you," the reference is likely to volunteer information about this particular ability before being asked. At least he will be more prepared for the question when it comes. His remarks will be more persuasive.

Reconfirm your responses in writing after the meeting

After any meeting with a prospect, it is courteous to send a note to show you are interested in his business. Follow-up letters are a good place to acknowledge major concerns again and reiterate your response. This is particularly true when you want to give an assurance or offer an additional proof.

Follow up by phone after a meeting to confirm that concerns have been resolved and to probe for new ones

A follow-up call after a meeting provides an informal opportunity to determine how successful you have been at responding to a prospect's concerns. If you say, "There were some questions about our ability to meet your schedule. Do you feel everyone is satisfied that we can?" the answer will help you decide whether you need to provide more evidence.

You should also ask a few open questions to make sure that no new concerns have come up. "What other questions came up after we left?" is a good one to start with.

13

Writing a Proposal

When discussions get serious, your prospect will usually want you to submit a written proposal. He may want one for any of several reasons.

- *It helps clarify his thinking* about his needs and how to meet them. A proposal that does this adds real value.

- *It provides him with a way to validate your understanding* of his issues, your credentials for dealing with them, your approach to dealing with them, and your terms.

- *It formalizes the commitment.* The proposal helps sort out marketing hyperbole from fact and commitment. The prospect realizes that most people are more cautious about what they put in writing than about what they say. He can refer to it later if there are any disagreements about staffing, scope, deliverables, timing, or fees.

- *It shows he has been diligent in his selection.* It gives him something to show to others interested in the selection of a professional to confirm what you will do and that you are the right one to do it.

- *It tests your responsiveness.* This is especially true if you have little time in which to prepare it.

- *It facilitates comparison of professionals* competing for his business.

The weight a buyer places on a proposal when he makes a choice can vary from heavy to almost none. You must always assume the former. Make it work for you by doing the following.

Offer to prepare a proposal when you think it will advance the sale
An agreement to accept a proposal signals a prospect's increased seriousness about retaining you. It implies that he has gone beyond general discussion to a point where he may be able to make a decision or that he is now willing to submit the proposal to someone else for a decision. If you sense you are getting to such a

point, offer to prepare a proposal. If the prospect accepts, it shows that you have read the situation correctly.

If he declines, you have misread him and must figure out how close to hiring you he really is. Try open questions, such as, "What would have to occur to make you feel ready to accept a proposal?" to determine what his concerns are.

A proposal may also be a way to help the prospect clarify his thinking. I recently used a proposal this way with the head of a consulting firm. We had talked three times about the sales training needs of the firm's partners. He could not clearly state what he wanted, and every suggestion I made ran into obstacles. He seemed to like me and to want to hire me, but he couldn't figure out exactly what he wanted me to do. To advance the discussion I sent an unsolicited proposal, suggesting that it might give him something to react to that which would clarify the problem. It did. Based on the discussion that followed I sent a substantially revised proposal and was hired.

There is a risk; the prospect may use your proposal as a basis for a formal Request for Proposals (RFP) sent to several firms. I usually take that risk, believing that if I really help the prospect do his job by helping him clarify his thinking, he will remember me later. Usually I am right. When wrong, I forget about it and move on to the next prospect.

Remember that it is primarily a marketing document
Yes, a proposal can have legal implications, especially if it doubles as a contract. You should be careful to avoid words that imply an unachievable standard of performance (such as saying that you will find the best solution or that you will ensure that something happens) and ones with a different legal meaning from their common usage ("time is of the essence" is such a phrase). Consult a lawyer for details. You should be careful not to promise services that you can't or won't deliver. But you must not let legal considerations blind you to a proposal's fundamental objective: selling your services.

A proposal also has operational and financial implications. Often, preparing a proposal helps the professional think through exactly what he is going to do when he gets hired and how he will make money at it. Do not confuse this benefit to you with what you want a client to get from your proposal. When you actually write it, much of the information you prepare to get you to that point should probably not appear in it.

Lack of clarity about goals is the single biggest reason for weak proposals. Remember that what you want it to do is sell your services.

Treat a proposal as part of a larger marketing effort
You have worked to gather information on the client's need. Review what you have learned prior to preparing the proposal in order to refresh your memory on details and nuances. If your knowledge has important gaps, try to fill them before you start on the proposal. The need to put your thoughts in writing often helps you recognize information gaps and provides a legitimate reason for calling your prospect to ask additional questions.

You have also worked hard to deliver specific messages to a prospect, messages you will want to reinforce in the proposal.

Decide what image you want the proposal to project

Should the proposal give the impression that it is simply formalizing an agreement arrived at with a handshake? Should it suggest that you want this project more than a dozen other competitors do? That you are creative? That you are reliable? Its form and appearance will convey these messages. Based on the circumstances of each sale, you need to decide what image you wish to project and build it into your proposal.

If the proposal is really just a formality, make it look like one. Keep it short. Consider a letter format. A major competition, on the other hand, demands something more elaborate. The choice of covers can make you look creative or reliable, expensive or economical. Choose carefully to match the image you want to project.

Desktop publishing technology makes it easy to customize proposals. If you have a scanner, consider using the client's logo on the title page. Design-oriented professions, in particular, have the freedom and resources to prepare covers and dividers with images that relate to the prospect.

Focus on benefits

Many professionals view the description of the work they will do as the core of a proposal, the real reason for its existence. But prospects don't hire you because of the task you are going to perform; they hire you for the benefits they expect to receive. Your description of the work you will do is only there as a proof, one of several proofs, that you will deliver benefits. Think of why people buy a specific car. They want reliable transportation, comfort, image, and many others things. Engines, interiors, color, and a vast array of other features are but means to acquire the benefits they want. It is the same with professional services.

If you have not done so, read chapter 11 on presentations where benefits are described in more detail. Pages 150 through 153 tell about linking your services to a prospect's core objectives and about differentiating your firm through consistent use of a central theme. These suggestions apply equally to both proposals and presentations.

Decide what services you should offer

In many cases you have some discretion in deciding how large a project and how full a range of services to offer. At one extreme you can offer only those that meet the prospect's most immediate need while mentioning that you can also help with later needs. The other is to offer a full-service package immediately. The choice you make between these two extremes or some compromise between them depends, in part, on the signals you have received from the prospect about his propensity to spend (see chapter 14 on fees). It also depends on the probability that the prospect well require the full range of services. If initial work might help the buyer decide that no further action is needed, the impression that you will provide this work objectively will be enhanced by a proposal that asks the prospect to commit only to the first portion. A small project can help the prospect get to know you without making a large commitment.

Throughout the proposal, amplify on your theme and the benefits you will provide

The standard parts of a proposal are only vehicles for you to show the benefits you are going to deliver and to differentiate yourself from your competitors. Each must fulfill these functions.

Cover letter

The cover letter should introduce your central theme and delineate the major benefits you will provide. It should not run more than a page and a half; a single page is better. This is the place to thank members of the prospect team who have helped you gather information needed to put the proposal together. If you are submitting a letter proposal, these points should be covered in the first paragraph.

Executive summary

If the proposal is thirty pages or more, you may wish to add an executive summary, focusing on the prospect's core objectives, the benefits you will provide, your primary credentials for providing them, and the major features of your services. Executives focus on core objectives and high-level benefits more than anyone else.

Project understanding

Variously called the "The Issue," "The Statement of the Problem," and "Background on the Problem," among other names, this section shows that you understand what benefits the prospect needs and why. Whenever possible, start with a statement that defines a high-level corporate objective. ("Allington China seeks to become the low-cost producer in its industry.") Then tie the need you will be addressing to the higher, corporate one. ("As a part of this effort, the Distribution Department seeks to lower its total operating costs by 15 percent.") This can be followed by a description of specific opportunities to meet that need. (In the example this might include references to reduced inventories, more efficient material handling, improved shipping logistics, etc.) At the end of the section, state simply that you propose to help solve the problems that you described. (Crosbie Consulting proposes to conducted the analyses required to help the Distribution Department reduce its costs by 15 percent.)

Background on your firm and engagement team

This section should prove that you have the credentials to do what you promise. If you have already delivered these credentials in a presentation or some other way, you may choose to keep it brief, but don't eliminate it completely. Prove...

- ...*your reliability*. You are not a fly-by-night organization. The firm or its staff know the business because they have been at it for a long time.

- ...*your relevant experience*. This is a good place to summarize relevant past experience with short client lists and one or two descriptions (one to three sentences each) of past projects. Refer the reader to an appendix for greater detail. If this section gets too long, the reader will lose the thread of your argument.

■ *...your expert's credentials.* A concise summary of honors received, publications, or other relevant expert's credentials may also be appropriate here. Place detailed resumés, if they are needed, in an appendix. Guidelines on how to prepare a good professional bio are located in appendix A.

Project outline

This section proves you have an approach that will deliver the promised benefits. In it you commit to certain work and ask the client to commit time and other resources. It should only be detailed enough to make the prospect feel confident that you will do the job. The level of detail required varies among buyers. The more technically oriented the buyer is the more detail he is likely to want to see. This is analogous to a contractor who wants more detail on the construction of a house he may buy than others might.

Make an effort to tie each major task described in this section to the benefits the client is seeking. When you begin to describe any information gathering you must do, tell the prospect how this will produce a benefit. If developing a consensus is important to him, mention that information gathering is the first step in developing consensus because it involves everyone in the process early. If the nature of the problems the client faces is not fully understood at the time the proposal is written, say that this stage will help ensure that you solve the right problem. Each task will cost the prospect money; tell him how each one will provide him value. Doing this will differentiate you from the majority of your competitors. The less experienced he is with buying your services, the more clearly he needs to be told. Exhibit 13.1 lists some common elements of a professional project outline. With a specific prospect in mind, see whether you can describe the benefit he will receive from each.

Exhibit 13.1

Relating Proposal Elements to Benefits

The column on the left lists elements common to proposals of many professionals, though the precise name for elements varies among the professions. In the column on the right, list the primary benefit(s) that a specific prospect will receive from each element. Note that on some engagements there are multiples of some elements (e.g. Analysis, Interim meeting, etc.).

Element	Benefit to Prospect
1. Information gathering A. Internal to Client	
B. External to Client	
2. Analysis	
3. Generation of alternative solutions	

4. Interim meetings	
5. Documentation	
6. Recommendations	
7. Final meeting	

Make sure to note key events such as major review meetings during this portion of the proposal.

Deliverables

This can be incorporated within the project outline or compose a separate section, but somewhere within the proposal you need to summarize specifically what the client is going to receive from you by the end of the engagement, or, this will be an ongoing service, at designated times. Examples of deliverables include presentations, reports, analyses, findings, recommendations, plans, and documentation of many sorts. This is a good place to summarize the overall value you are providing.

Assurances

Make clear that you will comply with any legal or other concerns noted by the prospect, which might include demonstrating that you have an affirmative action plan or that you will hold information provided to you in confidence.

Timing

The prospect needs to know how long the work will take and when key events will occur. If he is in a hurry, be sure to show that you are especially qualified to do the work quickly.

Fees

The prospect will want to know what the work will cost. You should quote fees clearly and concisely, avoiding any appearance of evasion. Prospects are extremely sensitive about professionals who promise one fee up front and ask for a larger one later. An unclear fee quote will create the impression that you may do this. See chapter 14 on fees for suggestions on how to construct them.

Authorization

At the end, the proposal should state clearly what the prospect needs to do to authorize your work. This can be done by signing a copy of the proposal so that it becomes a contract and returning it to you, requesting a formal contract, issuing a purchase order, or sending a separate letter of authorization.

Appendices

Use appendices for any information that is so lengthy it might distract from the major thrust of your proposal's argument. An appendix is also a good place to put any information the prospect is unlikely to read in detail but wants access to.

Full resumes of team members, detailed project descriptions, and proofs of the firm's financial stability are all good candidates for appendices.

Use simple language

The proposal should be easy to read. This means you must use simple language and comply with the rules of usage, grammar, and style. If you have concerns about your English composition skills, ask someone else to edit your draft. Review Strunk and White's *Elements of Style* (see appendix E for reference) once a year. If you do what this small book recommends, the quality of your proposals will improve.

Make it visually appealing

A proposal cannot sell for you if no one reads it. The easier it is to look at, the more of it people will read. Make it visually appealing. This means:

- *Have an attractive cover.* First impressions count. An attractive cover will induce a prospect to look inside.

- *Have a logical layout that is easy to follow.* Clearly mark transitions in subject with headers. If the proposal is over five pages, include a table of contents.

- *Avoid large blocks of text.* Keep paragraphs short, generally five sentences or less. Use bullets periodically; they provide relief from standard paragraphs and engage the eye. Leave ample margins.

- *Keep it short.* A short proposal is less intimidating than a long one. You can relegate back-up material, the kind of material a prospect is likely to leaf through anyway, to an appendix. Short is relative. Some clients or projects require large proposals. Yours should be shorter than the average submittal, whatever its length.

  You may choose to disregard this suggestion if technically oriented buyers will have a primary role in reviewing your proposal. Such people often decide who to recommend on the basis of detailed specifications that require longer submittals.

- *Use graphics.* Architects, interior designers, consulting engineers, and others in the built-environment industry use pictures of their work to interest readers. Most professionals can use diagrams, charts, tables, and other graphics to illustrate aspects of their proposals. Readers like it when you do. If you do not currently use graphics in your proposals and your proposals are more than three pages long, spend half an hour brainstorming about what you could include. Consider Gantt charts, flow diagrams, organizational diagrams, maps, and sample deliverables. See appendix B for guidance in graphics preparation.

If the prospect has requested a specific format, follow it

Some prospects send RFPs that ask for information in a specific sequence or format. In such cases, comply with the request. If you don't, you will appear unresponsive; you will offend the author of the RFP, who is likely to prescreen proposals before others see them; and you will make it difficult for a review committee to compare your proposal to others, which will annoy them. Most proposals that ignore requested formats lose jobs.

Occasionally an RFP will be so ill-constructed that you will find it difficult to follow the requested format without huge redundancies or confusion. If you must violate the format, stick as closely to it as you can and make it clear that you are doing so. For example, after a heading you might note, "This section answers questions 4, 5, and 11b of your RFP."

Customize boilerplate material

Most proposals incorporate boilerplate. There is seldom sufficient time to write everything from scratch, and content requested by different prospects tends to be repetitious. Use existing materials, but be sure to take the trouble to customize them each time. You must edit resumés to ensure that the most relevant experience is listed first and that material irrelevant to your prospect is deleted. Project descriptions often need recasting to emphasize their relevancy to a particular prospect. Often this can be done efficiently by including a heading, "Project Relevance," after which you list key similarities with the prospect's situation or key benefits you provided.

You must discipline yourself to make substantial changes, too. When rushed, you will be tempted to use an old work outline that almost but doesn't quite fit this prospect's situation. This often results in a weakly developed case for why you should be hired. Use the old material to help you plan your project outline, and then rewrite it completely for the prospect you are pursuing now.

Hand-deliver your proposal

Delivering your proposal by hand accomplishes several things. First, it shows the project is important to you. Second, it provides you with another chance to talk with the prospect about his needs. Third, it may give you a chance to present the proposal. A few professionals refuse to deliver proposals any other way.

If you can't deliver your proposal in person, follow up by phone to make sure it was received.

14

Quoting a Fee

You must get paid for your work or you will soon have to find some other way to make a living. Furthermore, not only must you get paid, you must get paid enough. The economics of a professional practice are so simple they can be reduced to the following formula:

$$P = (H \text{ times } B \text{ times } R) \text{ minus } C$$

Where:

H = total hours available
B = percent of those hours that are billable
R = hourly rate
C = costs

If you want more money, you can lower your costs, increase the percentage of your time spent on paid work, or increase your rate. You can also work more hours in a day, provided that you can get paid for some of the additional time. Most of this book focuses on keeping the percentage of your time that is billable high. First it shows how to get billable work; second it shows how to get it efficiently, so that you spend as little time as possible on nonbillable marketing. This chapter focuses on your pricing, which determines your hourly rate.

You are likely to find pricing persistently the most difficult part of selling. Professionals with years of successful selling behind them continue to struggle with pricing. From one direction they are pushed by prospects to get prices down, and from the other they are pushed by their cost structure to get prices up. If you have spent most of your career managing projects to a budget and have suffered through a few that have been underpriced, you are likely to focus on a cost-plus-profit approach. Many professionals do this; many lose sales because they do.

Another group of professionals become so enamored of winning a job that they lose sight of their costs. There is an old joke about an architect who inherited a million dollars. When a friend asked him what he was going to do with it, he responded, "Keep practicing until it's used up." Few of us have a million dollars to spend this way.

Try to set aside any biases you have about pricing as you read this chapter. The following principles about pricing will help you determine the best approach for your practice.

Your flexibility in setting a price is determined long before you quote a fee
Pricing starts when you select a profession and a specialty, when you select a market and when you select a strategy for pursuing that market. Some of this is now beyond your control, but not all of it. You may still have the freedom to define a specialty, shift your market, and choose a new strategy. If you wait to receive a Request for Proposal before you think about pricing, your fees will be lower than if you address the issue early.

First, you can create a niche where competition is lower, permitting you to capture higher prices for a while. This happens in product markets all the time, Apple Computer's creation of the desktop publishing market being but one good example. It also happens in the professions. I remember attending a breakout session of three hundred people at a conference for strategic planners. A principle from Boston Consulting Group spoke on time-based competitive strategies. When he finished, at least three quarters of the audience rose and tried to get a private word with him at the podium. Time-based competition was a new concept, and BCG had a temporary corner on the market.

On a less dramatic scale, this kind of differentiation is possible in almost any profession. One New Jersey accountant, for example, developed a specialty in the valuations required for divorce settlements. You must think about your experiences and the needs of your market and look for opportunities to establish a niche.

Second, you can select a market that permits higher margins. Analyze your past projects to see which have been profitable and which have not, and focus your attentions on the profitable part of the market. This can be hard to do, especially if you are in a business in which you receive many unsolicited RFPs, as is true, say, for information systems consulting in the government market. An RFP looks attractive. The prospect has a need and almost certainly has a budget. But if you must compete with thirty to fifty other firms for the work, you had better have a strong reason to believe that you can win before you waste time and money responding. In such an environment, prices are sure to be low. Some of the most important choices you make in marketing are what projects not to pursue.

Third, you can decide how you will take your services to the market. As I have noted earlier in this book, one consulting firm grew from $20 million in revenues to $100 million over three years because it developed a new strategy for taking its business to the market. Defying accepted beliefs about what works and what doesn't, the company developed a cold-calling strategy that allowed it to bid without competition on large projects. Complementing or replacing your current strategy for going to the market can sometimes reap big dividends. Part III of this book will help you determine what strategies might work for you.

The earlier you discuss a prospect's needs, the better chance you have of getting a good fee

Early knowledge of a need gives you the chance to learn more about the client, develop a relationship, and help him define a need. You may be able to presell him before the formal selling process begins. When this happens, you can sometimes get yourself sole-sourced for the project, or at least be the favored contender in a competition. This usually translates into a higher fee.

Yesterday I spoke with a consulting engineer who had been pursuing a university client for many months. Because it is a public institution, the university has to advertise formally for bids. When a project came along that my friend wanted, he wasn't worried about the competition that open bidding would create. "We'll get it," he assured me, "because we understand their problem better than anyone else. I know just what to put in our submittal to make us the right firm to do the work." His early relationship with the client allowed him to compete more on service than on fee.

Your marketing strategy will determine how early you get in. Pick it carefully.

The higher you sell in an organization, the better the chance you will have of getting a good fee

The CEO will pay more for your services than a manager will. Both will pay more than a purchasing agent. Many professionals will ask to speak to a senior executive as a part of the investigation required to define a project's scope and set a fee. The senior executive's contribution is usually valuable, and the professional has a chance to win an ally who will not be price-sensitive.

If your initial meeting is with a high-level person, he may seek to pass you off to a subordinate to talk further about your services. The subordinate is likely to be more price-conscious and may not want to hire you at all. When the boss suggests such a transfer, say something like the following:

> I would like to meet with Mr. X, and let me make a suggestion. Bringing in an outside professional can be threatening to a manager. He may wonder if you think he is doing his job right—professionals are often hired because of a boss's doubts. I can tell him how my firm can help him do a job, but it sounds self-serving for me to tell him we are needed. If you say there is a need, it begins the relationship on an entirely different basis and helps ensure that the project goes well later. Would you be willing to call the first meeting with Mr. X to get things started right? After that he and I can work out the next steps together.

Everything in this paragraph is true. The boss's sponsorship of the initial meeting with his subordinate will also help ensure a higher fee.

Don't quote a fee any sooner than you have to

Many clients ask for a quote during preliminary discussions, either because they want to avoid wasting your time and their own if you cost more than they can afford, or because they are just curious. Avoid giving a number. You can usually forestall further discussion by saying that your fees vary greatly depending upon the exact services provided and that you will have to learn more before you can give an estimate. If the prospect persists, ask him why he wants to know now. The answer may give you the information you need to deal with his concern appropriately.

When forced to talk about fees early in the process, give wide ranges. Saying that your fee will run between $50,000 and $100,000 tells the client that he won't get away for $5,000 and that he won't have to pay a million, but gives you plenty of room to determine the right price later. Be aware, however, that a prospect tends to remember the low end of the range. When you finally quote a figure, remind him of the full range before stating the fee.

Occasionally you may want to quote a range early in the conversation in order to qualify a prospect. You should do this when you seriously question the prospect's willingness to pay or when the cost of pursuit will be high relative to the final fee. While working in Chicago, I used to do this when a small prospect called me from California. I went to see those who weren't put off by the range I quoted, and I avoided several expensive trips to the West Coast for projects I probably could not have won and that would not have been worth much if I had.

You must determine the prospect's fee expectations

Often buyers expect fees to fall within a preconceived range. This is true whether or not the buyer has ever purchased the kind of service you offer. Once established, these expectations are difficult to change and are a major determinant of what the buyer will pay. They come from many sources. The buyer may have talked to your competitors, heard comments made by a peer, made an analogy between your services and some other kind of service he is familiar with or simply based his expectation on his budget or approval limits.

If possible, try to determine what that expectation is before you quote a fee. Sometimes the nature of a client provides a clue; an investment banking firm will expect to pay more than a discount retailer will expect to. Usually you have to infer a range from answers to indirect questions. You can ask:

- *How did you hear about my firm?* This is always a safe question, and the answer can help. A referral from a past client suggests a price expectation comparable to the fees paid by that firm.

- *Have you ever worked on a project like this before?* You may not have to ask this question. The answer may be volunteered in discussion about how long the buyer has been on his job or about the need for the service. The more experience he has, the better informed he will be. Information on specific firms he has worked with also tells you about his fee expectations.

- *Is there competition on this project and, if so, who is it?* You may not want to ask this question, and if you do, the buyer may decline to answer. On the other hand, he may volunteer it, or you may pick up gossip on competition through your network. The more competition there is, the better informed the prospect will be about pricing. A selection of high-end or low-end competitors also gives you a sense of the level of other quotes he is likely to hear.

- *What is your budget?* It is often inappropriate to ask this question, but sometimes your rapport with the buyer will allow you to do so. I did recently asked a buyer for his budget, and he told me, "Up to $x without approval, and up to $y with approval." In the built-environment professions, of course, the expected construction costs and building type provide indicators of the expected budget for professional services.

- *What benefits will your company get from this project, and why do you need it now?* These questions will give you a sense of the value the client expects to get from your work and his level of urgency. All other things being equal, the more value expected and the greater the urgency, the more the prospect will be willing to pay.

To change expectations, you must change either the scope of your services or the perception of value

When the prospect doesn't want to pay what you want to charge, you can either walk away or try to find a solution satisfactory to you both. Sometimes you can educate him on the value of your work, an onerous task, especially if you are up against low-priced competitors. In that case you must not only demonstrate the return he will get from your work but also prove that the return is much higher than he will get from the competitor. For many services this is difficult to do.

Your best bet is to redefine the scope of the service. You can then redesign and reprice the project. When I sold location consulting services, I sometimes had to compete against large construction companies that would practically give away the work in hopes of getting large construction contracts later. Once this happened with a price-conscious prospect planning to move a manufacturing plant. I knew the job would go to my low-ball competitor in a direct comparison, even though I believed my services were superior.

The CEO wanted to move in order to lower labor costs, because his company was losing market share to low-cost competitors. "What if moving the plant doesn't reduce your costs enough to make you competitive?" I asked, and told him a true story about a company that had spent millions to relocate, only to have the competition drop its prices still further and maintain a price advantage. The company went bankrupt. This captured my prospect's attention. I was the location consultant, and I was suggesting that a location change might not work! I recommended a low-cost feasibility study to determine whether the company should move, upgrade its manufacturing technology, reengineer its product, or do some combination of these three to meet the competition. I won the job, performed a service that dealt more accurately with the client's need, and, after three phases of work, earned a higher fee than if I had just sold a location study.

Redefining the scope often requires determining the underlying goal that the prospect is trying to achieve. If you understand that goal, you can sometimes see another way to achieve it that will allow you to win the project at a price you can afford. Another way to redefine scope is to ask yourself, "What does the prospect need to meet his immediate objectives?" If you define the scope this way, you can often reduce the work required and demonstrate to the prospect that you will be a good steward of his money, spending it only as it is needed.

Consider alternative ways to construct a price before you make a quote

The principal approaches for constructing a fee are:

- Cost-plus
- What-the-market-will-bear
- Competitive
- Value-based

Cost-plus pricing

This approach is most easily explained in the context of a sole practitioner. To estimate costs accurately, the sole practitioner must estimate his overhead for a year. This includes rent, utilities, insurance, labor, postage, office supplies, and all other nonreimbursable expenses. He must also estimate the percentage of his available hours that he can bill to clients, the remainder being overhead. With this information he can use the formula shown at the beginning of this chapter to calculate the fees he will have to charge to a targeted annual income.

Exhibit 14.1 provides an example. The consultant must charge $190 per hour ($1,500 per day) if he wants to make $150,000 per year. To price a project, he must estimate the number of hours it will require and multiply it by $190. This is typically done by listing each task to be performed and then estimating the hours required for that task.

Exhibit 14.1

Determining an Hourly Rate

Total available hours	2,080		
Nonbillable hours	- 1,040		
Billable hours	1,040		
Rate per hour	(a) x $125	(b) x $190	(c) x $250
Gross income	$130,000	$197,600	$260,000
Annual expenses	- 50,000	- 50,000	- 50,000
Net annual income	$80,000	$147,600	$210,000

Many larger firms build this kind of calculation into their hourly rates, so that in calculating a cost for a project, you only have to add in a figure for nonreimbursable expenses.

A cost-plus price can be structured either as a daily rate or a project fee.

What-the-market-will-bear pricing

Few professionals acknowledge that they charge on this basis, but many successful ones do. This approach will help you increase or decrease your fees, depending upon which you need to do.

If your calculation of a cost-plus fee results in a number that is more than the client will pay, you must either get your fee down or forgo the engagement. First, ask yourself whether you have defined the scope of the project correctly. What specific questions does the client want answered? What outcome is he seeking? What specific deliverables does he require? You may find that your cost is too high because you are answering the wrong question. This is an easy trap to fall into. My own hit rate increased markedly when I became more effective at defining client need. It resulted in selling more, smaller projects to the same client with higher total fees than I had been able to win in the past.

Next you must review the list of tasks developed when you originally priced the project to see what can be taken out. For each task, ask: Does the client really want this done? Is it necessary for the completion of the project? Is there a cheaper way to do it? Cheaper ways include using low-cost talent within your firm, outsourcing it, or asking the client to perform it. You may also be doing things by hand that should be automated, delivering reports instead of presentation summaries, or providing your services in other ways that are more expensive than need be.

Finally, ask yourself, "If I had no other choice but to do this project at price x, how would I do it to make it profitable?" Often this reverse thinking can lead to creative ways to get your price down.

What-the-market-will-bear pricing can also ensure that you do not underprice your work. Some clients and industries are simply willing to pay more than others. Believing that price is one measure of quality, they may pick a competitor if your price is too low. It takes chutzpah to ask for twice your normal rate, but if that is what the prospect wants to pay, you would be foolish not to ask for it.

Competitive pricing

Competitive pricing is much like the previous category, except that instead of using your beliefs about what the client is willing to pay to determine your quote, you use your expectation about what the competition will ask for. This can be risky, because few of us really know what a competitor is likely to charge. But if the client has chosen high-priced firms to ask for bids, you can quote a higher fee than you might otherwise.

Value-based pricing

When you charge a client a percentage of the expected or actual value received from your work, you are value pricing. This is how most professionals would like to price, but most don't, for two reasons. First, they may not be able to demonstrate the value of their services. What is the value of an accounting audit? What is the value of a good interior design? It is hard to prove. Second, the market may not let them. A prospect who requests bids from several professionals is, in essence, saying that she can get the same value from any of several firms and so will hire the one with the lowest price. True value-based pricers are typically those firms whose marketing strategy allows them to bid noncompetitively.

Even if you do not see an immediate opportunity to price in this way, it is worth seeing whether you can demonstrate the economic value received from your work. Firms that do this can often find ways to apply the information to win clients at higher fees. Here are some of those ways:

- *Performance pricing.* Some cost-reduction consulting firms get paid a percentage of what they save; some litigators and attorneys who do collections work earn a percentage of the money they get for their clients. Many professionals feel that they cannot maintain their objectivity with such fee arrangements and look down on those who price this way. Others, including such high-profile firms as Bain & Company, have no difficulty about tying compensation to value. Clients are increasingly looking for this type of pricing.

- *Providing testimony from past clients.* One consulting firm I know provides estimates of cost savings before beginning an assignment, supported by data on actual savings produced at other clients. References validate these data. It then asks for a fixed fee based on the value it forecasts it will provide.

- *Documenting value for a client.* Whenever possible a professional should show a client the savings or revenues that have resulted from his work. McKinsey & Co. is reported to go to great lengths to do this. This practice undoubtedly accounts for some of the loyalty its clients show; it makes the person who hired the firm look good.

A prospect is less likely to balk at a fee that is delivered in person
When you deliver a proposal in person, you can reinforce the value of your service. You can also observe that prospect's reaction to your fee, and explain and modify it as needed. The prospect lacks this support if you send the proposal by mail.

Bill your client as soon as you can
A client is willing to pay for a service he needs. He will also pay for one just completed, while the memory of value received is fresh. Once a project is completed, the longer he must wait to make a payment, the greater will be his reluctance to do so.

Get clients in the habit of paying from the beginning of an engagement. Asking for a sign-on fee equal to between 20 and 30 percent of the total expected fee is one way of doing this. It will also help your cash flow. Thereafter, submit bills at established intervals.

Conclusion
Too often professionals consider pricing only after a prospect asks them for a fee. By then much of their flexibility is lost. Pricing deserves to be one of the fundamental issues you consider when you develop a marketing strategy. Good negotiating after you submit a quote can seldom make up for being able to make a profitable quote in the first place.

15

When You Lose A Sale

I do not love thee, Doctor Fell.
The reason why I cannot tell;
But this alone I know full well,
I do not love thee, Doctor Fell.

This may be the best-known rejection of a professional in song or story. Presumably Doctor Fell did not get the business of the rhyme's author, and, if he was at all concerned about marketing, he would want to know why.

Unfortunately, like many notifications, this one is uninformative. I have never heard words so blunt as these myself, but like most professionals, I have been told that the chemistry with my competitor was better, a tactful version of the same thing. And just as in the rhyme, the person who delivers this message always says he doesn't know why. This chapter will help you get beyond such vague statements.

The market *is* a great teacher, and for reasons I don't fully understand, it teaches better when we lose than when we win. A debriefing on why you didn't get a job is the market telling you what you are doing wrong. Only a fool would ignore this source, the only one that really matters. Smart people want to get every drop of help that they can.

When you lose a sale, try to do the following.

Understand the prospect's mind-set.
When a prospect calls to give you the bad news, his words are influenced by recognizable inhibitors.

- *Time*. The call to you is a necessary distraction. The prospect wants to get it over with as quickly as possible so he can get back to the business at hand. His objective, then, is to keep the conversation brief, and he will choose the reasons he gives you for his decision accordingly.

- *Good manners.* Just as you would be reluctant to tell a casual acquaintance that he smells, prospects will avoid telling you anything that might offend.

- *Self-interest.* Prospects don't want an argument. The decision is made and irreversible. It is simplest to give you a reason that is unarguable.

- *Self-esteem.* Sometimes giving the reason would embarrass the prospect. If the project was wired from the beginning, or if the senior executive chose someone else for a selfish or petty reason, the notifier is unlikely to tell you. If he wasn't really party to the decision and doesn't know why his boss decided as she did, he may not want to admit it.

- *Confusion.* Often the notifier doesn't fully understand why the decision went the way it did. He only senses it.

- *Unconscious behavior.* Some people are extremely nonconfrontational. They seldom speak directly to anyone. This is a deep-seated psychological condition that you cannot change.

Given these inhibitors, the chances of getting good information on why you lost a sale are slight, unless you handle the situation carefully. Remember that the prospect feels about as comfortable telling you why you lost as you would explaining to a neighbor why he wasn't invited to your party.

Try to convince the prospect to talk to you like a Dutch uncle
A Dutch uncle is the person who has the relationship and feels the duty to give a vainglorious teenager stern and candid advice about his behavior. That is what you want the prospect to do. To do it, he must feel that he has the relationship and the duty. He must feel that doing so won't be too painful. Only such feelings will overcome the inhibitions that keep him from giving you good information. Getting him in this frame of mind underlies many of the following guidelines.

For starters, you must really want this kind of talking-to. You won't always like what you hear, and you will have to sit there and take it. When this happens, remember it is what you don't hear that hurts you the most. The person who talks to you like a Dutch uncle does it for your own good.

At its worst, a marketing problem is like a cheating spouse; friends know but don't tell you about it. One successful architectural firm almost went bankrupt after the president and primary marketer retired. His successor, who wanted to fill his shoes, took the lead in all the firm's marketing efforts, but his abrasive manner drove away prospects. He could have solved the problem with training or by transferring the marketing lead to someone else, but he didn't want to hear he had a problem. The accountant who told me this story had tried to fill the Dutch uncle's role and found that his help was unwelcome. Don't react this way. We all need Dutch uncles from time to time.

Try to set up a special interview for the debriefing
Before calling to give you the bad news, the prospect has decided what he will say to get the job done quickly and painlessly. At best he plans to give you partial infor-

mation; at worst, to lie. To push him beyond this initial explanation risks exposing him. He will withhold cooperation rather than let that happen. Also, if he must notify several other losers, he will be anxious to get on to them.

For these reasons you should not try directly to overcome resistance to getting good information during this first conversation. Rather, listen to his brief explanation and then try to set up a separate time for a face-to-face or phone interview, using words like the following:

> Obviously we're disappointed at the news; we really wanted to work with you. But we understand that you had to make a decision and wish you every success. If we can be of any further help, let me know.

> I do have a favor to ask. Once a project is lost, it's lost. The only thing we can get from the time and effort invested is information on how we can do better the next time. We have a set of debriefing questions that we like to ask when we lose. Could I arrange a half-hour conversation with you to go over them? It would be a great help.

These words inform him that you accept the decision and are not going to argue and that you bear him no ill will. They also let him know that the debriefing is a standard procedure, so that he doesn't feel singled out.

If he agrees to the meeting, schedule it immediately. He may say that he doesn't see what more information he can provide. If so, respond that you have found such meetings extremely helpful even when the prospect feels as he does and repeat your request. Once he gives you a commitment, thank him and get off the phone.

I have had prospects totally revise their explanation of why I lost a sale, during a follow-up meeting. This would not have been possible had I asked all my questions during the initial phone call, because reversing themselves so quickly would have embarrassed them. Of course, if the prospect insists on doing it then and there, you must comply.

Occasionally a prospect will agree to a meeting, ask you to call back in a week to schedule a time, and then not take your calls. Move on. He wouldn't have given you good information if he had met with you.

Claim any relationships that will get you better information

You may have a relationship with the prospect that creates an obligation on his part to give you better information. If so, use it. You can sometimes make claims on a relationship that would have been inappropriate during the sale. If the prospect has been a client in the past, for example, ask for a follow up meeting on the basis of the good work you have done previously. I once lost a sale at an insurance company that was the carrier for my firm. During the sale we never mentioned this relationship. We suspected the prospect knew of it and that he would take offense if we claimed it. Once we had lost, I felt differently. I politely pointed out the relationship—we had been right; he was aware of it—and said we had not felt that it was appropriate to make an issue of it during the sale, but that now I was making a request as a customer, not a vendor. I wanted good information on why we had lost the sale. He understood me and respected my earlier discretion. He gave me one of the best debriefings I have ever had, one that was instrumental in fixing several problems in my firm.

You may be able to make a claim on friendship. If the prospect used to be in private practice, you may be able to make the claim on the basis of his understanding of your need for this help. By making such claims tactfully, you are freeing the prospect to talk to you more candidly than he might otherwise, that is, to talk to you like a Dutch uncle.

Make it clear that no one will lose his job on the basis of what the prospect says in a debriefing

A prospect naturally fears that if he speaks candidly, his words will hurt someone. This is an unfair burden to put on him. No one should lose a job for making mistakes on a few sales. (Unemployment rates would rise steeply if this were a general practice.) Instead, you seek his help in identifying ways in which you and your teammates can improve. If I sense any hesitation, I usually say:

> This is not a witch hunt. That's not the way this firm operates. We all want to get better. That is deeply built into our culture. We can sit around and guess what went wrong and maybe even be right some of the time, but it means more when we hear it from someone in the market whose opinion we trust.

Plan your questions in advance

When you get a formal debriefing, use the prospect's time well by knowing what you want to ask. I always work from a questionnaire for two reasons. First, it ensures that I cover what I want to know. Second, if I am meeting face to face, it confirms my claim of a formal debriefing process.

A sample list of questions is provided in exhibit 15.1. Note that part A starts the interview with several open questions. These give the prospect the chance to say what is on his mind on any subject he chooses. Narrower questions might focus his response too quickly and bias his answers.

Exhibit 15.1
Debriefing Questionnaire

Company Name: _____

Interviewee: _____ Title: _____

Address: _____

_____

Interviewer: _____ Date: _____

Part A: Overview *Introduce with the statement: "I would like to ask some general questions first."*

1. Why did you select the other firm?

_____

_____

_____

_____

2. What did they do especially well during the sales process?

_____

_____

_____

_____

3. Where could we have been better?

_____

_____

_____

_____

Part B: The Sales Process *Introduce with the statement: "I would now like to ask how we compared with the competition in some specific areas." You may have to prime responses with additional questions, such as "Who did you talk with at each firm at this stage?" or "How did what each firm said make you feel?"*

4. Initial phone contact discussing the project:

_____

_____

_____

5. Fact-finding visit to your office:

_____

_____

_____

6. Your visit to professional offices:

_____

_____

_____

7. Brochure and other marketing materials:

_____

_____

_____

8. Presentation
   a. General comments:

_____

_____

_____

   b. Participants:

_____

_____

_____

   c. Format:

_____

_____

_____

   d. Visual aids:

_____

_____

_____

e. Q & A:

_____

_____

_____

9. Proposal
   a. General comments:

_____

_____

_____

   b. Appearance:

_____

_____

_____

   c. Understanding of issue:

_____

_____

_____

   d. Description of scope:

_____

_____

_____

10. Fees:

_____

_____

_____

11. Follow-Up:

_____

_____

_____

12. Additional Comments:

_____

_____

_____

Part C: Specific Concerns *Introduce with the statement: "To finish up, I would like to ask you a couple of questions on specific concerns about our performance that we had." Since these concerns are situational, you must develop these questions yourself.*

13. Concern A: _____

_____

_____

_____

14. Concern B: _____

_____

_____

_____

Once he has answered these questions and elaborated on any issues that they raise, I tell him that I want to review the sale from beginning to end, then ask the questions in part B. The answers to these questions help in two ways. First, they tell you about the relative importance of different issues. If he can talk at length about presentations but can barely remember proposals, it tells you that the proposals didn't weigh heavily in the decision. Second, they keep him talking, and when he talks, he gives information. Often he is unaware when he tells you something important. He may even provide a clue to something he is unwilling to say. That you presented with transparencies while everyone else used slides is useful competitive information, whether or not it affected this sale. In responding to these questions, the prospect will sometimes give you information that you can combine with information drawn from other sources to identify a problem. In the chapter on presentations I noted how the same criticism from two prospects combined with what I learned from a competitor when I saw him speak at a trade show taught me how to counter his presentations.

In part C, saved for the end of the interview, I ask any questions that test theories I have about the loss. What effect did a specific mistake have? Would it have helped if we had brought the president along? Questions like these might bias the interview if asked earlier.

Never disagree with or debate what you are told!

Never disagree in a debriefing, *never* debate. The instant you do, the prospect will clam up. He is giving you information as a favor, and disagreement implies that you don't appreciate it. He doesn't want to argue; he has better things to do.

This doesn't mean you have to agree with everything he says. You must only accept it as his understanding of what happened. If you don't see how he can feel as he does, choose nonargumentative language to learn more. "That's interesting. Tell me more." "I'm not sure I understand. Tell me more." "We certainly don't want to give that impression. Can you tell me what we did that gave it?" These words show you won't argue and that you are truly interested in learning more without implying agreement.

Write down what you hear

Take detailed notes on what you hear during a debriefing. Over the years I have learned that it is much easier to remember good news than bad. Note taking helps ensure that you remember both. Also, the full value of what you learn may only be apparent with time. As noted, a response may only be meaningful when combined with other information you may not yet have. I keep a file of post mortems and review them about once a year to refresh my memory and see whether they can tell me anything new.

Discount certain information unless you can determine what it means

An explanation of why you lost may be true or may simply show that the prospect feels inhibited about telling you the truth. Treat the following comments with caution.

- *You lost it on price.* Maybe you did. Then again, maybe this is the least-controversial explanation available. Try to find out how great the difference was. Ask the prospect if he has any opinions about why your price was higher. Did you misunderstand the scope?

- *Price didn't make any difference.* If the prices were close, this is probably true. If yours was high by a wide margin, it probably means, "I don't want you to think I'm cheap." You probably failed to justify the price differential with added value.

- *You were second choice.* And so was everyone else. Only accept this one if you get strong details about why you were second and someone else was third. Usually this statement reflects a well-meant desire to make you feel better and nothing more.

- *It was a close decision.* Maybe, but he probably just doesn't want you to feel bad.

- *Their chemistry with our people was better.* Sometimes this, like price, is simply an easy excuse to give, because it is difficult to argue with. Sometimes it is a kind version of the words used with Dr. Fell. There is a reason, but the prospect is uncomfortable telling you. In some cases, however, it is a true statement and the prospect really doesn't know why. He only senses it. That is because "chemistry" derives from his feelings

191

about how you look, how you behave, and what you say. He may be summarizing his reaction to many little things he is not fully aware of. Your detailed questions on the sales process may help draw out an answer. Look especially at whether your looks, words, and actions made you seem: a) compatible with the prospect's culture, b) as if you cared about him personally, and c) as if you would be enjoyable to work with. If this phrase is repeated often, get professional presentation coaching.

- *I wanted you to get it, but the others voted for your competitor.* Read this as, "I want you to like me." It is probably untrue.
- *I don't really know why. When things could easily go either way, it's hard to say.* This person is probably extremely nonconfrontational. If so, you will never get useful information from him. Try a few additional questions to confirm whether this is true. If it is, thank him and try to get a debriefing with someone else.
- *You presented well, but the others on your team didn't.* The prospect will find it extremely difficult to criticize the debriefer. To do so would require overcoming what he has learned about good manners since childhood. The debriefer always gets higher marks in a debriefing than his teammates. Don't let it go to your head. He is probably just being polite.

Debrief as many people as you can

If several people participated in the hiring decision, interview as many of them as you can. Each will have a different perspective, and some may feel less inhibited than others. Use your questionnaire with each.

Don't expect all debriefings to be worthwhile

Not every debriefing will provide you with helpful information, but not every one has to. If only 20 percent give you insights into what you need to improve, you can make tremendous progress. Most will help at least a little. Breakthrough debriefings are rare and only happen if you make a practice of debriefing every time you lose a sale.

Send a gracious thank-you letter

After your debriefing, or when you realize that you won't get one, send your prospect a letter thanking him for the opportunity to compete for his project. Tell him that you appreciate his time and help and wish him success on the project. Make it as personal a letter as you can; a form letter will be seen as one.

This is good manners and also good business. Your prospects today are probably pretty much your prospects for the future. You want to be considered the next time he has a need, and the chances of that happening will improve if you accept the loss graciously and retain a friendship. Every so often a competitor will foul up a job. It will be more likely to come to back you if you have accepted the first decision gracefully.

Put each loss behind you and go on to the next sale

The harder you worked to win a job, the closer you came to winning, the worse it feels to lose. You must learn what you can from it, put it behind you, and go on to the next one. Good marketers bounce back quickly.

Everyone who sells has slumps. When this happens to you, remember that marketing is a numbers game. Though skilled marketers will win more jobs than poor ones, even they have slumps. The rules of probability ensure that during some periods you will hit a string of unusually difficult situations, while at others sales come more easily. You are not necessarily performing better when you are hot. You may simply be luckier.

That is not to say that you should wait for the slump to pass and take no other action. You should increase your inquiries into why you are losing. There may be a good reason; a competitor may have found a new and exciting approach, or client needs may be shifting. But good marketers adjust to such changes and bounce back and win again.

I once had a losing streak where every prospect I touched seemed to choose a competitor or postpone his project indefinitely. It drove me crazy. I rethought everything I did, completely revamping my approach to the market. In a few months the slump ended and I began to win again. To my surprise a number of the projects that I thought I had lost came back to me. This forced me to make a decision. I could either abandon the improvements I had made on the grounds that my reason for making them now seemed invalid, or I could retain them, believing that the basic reasoning behind them was good even if they had been initiated for wrong reasons. I chose the latter and have never regretted it.

Professional markets are extremely competitive. You have to work constantly to stay ahead. This means you must always be looking for ways to improve. You must always be questioning what you are doing. Just don't question yourself.

Part III

From Tactics to Strategy: What Works and What Doesn't

I have devoted the first two parts of this book to specific marketing and sales techniques. The professional who wants to develop new business must become proficient in at least some of them. Marketers market. By doing the things described in the preceding chapters, you can become a marketer and you can sell. You will see results. Marketing is a numbers game, and anyone who speaks or publishes often, keeps in touch with past clients, makes cold calls, or performs other marketing tasks will get some business. The more skillful you become, the higher your batting average will be, just as with a batter if he practices his swing.

But that is not enough. Individual marketing events must be built into a larger strategy if they are to have a lasting and large impact on your career and on your firm's development. The better your strategy, the more often you will score, just as a batter will hit more often if he makes informed decisions about when to swing, when to pull, when to bunt, etc.

Strategies are implemented by the allocation of resources. When you decide to write three articles, give one speech, and hold a seminar, and at the same time decide not to send out any mailings, you are making a strategic decision, whether or not you recognize it as one. In a world of infinite resources this would not be a concern, because you could do everything you want to do, but for most of us time and money are scarce. Spending them on one task means we forego some other.

This portion of the book describes marketing strategies to help you select the right mix of tactics. We will look at strategies for both individuals and firms, recognizing that for the sole practitioner, the two are indistinguishable.

In researching these chapters I have made studies of several groups. First I have identified marketing stars in several professions, people who showed a knack for marketing early in their careers and developed into lead marketers and rain makers for their firms. Some of these individuals have been described in the case examples that began each chapter in the preceding portion of this book. Looking at the entire group, I have been able to draw conclusions about the development of successful personal strategies.

Second I have looked at a large number of firms in one profession, consulting, interviewing roughly fifty people in more than thirty organizations. These interviews have been complemented with experience and selective interviews with other professions and anecdotal information gathered over a twenty-year career.

You must take several things into account when developing a strategy. You will want to get the most out of the investment of your time and money. Chapter 16 explores ways to do so, describing the simplest of marketing strategies. Simple though they may be, such strategies have been the foundations of many professionals' marketing careers, including my own.

You will also want to look closely at yourself, assessing both your personal inclinations and abilities and any specific gaps in your skills or credentials that need filling. Chapter 17 provides tools for making such an assessment.

Next you must look at your services and market. As is shown in chapter 18, different kinds of services and markets lend themselves to very different marketing strategies. Pick the right strategy and you will see an ample return on your marketing; pick the wrong one and you will waste your time, as many have before you.

Chapter 19 looks at strategies for firms rather than individuals. It serves two purposes. For the manager of a firm or a large practice within one, it will provide insight into successful strategies for large organizations. It will also help individuals learn how their personal strategies must fit within the context of a larger organization.

These three different levels of consideration—your personal abilities and needs, the nature of your service, and the strategy selected by your firm—create a complex environment within which you must develop your own strategy. Any reasonable strategy is better than none. There is no single right answer. But some individuals and firms have found breakthrough strategies that have pushed them ahead of their competitors. A final chapter describes some of the elements of breakthrough strategies.

16

Simple Strategies That Can Help You Now

Professionals cite lack of time as the single biggest obstacle to marketing. You have to bill a high percentage of your time to earn a profit, leaving few hours for marketing. This means that you must use what marketing time you have efficiently and effectively. Experienced marketers squeeze as much impact as they can from each hour they spend on marketing. Two principal means for doing so are leveraging and running campaigns.

Leveraging

Leveraging is simply using the same hours to complete several marketing tasks. It offers you the advantages of a two-for-one sale. Examples include:

1. *Using a speech as a basis for an article.* The time you spent preparing the speech will greatly reduce the time required to write the article. Often a trade association that has asked you to speak will be glad to publish the speech in its journal. If not, someone else may.

2. *Giving the same speech to different groups.* This economy has been used by politicians and speaking professionals since time immemorial. A little reflection or research will often provide you with at least two or three additional groups who would be interested in the speech you have just prepared for one audience. If you can prove that the speech went well with the first group (with a thank-you letter or summary of speaker evaluations), you have ammunition to convince someone else to give you a podium.

3. *Using the same article for several publications.* You have to be careful of copyright limitations, as well as editors' fears of being scooped by competing publications, but if you are careful, you can often use the same article for different publications. Never offer an article to a second

journal without noting that it has been published elsewhere already. Never do so without informing the publication in which it first appeared of your interest in using it elsewhere. Often the editors of the journal in which it is first published will be happy to authorize reuse, especially if their journal is referenced as the original place of publication. As one example, I once published a speech on analyzing labor markets in a personnel journal and in one directed at corporate real estate managers. The latter were interested because labor markets were crucial to selecting new corporate locations. The journal directed at corporate real estate executives was willing to reference the publication in which my article had first appeared.

4. *Using a similar article for several publications.* You can often adapt a single article for quite different audiences. An article on reengineering for the metal-stamping industry might be very similar to one for the plastic injection-molding industry. Each will have examples from companies in the appropriate industry, and each may require a few changes in emphasis to customize it to a specific audience, but the underlying content will be much the same. In such cases you don't have to seek permission from the journal that published the first article before you offer it to a second, nor must you advise the metal-stamping journal about the previous publication of a similar piece in the plastic injection-molding journal.

5. *Giving a speech at a trade association meeting you will be attending.* If you are going to devote the time to attend a trade association meeting, you might as well apply to speak. You will receive greater recognition if you go as a speaker, and moreover speakers generally have an easier time meeting and talking with others at a conference than nonspeakers. It is understood that they are making a contribution to the organization, they have at least minor celebrity status (often evidenced by ribbons attached to their name tags), and they are participating as experts in a particular area.

6. *Conducting a survey at a trade association meeting and using it as the basis for a press release, article, or white paper.* This works particularly well if you have a booth at an exposition or are speaking to a large group. You will be there anyway, so you may as well use the opportunity to gain information that can be used for future marketing. By promising a copy of the survey results to those who provide their names and addresses at the bottom, you can also generate a list of qualified leads.

7. *Using a press release as a basis for an article or speech.* Once a press release has been used or rejected by the media, get as much additional value from it as you can.

8. *Using an article that results from a press release and mentions your firm as a mailer.* This is a good way to remind your market that you are seen as an expert by the media.

9. *Using a reprint of an article you wrote as a direct-mail piece.* This saves the time of creating a mailer.

10. *Turning a speech into a white paper and using it as a direct-mail piece.* This is the same as No. 1, except that you do your own publishing. This can be done when you do not have time to wait for publication or when a speech is unpublishable for an acceptable reason—such as that it is focused on too narrow an audience for a publication to find attractive.

11. *Asking a network contact to speak at a seminar.* You help the that individual, whom you are trying to cultivate, by providing market exposure. At the same time you gain a speaker for your seminar.

12. *Asking a client you want to build a strong relationship with to speak at a seminar.* He may enjoy the recognition, and you gain a speaker.

13. *Asking a client you want to build a strong relationship with to share a podium with you.* He may welcome the exposure, and you will get to work with him while preparing the presentation. Working together builds relationships.

14. *Asking a client you want to build a strong relationship with to author an article with you.* He may appreciate the exposure, and the joint authorship will enhance your credibility.

Whenever you undertake a marketing task, it is worth reflecting on how the time you are expending can be leveraged. But leveraging does not apply to marketing tasks alone. You can also leverage nonmarketing activities. Here are some examples.

■ *Turning a business contact into a network contact.* Most professionals have contact with vendors, subconsultants, clients, and other professionals who serve your clients. Some of these people can be useful network contacts. When you identify people with this potential, see whether you can help them, and follow the other networking rules that will allow you to make them a part of your network. For example, a New Jersey accounting firm that handled the personal accounts of several attorneys at a New York law firm held a party for the law firm's partners to inform them of the accountants' corporate experience. When one of the lawyers later needed to refer a corporate client based in New Jersey to an accountant, he referred it to the firm that had held the party.

■ *Using research conducted for a client as the basis for a speech, press release, or article.* This is the most common leveraging technique. Some forms of research, like surveys, lend themselves to this kind of use. Whenever a survey is contemplated for a client, its marketing value should be considered *before* you design the survey questionnaire, in case a few questions need to be added to increase its marketing value.

- *Using research as a basis for cold calls.* If you have surveyed companies who might make good clients, offer to discuss the results with them as a reward for participating.

- *Turning a training session into a speech or an article.* If you train other professionals, you may be able to leverage the work required for a half-day training session into a speech or article.

- *Turning an internal training session into a seminar.* Of course, you will not want to give away company secrets. If you can avoid doing so, the internal training program you have created can sometimes have marketing value.

Experienced marketers make the most of the nonmarketing work they do for marketing advantage.

Finally, there may be things you do for social reasons that can be leveraged into a marketing activity. The combination of business with golf provides a hackneyed but real example. I once helped a social acquaintance sell a training assignment through an introduction and endorsement. She has since become a useful business contact and a part of my network.

Campaigns

A campaign increases the impact of your marketing by delivering your message several times to the same people. It helps your market retain your message and associate it with you. Many of the leveraging techniques described in this chapter can be used to create a campaign. For a successful campaign you must have a target market, a message, and a series of events to deliver the message to the market. A campaign I directed at the insurance industry included four articles, a speech, a direct-mail program, and cold calls. Over two years, work from this industry went from almost zero to 20 percent of the revenues of the office I was working at.

Several kinds of campaigns are commonly used by professionals.

- *Direct Mail.* Perhaps the most obvious example is a direct-mail campaign. A single mailer is seldom adequate to imprint a message about your firm on the minds of recipients. As noted in the chapter on direct mail, you will generally need to deliver your message three or four times over a short time to have an impact.

- *Speaking.* In businesses characterized by a large number of regional associations, a campaign to speak at a large number of them can be an effective method of building your reputation and developing leads. As noted previously, you can leverage the time required to prepare for such a campaign by using the same speech over and over.

- *Cold calling.* This is particularly important when you have a market that consists of a relatively small number of large organizations to whom you want to deliver a specific message. In such cases, direct contact is probably the most cost-effective method. An architecture firm developed a strategic alliance with a mechanical, electrical, and plumbing engineering firm to deliver a specialized service to the pharmaceutical industry. Cold calls at each company in the industry were an important factor to the alliance's success.

Many campaigns are based on more than one marketing technique. A firm that has developed a specific skill, service, or knowledge base will wish to get the word to the market repeatedly through a variety of methods.

17

Self-Marketing: Experts Make Themselves

Larry and Alice were both in trouble—for different reasons. With one year on the job, Larry was 50-percent billable, when the target for entry-level professionals was 75 percent. Project managers didn't find him productive and weren't anxious to have him on their projects.

Alice, a senior project manager, billed over 80 percent of her time, putting in long hours every day and on weekends. Given her experience and compensation, she should have been bringing in new clients, but she never found the time. She was always too busy producing work—some of it work that Larry should have done.

The head of the practice met with each separately and began by asking them how they thought they were doing. Larry's response was enlightening. An ambitious young man, he perceived that long-term success in the firm would be based on marketing. He was anxious to prove himself in this area. The practice leader educated him on the economic logic of the firm and showed him why, at this stage in his career, his most crucial need was to market himself internally to project managers by demonstrating high productivity, remaining highly billable, and developing the experience that would, in a few years, permit him to market effectively on the outside.

The practice manager next sat down with Alice. She perceived that she was doing well, though she was concerned about the long hours. The manager reviewed the economic logic of the firm with her, showing that at her level a certain amount of selling of new business was required. She protested that she didn't have time, and he committed to lighten her work load.

Within six months Larry had transformed himself into one of the firm's most productive associates. His labor was eagerly sought by several project managers, he billed over 80 percent of his time, and he still made time for a little marketing. During this same period, Alice made little progress. Though the

*practice leader steered new work to other managers, he found that Alice volun-
teered to relieve others of some their burdens, informally taking on the work he
had tried to protect her from. When he mentioned this to her, she protested that
the work had to get done and that she had been obliged to help the other project managers.*

*When the firm had to lay off employees because of a downturn in busi-
ness, Larry kept his job and eventually developed into a fine marketer. Alice lost
hers for the simple reason that at her compensation level the firm could not afford her unless she brought in enough business to support herself. There were
other capable managers who could run projects.*

Events like these are common in large professional service organizations. Careers are made and broken by the compelling logic of a market that demands high
production of professionals at the same time that it demands sales. It is a logic that
relentlessly weeds out many fine professionals like Alice, allowing only a few the
chance to reap the rewards of becoming a partner with a major firm. The logic
works equally well for the sole practitioner, who must both sell and produce work
to stay in business.

Interested in developing talent for professional firms, I once wrote down a list
of all the successful marketers of professional services I knew well and reviewed
their careers to see whether I could identify any commonalty in their histories. My
objective was to learn from the experiences of these stars and find a way to transfer
it to others.

I learned the following:

1. The stars were universally high producers early in their careers.

These people threw themselves into client work early in their careers. Sought after
by managers because of their productivity, they rapidly developed a strong experience base. They sought independent experience in which they could work directly
with clients and were eager to demonstrate an ability to manage client relationships. As a young lawyer, Mike Schell, now a partner with Skadden, Arps, Slate,
Meagher & Flom, preferred to work on the firm's less prominent merger and acquisition projects instead of the large and more prestigious ones, which were followed
carefully in the business press. "On the big projects I would have been the fifth face
on a six-headed totem pole and likely would have had little contact with the client.
I felt I got a lot more out of the smaller projects where I could be a principal player,
work directly with the client, and have a central role in all the work."

In most firms, professionals who can demonstrate an ability to earn client
confidence are given increasing responsibility. As a partner at another large firm put
it, "Finding young people who are acceptable to clients is a key issue for the partners, because if you don't your time is fully taken up by existing clients and you
can't do any marketing." The stars filled this need.

The experience they gained by working many projects allowed them to talk
more knowledgeably to prospects when they had the opportunity and to develop

their own anecdotes, so essential to marketing services. Because of this knowledge base, they were included on sales teams early, increasing their market exposure.

2. The stars showed an intense interest in marketing early in their careers.

These people were more than reliable producers of work and managers of client relationships. They also had a strong desire to bring in new business. Each developed an approach to marketing and stuck with it. Each found special ways to assist in the marketing effort. Some became superb relationship marketers, deliberately converting one-time projects with clients into long-term firm relationships. Several became skilled networkers, bringing in leads from their contacts outside the firm. Others used other techniques, but each had a concept of how he or she could bring in business, and worked at it steadily. Others in their firms soon viewed them as specialists in specific marketing activities. When opportunities requiring these activities arose, they were asked to participate.

3. They took great care to credential themselves.

All of the stars updated their bios regularly, ensuring that this most fundamental of marketing documents reflected their full experience. This was particularly important early in their careers, when each additional assignment significantly expanded their experience base.

Their craving for credentials showed itself in different ways. One had earned degrees in architecture, engineering, and business and was working on his CPA accreditation when workload resulting from career success forced him to reassess his priorities. Another was a joiner of associations and became known as an expert among the members with whom she worked on committees. Several published or spoke frequently.

4. All found ways to improve their firms' services.

Sensitive to client needs, the stars were more interested in making their clients happy than in rigid rules about how to do an assignment. They responded to client concerns and, in doing so, found ways to improve their firms' services. One consultant developed an add-on service that eventually became a substantial revenue source. Another overhauled the way cost comparisons of alternative solutions were made. An architect enhanced his firms' programming effort by developing specialized knowledge of a specific building type. An attorney solved a legal problem in a way that the partner in charge of his project doubted would work.

These improvements didn't just help clients. They lowered production costs, increased revenues, or increased service value without increasing costs.

5. They became specialists.

Early in their careers the stars were seen as specialists, often, though by no means always, in areas in which others in the firm showed little interest. This had crucial benefits. First, they were increasingly selected to work on projects requiring their specialty, because they were easy to market to clients, thereby further increasing their knowledge in the area. Second, as experts they gained selling and marketing opportunities because they were the logical individuals to speak for the firm on the subject of their expertise. Many of the stars developed two or more expertises during their careers, adding one after another.

In all the professions it is increasingly important to develop such specialization both as firms and as individuals. A specialization is often a prerequisite for an emerging marketer to get opportunities to sell. Take these examples.

- An attorney was brought into a firm specializing in bankruptcy law to broaden its commercial practice. At first he billed himself as the individual who did all of the firm's nonbankruptcy commercial work. This did not work well. It proved so hard to claim expertise in such a wide area that even his partners couldn't figure out how to pitch him to their clients. When he began to develop an expertise in labor law, the situation changed. He became a credible expert. The other partners began to refer him business.

- An architecture firm established a program to develop specific second-tier personnel as marketers, but found that it only succeeded with specialists, including one who had not been identified for development. The need to succeed at sales was so great that senior personnel almost always bumped the generalists from sales calls and presentations, because the seniors were perceived to have a higher probability of winning. Specialists seldom got bumped, because they had knowledge and credentials that the seniors didn't.

- A partner at a Wall Street law firm found that he could get opportunities to speak and to meet with clients because of his specialty in a specific area of securities law. Sometimes the work that resulted had little to do with this specialty, but the specialty got him in the door ahead of competitors.

The stars saw the benefits of becoming specialists and didn't resist the label, as some of their peers did. They didn't resist concentrating their work in one or two areas at the expense of broader experience.

Beyond these points there was little the stars had in common. Certainly all were ambitious, but seemingly for different reasons. Some wanted money, others recognition, and still others seemed to work so hard largely for the fun of building a practice. Some were extroverts, some introverts; some highly polished, and at least one somewhat folksy. A few were good managers, others were not, but they all brought in business.

The characteristics of the stars can be used by other professionals seeking to develop a personal marketing strategy. In the often-quoted line from Robert Louis Stevenson, everybody lives by selling something. At different points in a professional's career, he sells different things to different people. Early in his career a professional in a large firm *sells his production skills to partners* and other senior personnel in the firm. People seen as unproductive seldom last long enough to prove themselves as external marketers. Somewhat later in a career the professional is asked to participate in client meetings and selective sales presentations. This happens first when the client wants "to see the one who actually does the work." In these circumstances the professional's primary task is to *sell himself to existing or prospective clients*. Still later in his career the professional markets projects that will largely be done by others. At this point in his career he must *sell the firm to prospective clients*.

Defining the track this way explains why star marketers bill so many hours early in their careers. They know that this is the best way to sell themselves to senior firm members and earn opportunities on the assignments that most interest them. Skills and experience gained from working these assignments form the basis for credentials, and credentials form the basis for marketing.

I have refined this career track into the following four-step hierarchy of development needs for the aspiring marketer.

1. *Skills.* These are gained through training, often on the job from more senior professionals, though they are sometimes self-taught. They are demonstrated by an ability to complete specific tasks efficiently and effectively. They can be technical skills, such as a particular analytical ability; process skills, such as the ability to gain consensus; aesthetic skills in some professions; and marketing skills.

2. *Experience.* This is gained by doing many assignments with limited guidance from more senior professionals and is demonstrated by an ability to apply a skill to new situations. Having it means you can be sold to others in the firm and to prospective clients as a key player in a project team.

3. *Knowledge.* Gained by thinking about experience and through research, it is developed largely on one's own or through discourse with other experienced professionals. Knowledge is demonstrated by an ability to draw inferences from experience that go beyond technical proficiency. Knowledgeable professionals are the ones who expand their companies' practices by modifying old services and developing new ones, and by devising marketing programs.

4. *Expertise.* One message stands out from the experiences of the stars: *Experts make themselves!* Gained largely by the professional's promotion of his or her knowledge, experience, and skills, expertise is demonstrated by a recognition of your status as an authority by others. Note that an expert doesn't have to have the most experience in a field; he or she simply has to promote his or her experience more effectively than others do.

To develop a personal marketing strategy, you must first determine where you are on this hierarchy. Exhibit 17.1 is a simple form that you can use as a tool. Make copies and fill out the form for each area in which you want to present yourself as an expert. This can include expertise by industry (banking, automotive, not-for-profit, etc.), functional area (securities, human resources, tax accounting, power plant design, sales force compensation, etc.), process skill (negotiating, managing, facilitating, etc.), and marketing (public speaking, article writing, networking, etc.). Define specializations as narrowly or as broadly as makes sense given your firm and market. So, for example, an insurance industry specialization might benefit by being narrowed to property and casualty or life and health companies, to mutual or publicly held companies, to large or small companies, or some other segmentation.

Exhibit 17.1
Personal Evaluation Form

Area of Expertise: _____

Target Market: Who would be interested in this area? Note types of clients, others in the firm, outside business contracts, etc.

_____

_____

_____

Expertise: What proof do you have that you are an expert? Include degrees, certifications, number of past clients in the area, publications, memberships, speaking platforms, testimonial letters, etc.

_____

_____

_____

Knowledge: What specialized knowledge do you have as a result of your experience? Is there anything that differentiates your knowledge from that of others with similar experience?

_____

_____

_____

Experience: What experience do you have on which knowledge can be based? Include client work, previous employment, and any other appropriate experience?

_____

_____

_____

Skills: What specialized skills do you have of value to the market? Include both technical and process skills.

_____

_____

_____

If you find yourself thinking, "I can do it all," beware. Maybe you can. But that is not the point of this exercise. Now you are trying to evaluate your level of expertise in specific areas, and expertise is defined by your markets' view of you, not your own. You can start anywhere on the form you wish; I often find it best to begin with *knowledge*, since this category best describes what I would like to sell.

Do not be concerned if you have little to put down in some categories. The main purpose of the exercise is to identify gaps you must fill. If your credentials are weak, you now know that they must be improved, and a first step in your marketing strategy should be to do so. Credentialing activities include writing and speaking. I would also recommend writing and speaking if your knowledge is weak, because doing these things will force you to articulate what your experience has taught you. If your experience is weak, you must find a way to increase it. Perhaps you should ask senior people in your firm for the opportunity to work on projects that will develop it. In the architectural industry firms can gain experience through teaming arrangements where one team member offers geographical proximity or client access or superior design, while the other brings experience and expertise. A series of successful team arrangements can give a firm the experience needed to become an expert and dispense with further teaming. If you lack skills, you must seek further education.

Exhibit 17.2 shows a personal evaluation form filled out by an architect who specialized in research laboratory design. Note that his expertise is based, among other things, on working on twenty laboratory projects. Other individuals may have more experience than he does, but that is not a major concern as long as he promotes his experience better than they do or can differentiate what he has to offer in ways of importance to his clients. Others may also have written more expensively on laboratory design. How he uses his publications for marketing is more important than the quantity he has produced. Nevertheless, this individual might conclude that he needs more publications or speaking opportunities to further enhance his stature at this point in his career. He might also place a priority on building nonpharmaceutical experience, or decide to specialize further in the pharmaceutical industry.

Exhibit 17.2

Sample Personal Evaluation Form

Area of Expertise: Research laboratory architecture

Expertise

- List of 20 laboratory projects
- Reprint of article on laboratory design in *Industrial Research & Development*
- Member of ISPE
- List of five speaking engagements
- Juror on panel to select "Laboratory of the Year"

Knowledge:

- How to program a research laboratory
- Implications of changing technologies on laboratory design
- Language used by researchers when discussing facilities issues
- Typical facilities concerns of researchers and alternative design solutions
- Names of leading specialists needed to support work

Expertise:

- Work on 20 laboratory projects (15 pharmaceutical)
- Work with most noted research lab design consultants

Skills

- Architectural programming
- Laboratory layout
- Consensus building
- Explaining laboratory requirements to nonspecialist architects

---

Next use the material from your Personal Evaluation Form to create a bio for yourself describing your expertise in a particular area. This bio can be used when you are selling yourself to prospective clients, seeking speaking engagements, and being introduced at speaking engagements, as well as for other marketing purposes. If your firm has a standard format, use it. If not, invent your own. Appendix A provides guidance for doing so. Review the bio. Does it sound convincing? Do you have enough credentials, and have you used them effectively to prove your expertise? What does it tell you about the self-marketing that you should be doing?

Creating a personal marketing plan

The personal evaluation is an important first step to creating a personal marketing plan. Such a plan must do four things:

1. Build your credentials
2. Disseminate those credentials to prospects
3. Get you information on prospect need
4. Get you face to face with prospective clients

The first part of this book is devoted to marketing techniques that can help you achieve these objectives. A strategy selects a mix of activities to achieve all of them. For example, publishing articles is an excellent way to accomplish item 1 and will help with item 2, but it does a poor job of getting you information on prospect need or getting face to face with prospective clients. That is why a marketing strategy can seldom be built on one technique. In selecting a mix of techniques appropriate for you, you must consider several things.

First you must consider where you are at in your career and what your existing credentials are. Younger people must concentrate more on building experience and credentials. Their experience, as reflected by their bios, often looks thin. Often they are not expected to bring in much business, and so can devote more time to building their experience, credentials, and reputations. Seasoned practitioners have experience and are often under more pressure to bring in work. Building experience is usually less an issue than using what experience they have effectively to win new clients. They need to spend more time on generating leads and getting face to face with prospects.

Second you must reflect on your personal abilities. Do you write well and enjoy it? If so, article writing offers a possible avenue. If not, you must either find writing help or abandon this approach. Do you like the idea of public speaking, or does it make you acutely uncomfortable? Are you a sociable person, a natural networker? If so, networking becomes a particularly attractive alternative. It sometimes pays to ask others, people whose judgment you respect, what they think you are best at. Friends can provide a reality check.

If you review the case studies that begin each chapter in the first part of this book, you will see that most of these star marketers began by doing something that came easy to them, relative to the alternative approaches. Most built upon one key ability, adding others as their skills and reputations developed. Doing something for which you have a natural ability will help you market efficiently early in your career, when the demands to remain highly billable are greatest.

Third, you must be sure that the marketing tasks you set yourself are achievable. Because you must produce work at the same time that you seek to develop new business, a large portion of your marketing effort must be interruptable. Few professionals can afford the luxury of dedicating themselves solely to marketing for a three-month period. They work on a marketing project in fits and starts, because they are always being interrupted by the demands of paying clients. If your marketing plan does not take this into account, it will fail.

A primary focus in the first part of this book has been to show how specific marketing tasks can be structured so that they are interruptable. Many of the formulas described in the chapter on article writing provide a structure that makes it possible to write an article in pieces, when a canceled meeting gives you an unexpected half hour, or while in a plane, or between 7:00 and 8:00 a.m. before the phone begins to ring. Similarly, Chapter 3 on networking describes techniques used by others to maintain a networking effort in spite of production demands. Your personal strategy should include activities of this type that allow you to make incremental progress.

That does not mean you should always steer clear of large projects. Writing a book is a major marketing achievement for many professionals and a worthwhile goal. However, it is also a huge undertaking requiring many hours of work over an extended period. Even after you finish writing it, a year can pass before you see it in print. Writing a book can easily be a two- to three-year process. If authoring a book represents the main focus of your marketing effort, you will have to wait a long time before you see any results from your work. Thus, if you depend upon your marketing to bring in business, you must employ some additional methods to carry you while you wait for the book to appear.

Depending on the level of support you can call on, other marketing activities can also require long periods before you see results. Preparing a two-day seminar, which requires arranging for speakers and facilities, preparing content, acquiring a mailing list, preparing a mailer, sending the mailing, and many other tasks, is also a major undertaking for an individual. Yet you see no benefits from all that effort until the seminar is completed. No new business can be expected from any of your work until then.

Compare these activities to making a cold call on a prospect once a week. Each visit has stand-alone value—you learn about a particular prospect and deliver a message. Even if your program is interrupted by production needs, the value of visits you have made remains and may result in new business. Incremental benefits can come from direct mail, speaking, article writing, public relations, and networking campaigns. With so many approaches to choose from, every personal marketing plan should include techniques that permit incremental benefits.

Finally, your personal marketing plan must take into account the special characteristics of your market and services. This is so important a subject that the next chapter is devoted to it.

With these considerations in mind, review parts I and II of this book and set out five key goals for yourself for the next year. They should be so stated that your performance can be measured. Examples of such goals might include:

- Publish one article.
- Meet with twenty other partners in the firm (roughly one every two weeks) to discuss cross-marketing opportunities.
- Devote one hour every Tuesday morning to making networking telephone calls.

Create a separate page for each goal in a log and establish tasks and completion dates required to complete them. For example, since most articles take an average of six months to appear in print, you must submit one or two finished pieces over the next five months to have reasonable assurance of meeting the goal of publishing one within a year. Set a deadline for submittal and work a schedule back from there. If you are going to meet with twenty other partners to discuss cross-marketing, you must schedule time for setting the appointments. You need as much discipline in structuring your marketing work as you do in working for your clients. Monitor your progress toward your goals twice a week.

18

Market-Based Strategies

Charlie found the secret—a new way to sell his firm's services that would bring in millions of dollars in additional fees. He learned of it from an ebullient, somewhat eccentric consultant who had devised the method. A cautious man, Charlie checked the system out with other firms who had used it. Their responses convinced him. They had seen a dramatic increase in sales from the approach, which relied on sophisticated telemarketing techniques to get senior marketers in front of prospects.

Charlie pushed hard to have the system adopted at his firm. He arranged a meeting between his boss and the marketing consultant. He pitched the system to his partners. The consultant was hired and the system put in place. One year and many thousands of dollars later the firm abandoned it. It had not produced a single new project in all that time. What had gone wrong?

While researching this book, I asked many professionals what they would like to see in it. One said, "I'd like to know what works and what doesn't. I've spent money trying a lot of things. For many of them, I don't know if they paid off or not. For others that clearly didn't work, I don't know if it was because of my execution or because they just wouldn't work for (a firm in my practice)."

My friend's concern is valid and, I suspect, common. One hears a lot of conflicting statements about marketing techniques in the professions. A few I have heard include:

> *You really can't market this business.*
> *Cold calling doesn't work for law firms.*
> *Cold calling doesn't work for consulting firms.*
> *We built our (new law) office by cold calling.*

> *Our cold calling program is the source for almost all of our new (consulting) clients.*
>
> *We network with a lot of people, but I really couldn't say how valuable it is.*
>
> *Networking doesn't work for someone new in the profession because all of the best relationships have been taken.*
>
> *Clearly the quantity and quality of leads we get from networking are better than from any other source.*
>
> *We had a publicity program, but it didn't produce any results.*
>
> *Getting your name mentioned in the press is one of the most important things you can do.*
>
> *I spend a lot of time and money putting together a newsletter twice a year, but I don't know if it does any good.*
>
> *(Our newsletter) is the spearhead of our whole effort to keep our name constantly in front of our clients.*

Many of the conflicting views result from treating a whole profession as the basic unit for analysis of what works and what doesn't. Because each profession is so diverse, approaches that work for one firm or practice often don't for another.

Take, for example, the two characteristics of client need shown in exhibit 18.1. The vertical axis shows the frequency of need. Companies need accounting audits annually. Compensation analyses are also required frequently. Some have an ongoing need to investigate all prospective employees. In contrast, most companies select sites for major new facilities at most once every three or four years. If lucky, they will never need assistance from a bankruptcy attorney or from a consultant who will help them recover from a disaster.

The horizontal axis shows the confidentiality of the need (not to be confused with confidentiality of the actual work performed by the professional). Everyone knows that companies have an annual need for audits, that they must conduct compensation analyses frequently, and that they would like to reduce their costs. No call for secrecy there. Likewise, when a disaster occurs, it becomes public rapidly. Other needs for services, however, must be confidential. Companies will often confidentially identify a replacement before firing an executive. Those that are planning a move know that if word leaks out, their employees will be upset, they will be subjected to political pressure to stay, and real estate prices may rise in the areas where they want to buy a site. Many firms do not want it known that they hire an investigator to check out the people they plan to hire. If they are suffering from financial troubles and fear bankruptcy, they will want to minimize publicity and the associated risk of scaring customers and creditors.

Exhibit 18.1
Characteristics of Prospect Need

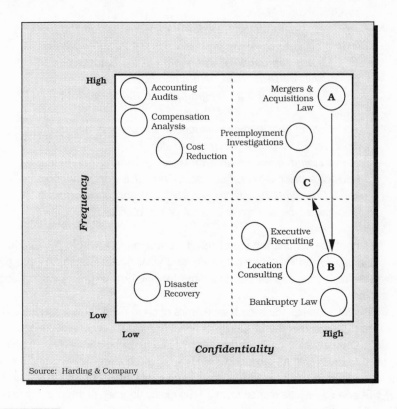

Source: Harding & Company

Over time, the characteristics of prospect need may change. During the major boom in mergers and acquisitions in the 1980s, some companies were under constant threat of takeover, while others were almost constantly seeking acquisitions (Circle A). During the recession that followed, M&A activity declined precipitously (Circle B). With current recovery, activity has increased again (Circle C), though not to the level seen in the eighties.

Companies falling in different quadrants of exhibit 18.1 face different marketing challenges, even if they are in the same profession. (See exhibit 18.2.) The more frequent the need a company has, the more loyal it tends to be to the firm it works with. Working together regularly, client and professional establish deep relationships. The less frequent the need, the lower the loyalty. The more confidential a need, the fewer firms a company is likely to talk with before making a selection. By comparison, pursuit of publicly known needs can be a free-for-all. These differences result in very different marketing concerns that require different marketing approaches for companies in the different quadrants.

Exhibit 18.2
Key Marketing Challenge Based on Client Need

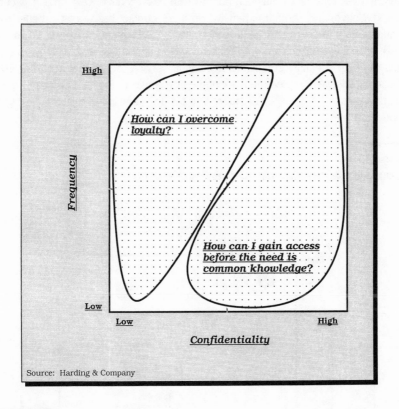

Source: Harding & Company

They also explain why the cold-calling program didn't work at Charlie's firm when it had at others. The firms where it succeeded sold solutions to a need that all prospects would readily acknowledge and that occurs with moderate frequency. These combined characteristics resulted in prospects who were not unduly loyal to any one vendor, a relatively high probability of identifying a need on each call, and a willingness to talk about that need. Charlie's firm solved infrequent, confidential problems. The probability of calling a prospect at the time it had a need were slim, the chances of reaching someone within the company who knew about the need slimmer still, and the likelihood that anyone would talk about such needs with a total stranger almost nonexistent.

The degree to which technique selection varies by firm is further illustrated in exhibits 18.3. and 18.4. The former, developed for a location consulting firm (a firm that helps its clients find locations for plants, offices, and warehouses), arrays a variety of marketing techniques against two factors, the cost per contact and the adaptability of the technique to the infrequent and confidential needs of its clients.

Cold calling is expensive and adapts poorly to the conditions of this market. It is also difficult for this firm to make relationship marketing work, because there are few business reasons to maintain contact with past clients once a project is completed. Networking, though expensive on a per contact basis, adapts better to a market with infrequent and confidential needs; the location consulting firm's network of real estate brokers, employee relocation specialists, and strategy consultants can help it identify companies needing its services before that need becomes public knowledge. Because the work of the firm results in job gain or loss in many communities, it finds it easy to attract free publicity, making this technique highly productive.

Exhibit 18.3
Technique Selection Criteria For Location Consulting

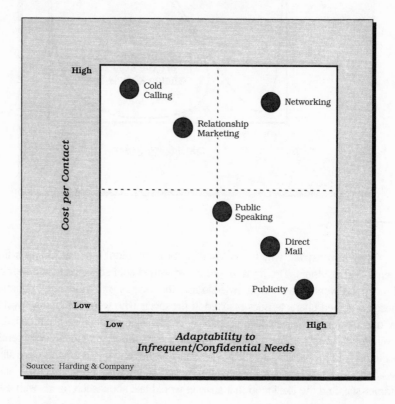

Source: Harding & Company

Exhibit 18.4 shows how a utility consulting firm (one consulting in many functional areas to electric power, natural gas and telephone companies) faces a very different situation, because the needs of its market are frequent and public. In this case relationship marketing with existing clients is highly adaptable and quite cost effective, because the consultants have frequent business reasons to meet with their clients. Cold calling also works well, though it is expensive, because the firm can count on a relatively high percentage of the prospective clients it contacts having a need for the firm's services and on their willingness to talk about these needs. Publicity is less adaptable to the utility consultant's situation than it was for the location consultant, because the subject matter the utility consultant deals with is of less interest to a broad public. This means that the firm has to work harder and incur greater expense to attract publicity. The cost per contact from publicity is therefore higher in this case.

Exhibit 18.4
Technique Selection Criteria For Utility Consulting

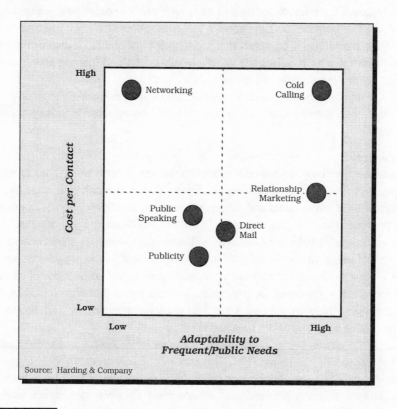

Source: Harding & Company

Analyses like these will not select techniques for you, but they do provide insights into why some techniques work well and why others don't. More importantly, they help you identify specific obstacles that have to be overcome to make a technique work.

Confidentiality, frequency of need, and cost per contact are not, of course, the only variables that influence what marketing approaches will work and what won't. Others include the average revenues per sale, the degree of geographic dispersion of your market, whether your firm's name is known, the number of competitors in your area of expertise, the size of your firm relative to others in the profession, and the characteristics of the industry you sell to.

The dynamism of professional markets ensures that almost every rule about what works and what doesn't will have exceptions. General statements, as long as they are seen as general, do hold. Here is how market and service variables generally affect the desirability of alternative marketing approaches.

Cold calling
Cold calling costs more per contact than any other approach. This means that it works best if the value of adding a client is high, either because your engagements cost a lot or because you can expect a long-term relationship once you have been hired. It works best with needs that are frequent and public. It also works best when your market is sufficiently geographically centralized that the time and expense of making a single visit is low.

When these conditions do not prevail, cold calling is less likely to work. Also, when there is extreme loyalty to another firm, cold calling alone is unlikely to overcome it.

Publicity
Some practices have more media appeal than others. When I worked at a location consulting firm helping companies like Toyota, United Technologies, and Citicorp select sites for new plants and offices, we received media attention because our work resulted in new jobs and taxes. Yet a firm that supported us, one that consulted on the movement of furniture and equipment, received little, because its work had little apparent impact outside the company that was moving. Services that are difficult to understand also have low media appeal, and so do those of interest to very small segments of the population. The larger your firm relative to competitors in your profession, the easier it will be to attract attention, because the media tend to seek comments from large organizations.

While all this is true, public relations is a far more flexible and resilient marketing approach than many others. You may not be able to gain access to major national media unless your service meets some of the preceding criteria, but you can still get attention from regional or trade press. Creativity, persistence, skill at helping reporters, and careful selection of media targets can ensure almost any firm media attention.

Relationship marketing
Relationship marketing works best when the need for your services is frequent and, at times, intense, resulting in a business reason for maintaining contact around which you can build a relationship. Lawyers who represent unions, for example, find that intense, close work during an election followed by the frequent contact

needed to deal with ongoing legal needs provides a strong basis for developing relationships.

Relationship marketing works best for geographically centralized markets, because it is easier to keep in regular, face-to-face contact when distances are short. It is particularly valuable if perceptions of service quality happen to be low in your profession, because then it serves as a differentiator. I know of an MEP (mechanical, electric and plumbing) engineering firm that has built a strong niche for itself on this basis.

Networking

Among the most resilient and flexible of marketing techniques, networking works for a large number of firms. It will work best if your market is geographically centralized or if those who service client needs related to your own are centralized. New York, for example, as the mecca of the securities industry, has a well-functioning network of professionals that service publicly held corporations throughout the United States. For firms located elsewhere, this network can be more difficult to access.

Networking also works best if you can capture a strategic relationship that provides leads exclusively to you. Networks can function so efficiently that leads and introductions flow rapidly through a profession. Every local law firm is likely to refer two or three accountants rather than one. By giving out the lead to several firms, it hopes to receive leads from each of them in return. The same practice applies when accountants refer lawyers or when banks refer either lawyers or accountants. All would like to receive exclusive leads from banks but seldom get them.

The more specialized the service a firm offers, the fewer competitors a network contact is likely to be able to refer when he uncovers a need. The improved ability to capture a strategic network is one of several reasons for specializing. The greatest beneficiary of the formal networking group I belong to is an independent consultant with a specialized niche in an area of purchasing. Because almost all companies can use his services, and because the other members of the network know no one else who offers them, he receives a larger number of leads than anyone else in the group.

Exclusivity can also be formally arranged between two firms, and many have made major marketing leaps because they have captured such a relationship. When exclusivity is agreed to, there are often market pressures to violate it. This means that some ability to enforce the arrangement may be key to its success. This is the case when an accounting firm acquires a consulting firm and establishes an internal network. Alternatively, it may result from a special and powerful tie unobtainable by others, such as the relationship between McKinsey and Company and its alumnae which it has helped place at client companies. Firm-to-firm commitments will be discussed more fully in the next chapter. But individuals can also arrange them.

When the need for a service is infrequent or confidential, networks can also be an effective way to reach a market. This is especially true if you can identify someone who has an ongoing relationship with a prospect and thus is likely to learn about a need when it occurs. For example, a disaster recovery consultant will usually develop networking relationships with property and casualty insurance companies.

Working a trade association

Trade associations help you overcome the difficulty of networking in a geographically dispersed market. At least once a year the members come together at the same place, and committee work provides reason for more frequent conversations. Because all associations feel pressure to bring in new members, it can be hard to establish exclusivity at such a group.

Seminars and conferences

Because seminars and conferences are marketed through direct mail, and direct mailings usually have low response percentages, success requires a large list of prospective attendees relative to the size of the audience you require. Such a list requires a market with at least one of the following:

- *Frequent and expected need.* If I know I am going to have a need and that I will have it soon, I have an incentive to find out how to deal with it. You can probably identify a list of people who will have to address such a need.

- *An infrequent need being faced by many firms all at once.* This can result from a change in laws. For example, one law firm drew two hundred Mexican companies to a conference on the North American Free Trade Agreement. It can also result from a fad. Numerous seminars and conferences have been run on management fads for zero-based budgeting, benchmarking, and reengineering. In such cases you can probably identify a list of people who might have an interest in a timely seminar or conference.

In contrast, it is much harder to attract an audience of prospective clients for a seminar on preparing for bankruptcy or tornadoes—examples of infrequent, difficult-to-predict needs.

Seminars and conferences also work best when mid- and lower-level personnel can have an influence on the purchase of your services, since these groups make up the bulk of most seminar audiences. Because most seminars are marketed through direct mail, you must also be able to identify logical categories of buyers for whom you can acquire lists.

Public speaking and article writing

The more audiences you can identify that might have an interest in your message, the more likely public speaking will work for you. Some fields offer many more audiences than others. Economic development consultants, for example, can speak to several national trade associations, five or six associations serving multi-state areas, state-level groups, groups serving portions of large states, and individual economic development organizations and chambers of commerce. Many of these groups will pay expenses and an honorarium to someone with a message. An accomplished speaker can obtain as many opportunities as he can handle. By comparison, a professional who specializes in work for electric power utilities will have many fewer opportunities. By necessity, public speaking will make up a smaller portion of his marketing mix.

The same logic holds for article writing. For some practices there are many possible outlets; for others, few. The more geographically dispersed your market, the more attractive both of these approaches will be, because they allow you to reach a wide audience at modest cost. Similarly, the less frequently a prospect is likely to need your services, the more you will wish to stress public speaking and article writing because attendees and readers will self-select on the basis of interest.

Direct mail
Because direct mail can be used to achieve several different objectives, it can produce value for most firms. As a lead-generating vehicle, it works best in geographically dispersed markets for services of moderate or low value. Because of its low cost per contact, it offers an affordable way to reach a large, dispersed market. As a way to remind past clients and prospects of your services and continued interest, it can work with any market.

What you must do
Services and markets vary greatly from firm to firm, and these differences must be taken into account when developing a strategy. A law firm specializing in family law faces a very different market from one specializing in securities law. An architect who designs nothing but public schools must market in very different ways from one that has built an international reputation for design excellence. An information systems consultant sells in different ways from a turnaround consultant.

You cannot select the right strategy for your market unless you know your market and service. A surprising number of professionals don't. A traffic engineer once told me how surprised he and his partners were when they first did an analysis of their client base. The results, calculated on actual contract dollars, differed substantially from the partners' perceptions. They were far more dependent on a small number of clients than they realized. The analysis demonstrated that the firm needed to diversify while devoting extra attention to the limited number of key clients that supported it.

Long ago I did a study of the geographic spread of consulting clients of the firm I was working for. Viewing ourselves as an national organization on the brink of becoming international, we were chagrined to learn that 80 percent of our business came from within a three-hour drive of our offices. The story that begins this chapter provides yet another example of a firm that did not fully understand the implications of its market on the effectiveness of alternative marketing approaches.

We all have a tendency to fool ourselves into believing our firms are bigger and more broadly based than they actually are. These self-deceptions can hurt us badly if we act as if they were true. Similarly, a growing firm may not realize immediately that its new size changes the market it sells in and the marketing opportunities available to it. If you have not done an analysis of where your business comes from, do so now. Here are some questions to answer.

Questions on business mix

- What percentage of my business do I get from different kinds of clients (by industry, by geography, by service, by size of company, by title of the buyer, etc.)? What kinds of clients are most profitable? What has the trend been?

- What percentage of my business do I get from my three, five, and ten largest clients? What has the trend been?

- What is the average size of my contracts? What percentage of my business do I get from contracts within specific size ranges ($5,000–$15,000, $15,000–$30,000, ...You must set ranges that are meaningful for your firm)? What has the trend been?

- What is the average size of my total billings to specific clients for a year? What has the trend been?

- How would I like to change any of the above? Rank these changes in order of importance.

Questions on service and market characteristics

- What are the characteristics of my service and market?

Answers to some of these questions will depend on the information you collected on your business mix. Fill out exhibit 18.5 for each major service you offer. This exercise will help you select a mix of techniques that you can work at consistently over time. Remember, it is through consistent work over time using techniques suited to your practice that you get results.

The exercise is designed to stimulate your thinking, not to be a recipe for a strategy, because strategies do not lend themselves to recipes. Neither should it be used to preclude ever using a technique. Perhaps the exercise suggests that cold calling or seminars do not show high promise for your practice. This should not prevent you from using them once in a while, if circumstances seem to recommend it; we all need to preserve a healthy opportunism when marketing. They should simply not be a part of your strategy.

Questions on your current marketing effort

- Where have your leads come from (publicity, client referrals, direct mail, network contacts, etc.)? What has the trend been?

Several firms I have worked with have protested that they don't know where most of their business comes from and that the information is unobtainable. In each case a focused effort has produced the information. If you don't know the answer to this question, you probably haven't tried hard enough to find it out. Of course, a lead can come from several sources at once (say, your reputation and a speech). If this is the case, and the client cannot tell you which was most impor-

Exhibit 18.5

Practice Assessment Based on Market Characteristics

Rate the suitability of each marketing approach for your practice.

Low-Flexibility Techniques: Ratings should average 2 or lower to warrant using as a central part of strategy.

Cold Calling

a. Frequency of need

1	2	3	4	5
At least annual				Less than once every three years

b. Confidentiality of need

1	2	3	4	5
Always highly public				Always highly confidential

c. Value of sale over next three years (You must create your own scale, depending upon the size of your firm.)

1	2	3	4	5
High				Low

d. Geographic dispersion of market (Relative to location of salespeople)

1	2	3	4	5
Highly concentrated				Highly dispersed

Relationship Marketing

a. Frequency of need

1	2	3	4	5
At least annual				Less than once every three years

b. Intensity of contact

1	2	3	4	5
Requires frequent, intense contact				Requires infrequent contact

c. Value of sale over next three years (You must create your own scale, depending upon the size of your firm.)

1	2	3	4	5
High				Low

d. Geographic dispersion of market (Relative to location of salespeople)

1	2	3	4	5
Highly concentrated				Highly dispersed

Medium-Flexibility Techniques: Ratings should average 3 or lower to warrant using as a central part of strategy.

Seminars and Conferences (either (a) or (b) must apply, but not both)

a. Frequency of need

1	2	3	4	5
At least annual				Less than once every three years

b. Time sensitivity of need

1	2	3	4	5
Many people need to know now				Few people need to know now

c. Confidentiality of need

1	2	3	4	5
Always highly public				Always highly confidential

d. Geographic dispersion of market (applies to short seminars, only)

1	2	3	4	5
Highly concentrated				Highly dispersed

Trade Associations

d. Geographic dispersion of market

1	2	3	4	5
Highly concentrated				Highly dispersed

High-Flexibility Techniques: *Warrant using if other approaches are inappropriate and rating on single factor is not 4 or 5.*

Networking

a. Geographic dispersion of market

1	2	3	4	5
Highly concentrated				Highly dispersed

Publicity

a. Media appeal of practice

1	2	3	4	5
High				Low

Public speaking and articles

a. Number of identifiable forums

1	2	3	4	5
Many				Few

---

tant, use your best judgment to assign a weight to the importance of each. What is the trend for each source?

Questions on the competition

- Who are your major competitors? How many projects have you lost to each of them? Why? Has the number and mix of competitors been changing?
- Where do your major competitors get their leads from? How is their business distributed among client types?

This is harder to learn, but you don't need precise answers. Ask the competitors' former employees. Ask others who know them, such as past clients and vendors.

What does all this tell you about the strategy you should be adopting?

19

Your Firm's Strategy and You

Unless you are a sole practitioner, whatever strategy you develop must fit within the larger strategy of your firm. Since few firms clearly articulate their strategies, your first problem is to determine what your firm's is. Start by identifying who the rain makers are and what they do.

Few metaphors are more persistent in the professional services than that of rain making. To be called a rain maker is the highest accolade that a member of an accounting, architectural, law, or consulting firm can receive. For those believing that metaphors tell a lot about organizational culture, this is an interesting one. Literally, a rain maker influences the forces of nature through magic and a special relationship with deities. Because rain is essential to life, the power is as awesome as it is mysterious. Those who are supremely successful at bringing in business to professional organizations are often viewed with the same kinds of feelings. By contrast, in my experience the rain making metaphor is totally missing from the marketing and sales organizations of business entities outside the professional services. In manufacturing, insurance, and general-service industries, the term "super-salesman" is more likely to be used, and there is generally a much greater sense that the skills can be learned and applied by others.

I once had the opportunity to discuss marketing strategies with more than fifty representatives of over thirty consulting firms, and the results provide interesting insights into the state of the art of marketing among consultants. Since then, work with lawyers, accountants, architects, interior designers, and consulting engineers has shown that what I learned applies in varying degrees to other professions too.

From my interviews it was apparent that even among successful senior executives in many firms there is a noticeable lack of confidence in the ability of most people to market professional services effectively, and in a few cases even a lack of interest in the issue. True rain makers are scarce. Why?

The interviews suggest that there are currently four competing models for business development within the professions. See exhibit 19.1.)

Exhibit 19.1
Business Development Models

	Key Concept	Primary Source Of New Clients	Firm Marketing Support	Firm Growth Strategies	Keys to Individual Success
Builders	Rely on relationships built over time	Referrals or luck	Sporadic or none	Add partners with books of business	Develop base of clients over time
Artists	Business development is an art that can't be managed	Partners' marketing efforts	Incentives and sanctions	Add partners each with sales objectives	Learn to speak, network, publish, etc.
Miners	Mine existing relationships by cross-marketing	Selling more product to existing clients	Incentives, sanctions, internal seminars, etc.	Increase cross-marketing opportunities by adding practices	Develop internal relationships to gain client exposure
Sellers	Sell consulting services the way you would other products	Produced by sales force	Centralized marketing and sales effort	Add salespeople, provide more sales training	Behave like a consultative salesperson

Builders

This view was most clearly articulated by the head of a small firm, who stated:

> *It's difficult to market this business. Each of our four partners has ten to twelve old clients that they have built up over the years and who bring us most of our work. We do some mailings and article writing, which occasionally bring something in, but the best source of business is past clients and their referrals.*

Some of those who hold this view feel that marketing is not an effective means of generating new business. They talk about how difficult it is to "make the phone ring." Rather, the firm is best served by responding to inquiries for services from those who know the firm or have been referred to it by others who do. At best, such people are relationship marketers by default. Others acknowledge the

227

potential to develop business in other ways, but focus their own efforts on relationship marketing because they are most comfortable with it. Believing that *most* business comes from past clients, that is where they expend their energies. Many are more focused on doing good work than on the other aspects of true relationship marketing. It follows that outreach marketing efforts are minimal, sporadic, and geared more toward name recognition than lead generation.

When a firm adopts this approach, the outlook will usually be reflected in hiring practices. These firms will only hire senior people who can bring a book of business to the firm and will promote only those who have been with the firm long enough to have gradually built up or inherited a block of clients. Implicit in this firm model is the belief that rain making is magic and magic does not exist. Sometimes new business "drops over the transom"—a second common metaphor in the professions, implying that it is impossible to determine where most leads come from and therefore impossible to plan marketing effectively—but most is the result of a lifetime of building and maintaining relationships through doing projects.

Many professionals still expound this view, especially lawyers and consultants. It is less common among accountants and is hardly ever found among professionals in the built-environment industry (architects, interior designers, and consulting engineers).

Artists

This model was most clearly articulated by a principal at one firm, who said:

> Our marketing strategy is very simple. Partners and every other level in the firm have a certain amount of business that they are expected to bring in. If you don't bring it in you don't last long. This tends to result in the promotion of strong marketers.

This model is broader than the first because it accommodates not only the individuals who have developed a block of business over a career but also those who have proven they can bring in new clients. Yet marketing is seen as a very personal thing, almost an art, heavily dependent on individual abilities and motivation and on market factors relevant to individual practices. For this reason, only those who have practiced in an area for many years and who have an undefinable flair for generating new business are considered able to market. If none of the senior members of a practice demonstrates this flair, the practice ceases to grow. The firm can exert very little influence over the marketing effort except through incentives and sanctions. In such firms, good speakers speak, writers publish, and networkers network independently of each other.

Practice leaders successful at business generation in such an environment are the archetypal rain makers, making their magic in ways often unclear to the rest of the organization. The firm limits its support at most to providing central public relations and similar services that partners can avail themselves of, and perhaps some institutional advertising. In short, there is no firm-wide marketing strategy or effort.

Those operating under this view of marketing will often grumble about a ritual that is common to all of them and already referenced in the introduction to this book. At the beginning of each year, professionals develop individual marketing plans that represent their commitments to activities they will undertake. At the end of the year only a handful have actually completed their assignments, the rest pleading lack of time due to client demands. This happens year after year, with the same results and the same small group of professionals completing their assignments. The frustration of this ritual epitomizes the lack of control that management feels over the marketing effort. You can't force a nonartist to produce art.

The ritual also reflects the world view of the firm. With no central marketing plan and a lack of central control (and confidence) in marketing, the firm focuses on billability to ensure profitability. Any professional whose billable hours drop below standards is quickly called to task. In contrast, there are few immediate sanctions for failing to complete individual marketing plans in such an environment. These are imposed only when revenue falls short and staff must be cut. Marketing one's way out of budget problems is not perceived as a realistic option, though several firms increased the number of partners and/or offices, each with a revenue target, in an effort to force up sales.

Miners

> *We were acquired by (a large accounting firm) two years ago and now about 60 percent of our business comes from referrals from the audit partners. The relationship of these (individuals) to their audit clients is incredibly strong. They hear about needs early and can get us in.*

So said the head of one consulting organization, summing up the miners' outlook.

Though the growth of accounting firms' consulting practices offers the most obvious example, the classic McKinsey strategy of relying on firm alumni who have gone to work at client and potential client companies provides another, as do the strategic alliances that some individuals and smaller firms have put in place. Architecture/engineering firms provide another example.

Firms adopting this approach seek to maximize the value of existing relationships and the marketing prowess of true rain makers by increasing the number of services sold to each client. In this way existing relationships are mined for additional revenue, with internal cross-marketing efforts dominating such firms' marketing programs. The job of earning the trust of partners who must place at risk a valued relationship by introducing new services offered by a different profit center is by no means an easy task. Doing this across a large organization with many thousands of potential relationships is complex and difficult. Management encourages this process not just through incentives and sanctions but also through internal seminars and literature, support for informal contacts, and the establishment of guidelines. The ability to master the complex relationships, procedures, and politics for making contacts and cross-billing in such an environment is one key to personal success.

The phrase "over the transom" is also employed in several of these firms, but its usage is extended to cover unexpected business from elsewhere in the firm. Even in this environment the correlation of marketing effort to leads is often seen as weak.

Intrafirm struggles for leads also produce interesting language. There is often debate over who "controls the client." In a particular marketing event, the phrase is used by those who want access—seldom by those who have the strongest relationship at the prospect company. As it is typically used, it implies, "since you control the client, you ought to be able to get us in." It is an example of how the sloppy use of language can result in unclear thinking, since the principal contact at most controls a client *relationship* rather than the client. These are two quite different things. On the other side, the relationship partner will sometimes become so protective of his client that he will hamper others' marketing efforts and will even refuse to bill a client for services provided by another profit center with the client's full agreement.

The phrase "cross-marketing" also appears among firms using this strategy. Unlike others cited, this term does imply that the firm can manage marketing. Examples of the tremendous success of the approach, which include Arthur Andersen, provide compelling proof that it can.

Sellers

Acceptance of this view varies greatly by profession. It is embraced (in modified form) by many architectural firms, who employ business developers to develop relationships and opportunities that can be closed by professionals. Most lawyers would still reject it. A few consultants and an even smaller number of consulting firms believe that consulting services, like other products and services, can be sold. One or two firms even employ professional sales forces, and a few of the salespeople have sales rather than consulting backgrounds. As one salesperson put it:

> We have designed a marketing and sales program to bring in our desired sales results. It's implementation-oriented and focuses on (specific industries) and uses a specific methodology we have developed. It has helped our revenues grow from $20 million in 1987 to over $100 million in 1990.

This is a radical approach for the professions but one that is gaining increased acceptance. Marketing efforts at these firms focus on a multistep process beginning with sophisticated telemarketing or direct-mail efforts to gain access to senior corporate executives, followed by highly consultative sales meetings. Efforts usually focus on the sale of low-cost projects that provide an introduction to the firm's services and also offer an opportunity to explore an issue that has potential for a larger project. The most advanced firm I spoke with knows on average how many dialings telemarketers must make to arrange a sales meeting and how many sales meetings are required to meet annual sales targets. In other words, it behaves like other sales-driven organizations. Interestingly, a salesman at this firm who sells over five million dollars of consulting services annually to new accounts had never heard of the term "rain maker." He views himself as a skilled salesman. This is another sign of the evolution to a more traditional sales model.

In organizations fully adopting this model, marketing and sales tend to be centralized functions with direct responsibility for producing new business. Firm management feels sufficiently in control of the marketing process and has enough confidence in its contribution that billability is not expected of marketers and sales people.

The existence of alternative models, sometimes competing with each other within a single firm, raises the question: How do individuals or firms select one model rather than another? I recall an anthropology professor's once telling me that belief in water witching in the American Southwest correlated highly with the shallowness of the underground water table. In other words, the more likely a person was to find water anywhere he put a shovel in the ground, the more likely he was to believe that it could be found with a forked stick. This might explain some of the differences in choice of models. For example, of all the people I met, one of the strongest advocates of the feasibility of selling consulting services proactively, and one of the two most confident in his ability to do so, also freely admitted that because of environmental circumstances, demand for consulting services in his practice area far exceed supply. To suggest that this phenomenon explains all of the differences in belief, however, is overly simplistic and does damage to reality. It does not explain, for example, why firms with competing practices sometimes adopt different models.

Ample evidence suggests that many builders are inheritors of practices originally developed by someone else. This was true in every case in which I could explore the history of a practice with some objective third party. By definition a true rain maker generates far more business than he can handle himself, and so develops a practice that keeps many others busy. Some members of the team develop strong enough relationships with clients to inherit them from the rain maker when he leaves the firm or becomes too busy to handle them. These successors tend to be excellent reactive sales people without being good lead generators.

Sometimes firms rather than individuals inherit, especially when not just relationships but also a strong reputation for expertise in an area is involved. A good reputation can generate over-the-transom business for many years. An example of this was described by the president of one firm:

> *(A specific practice) was developed by (someone) we hired from private industry. He had a strong reputation and a lot of contacts. He spoke often and worked hard at developing the business, so that it now represents 40 percent of our sales. Finally he got an offer he couldn't refuse from his former employer and left. The practice has stopped growing,*

and the top people in it don't really do much marketing, saying
they never have time for it. They survive because the phone
keeps ringing.

The interviews suggest that this transition from a proactive to reactive mindset happens often, if not always so obviously. Why should this be so?

First, as I noted in the introduction, professional service firms generally do a poor job of training marketing and proactive sales skills. Although a substantial effort is devoted to training in technical skills in both classroom and master/apprentice formats, very little time or money is expended on marketing training. They get what they pay for. Marketing and sales-driven organizations in other industries spend vast amounts in these areas.

Second, there is tremendous pressure for a successful marketer to continue marketing rather than delegating some of the responsibility, as developing new talent requires. There is pressure from the firm, which is anxious to put its best effort behind each sale, but there is also pressure from the market. As the founder of a highly successful architecture firm put it, "It isn't good for the firm for me to do as much of the marketing as I do, but people want to see the one whose name is on the door. Already competitors are saying that I'm reducing my participation in the firm's affairs." Of course, some individuals may also feel threatened by the emergence of strong marketers among their subordinates, or they may not be interested in marketing succession.

Third, in my experience many professionals simply don't like to market. The professions attract people with strong analytical or creative abilities who receive tremendous psychic income from client relationships in which they enjoy the power of expertise. They often have a low tolerance for boredom and rejection. Much of marketing is relatively simple conceptually but requires consistent and persistent implementation over a long period, during which rejections are frequent. Many professionals shun marketing tasks with these attributes, some seemingly adopting a model that justifies this behavior. This theory is supported by the ease with which some builders disparage, ignore, or explain away examples of individuals or firms that have successfully developed large blocks of new business. This rejection of marketing is epitomized by a story told to me by an accountant about a fellow partner:

> *George ran our government practice and believed there*
> *was only one way to market it—by working on close relation-*
> *ships with clients. He was good at that and denied anything*
> *else would work. He wouldn't let any of his people do any*
> *marketing at all. Even when we brought business in to his*
> *practice through some other means he wouldn't acknowledge*
> *any other ways to market. It used to drive us crazy, because*
> *we knew we were missing opportunities.* (When asked, the ac-
> countant noted that George had inherited the practice from a
> true rain maker.)

Finally, many professionals may not find it financially attractive to produce above a certain level of business. An individual whose objective is to live comfortably solving interesting problems can live a good life as a professional without generating huge amounts of revenue from new clients. If he does good work and supports himself and his practice, it can be difficult for the firm to get him to do more. Similarly, a partner with a high income may not find the cash incentive provided for helping someone else in the firm sell a project to one of his clients worth the risk to his relationship that the sale entails.

These four deterrents to broad-based marketing within a firm tend to compound each other.

What is most striking from the survey is the lack of marketing sophistication in many firms. At the same time, frustration over marketing issues remains intense. The domination of a specific model within a firm often seems to result more from historical accident than decision, and often there appears to be a struggle between different views of marketing as personified by specific advocates. Individual professionals go their own way within broad parameters allowed by the firm. Moreover, even professionals who espouse an aggressive marketing approach often behave quite differently. What is to be made of such a muddle?

For you, the individual who wants to market, it means that you must take into account the marketing outlook of the firm and the individuals you report to in constructing a strategy. If a builder mentality prevails...

- *...expect to receive little or no resources for marketing.* Focus your efforts on things you can do cheaply, like article writing.
- *...go around the individual,* without saying anything negative about her, to get a commitment from higher in the organization to devote some time to marketing. Otherwise your marketing efforts will be fought as wasteful.
- *...consider relationship marketing.* Builders will accept time spent in direct contact with clients more easily than any other marketing time.
- *...expect no emotional support for your efforts.* You will benefit from the client relationships you establish and must provide your own motivational support until you get them.
- *...don't waste your time trying to convert a builder* to some other point of view unless you have evidence that she has an open mind.

If an artist mentality prevails...

- *...focus on your personal marketing plan* and what the market suggests. In this kind of firm you will have freedom to operate almost as an independent entrepreneur when it comes to marketing.
- *...establish a specialization.* You will maximize your freedom of action if you focus your efforts on a service or market segment not currently being marketed by someone else. Within the free-wheeling firms adopting an artist approach, turf wars are common. The more you can insulate

yourself from them by establishing a niche, the less your marketing will be interfered with.

If a miner mentality prevails...

■ *...learn how the internal network works.* The opportunity to generate leads and new business through this captive network is one of the primary benefits to belonging to a large organization, where miner mentalities are most likely to prevail.

If a seller mentality prevails...

■ *...build your personal credentials first.* Professional salespeople will provide the most opportunities for client exposure to those in the firm who will look attractive to prospects. The better your credentials, the more they will want to put you in front of prospects.

■ *...build your sales skills.* (See part II.) If your firm has a professional sales force, most of the lead generation will be done by professional salespeople, relieving you of this burden. The salespeople will most need help in advancing and closing business and will provide the most opportunities to people who have skills in these areas.

■ *...consider sales as an independent career path.* In these organizations, people who sell are likely to be different individuals from those who do other tasks. Look at what the career means in your organization. How much contact do salespeople retain with a client and project once a project is sold? It varies. How are salespeople compensated relative to others in the firm? It can be a rewarding career in many ways.

20

Creating a Breakthrough Strategy

Any good strategy, implemented diligently, will increase your success in the market. If you simply do what your most effective competitor does, you will reduce his market success and increase your own. The best strategies do more than this. They help you grow your business rapidly, surging past competitors, because you do something distinct that captures strategic advantage.

As you might expect, breakthrough strategies are difficult to develop and may not even be possible some of the time. They are certainly more possible than most people believe, however. At any given moment in any practice, at least one competitor is probably benefiting from such a strategy. This fact begs the question: If one competitor can, why can't others?

Often, but by no means always, breakthrough strategies are developed in pieces. A firm finds one unique advantage, later combines it with another, and for a time captures a special place in the market.

These strategies result naturally from our capitalist system, which relies on competition to keep prices low. Clever business people have always sought to avoid the price-lowering tendencies of the market by seeking ways to avoid competition. That people will temporarily succeed in doing so through innovations that are both legal and beneficial to clients creates much of the dynamism of the system. Successful rain makers have found ways to avoid or reduce competition in four areas.

- *Markets.* By specializing in a specific market, they differentiate themselves from broader-based competitors. They sometimes intentionally seek out untapped, emerging markets for just this reason. Over the past ten years U.S.-based professional firms have capture dominant roles in international markets in this way.
- *Services.* Professionals have introduced unique services that offer market advantages until they are imitated. Fads in consulting (business portfolio

235

strategies, total quality management, time-based competition, reengineering) have provided firms with temporarily unique market offerings. Service-based strategies are strongest when built around data bases or other difficult-to-replicate resources.

- *Reputation.* Professionals have found means to develop brand identities stronger than their competitors'. Often, but by no means always, this is through some special publicity effort. The brand identity pulls in leads from prospects. It also eases access when a professional initiates contact with a prospect.

- *Market access.* Professionals have developed channels to the market that provide them with special access to prospects and information about them.

Professionals who have differentiated their services in more than one way have done particularly well, because their uniqueness has been more difficult to imitate. It is easy to identify examples in many professions and for firms with varying degrees of visibility.

- Skadden, Arps, Slate, Meagher & Flom specialized in mergers and acquisitions law. Early in the firm's history this service was almost unique, because large firms spurned such work. The firm also gained a special reputation based on a combination of superior performance and unique publicity; while other firms viewed talking with the press as improper, Skadden viewed it as a marketing tool. Its special reputation brought in leads. During its history the firm has also had special access to its markets based on networks, first of other law firms and later of investment bankers.[1]

- Bill Kaffer, a partner at Theodore Barry & Associates, a mid-sized consulting firm with experience in the electric power industry, foresaw the trouble that power companies would run into in the construction of nuclear power plants and ensuing government intervention. Building on past firm experience, he saw an opportunity for a practice that would help electric power company managements prepare for intense government scrutiny when they sought to include nuclear power plant construction costs in their rate bases. He took this special service to the market with a strategy unusual to consultants—cold calling. With a unique offering and marketing approach, the firm captured a large share of a profitable new market.

- Another consulting firm established a specialized channel to its market. Management recognized that professors in business, economics, and other fields received leads for assignments they could not handle alone. The firm established an exclusive network of professors, paying them professional fees for new business. The firm's knowledge of the special handling that this network required became a strategic asset.

- A small architecture firm developed a special methodology for preparing design/build specifications for prisons. Combined with the company's already strong network of contacts with corrections officials, this methodology helped the firm grow rapidly even during an economic downturn.

Over time, market advantages tend to diminish, either because the market changes (for example, the financial rewards of mergers and acquisitions fall off) or because competitors imitate successful firms. To maintain their revenues and profits, professionals must constantly seek new niches and approaches to the market. New niches diversify revenue sources and reduce the impact of downturns.

Often new niches derive from the current strategy. As a professional succeeds with a specific strategy, several things may happen. Clients may give her ideas for new services and opportunities to develop them; these services sometimes become the core of a new strategic initiative. A strategy that results in success in a market may also give the firm special knowledge of and access to that market. It can then sometimes sell other services there. Third, work with a specific market may result in the development of marketing channels that can be used to sell additional services. Finally, one reputation-building effort may lead to opportunities for others. When one of these things happens, a professional may be able to develop a new initiative.

The most successful professionals realize that market advantages are transitory and look constantly for additional ones. Once again, examples are numerous.

- Skadden, Arps used its clients' willingness to pay retainers in the event that they should face a takeover battle to expand into other areas. Retainers could be applied to any legal service purchased from the firm. This was the foundation of much of the firm's broad-based corporate practice, which has reduced the impact of the decline in merger and acquisition projects.[2]
- The Fantus Company (now PHH Fantus), a location consulting firm, realized that the information it gathered from helping select sites for plants and offices would be valuable to economic developers. Its work provided it with extensive contacts in that market, and it developed a successful economic development consulting practice.
- Large accounting firms realized that their audit work gave them advance warning of data processing consulting needs and access to decision makers. Adding information systems consulting was an outgrowth of these conditions.

In this way one specialization or market strategy can lead to another.

To develop a marketing strategy, then, you must identify unique or at least unusual markets you can serve, services you can provide, vehicles for developing your reputation, and channels that will provide you access to and information about prospects. Developing a breakthrough strategy requires creative thinking. Often this kind of thinking is best done with a group, so if you are a member of a firm, you should probably involve others in the process. Either on your own or as a facilitator of a group, try the following exercises, which should require no more than two hours for your first try.

Brainstorm on markets and services

Make a list of as many fundamental changes occurring in your market as you can think of. These include changes in product, in manufacturing, in distribution, and in customer service technology; additions of new and losses of old competitors; reactions to changes in laws or regulations; changes in the degree of vertical or horizontal integration; and any others you can think of. Create this list now. Once you have done so, make a file for it and update it every time you hear of new changes. Review it every month or so.

Next, for each item on the list, ask yourself what needs these changes will create that your clients don't have now or have at low levels. What services will these needs require? Which of these services might you be able to provide?

Make a second list of the information you collect as a by-product of your core services. Who else might find this information useful? How would you have to improve the information (for example, by creating a true data base, by collecting it on a more thorough basis, by wrapping consulting services around it) to make it attractive to another client base?

When you have completed this exercise, set it aside while you complete the following ones. You will come back to it later.

Look for marketing voids

That a dog didn't bark was a vital clue in one of Sherlock Holmes's cases. In this case his brilliance was demonstrated by his ability to see what wasn't there while everyone else was focusing on what was. You can do this too, with a little practice.

Make a list of all the services prospects ask for that you don't provide. Add to it each time you get a request. Review the list and ask yourself how you would provide this service if you had to. If there are aspects of your services that you think no one in the industry does a particularly good job of providing, look at them carefully. Any aspect of your services that members of the firm must talk around during a sales meeting is a candidate for inspection. What would you have to do to enhance these aspects?

Next, create a list of all of the truly creative marketing ideas you can think of, regardless of what service or product they supported. Every time you hear of a clever marketing idea, add it to you list. You should review this list from time to time too. When you do, ask yourself whether the concept underlying the idea has been tried in your practice area. Assume you had to apply it to your practice, what would you have to do to make it work?

Set the results of this exercise aside and go on to the next one.

Break the rules

Next, make a list of the rules that govern the marketing of your services. They exist in every field. Listen for them when you talk to others. Statements like, "You can't sell accounting services by cold calling" or "Quality consulting firms don't base their fees on performance" or "Architects are the prime contractors for design projects, and consulting engineers work for them" or "You can't work both sides of the street" or "If we sold that kind of business, it would destroy our existing business" are examples of such rules. (Each of these rules has been broken by at least one firm who has gained market advantage by doing so.)

Once you have listed the rules, write out the arguments that underlie each one and see what counter arguments you can think of. For example, the arguments I have heard that underlie the statement, "Quality consulting firms don't base their fees on performance," include:

- **Argument 1**: The consultant may lose objectivity and recommend quick fixes that maximize his fees but are bad for the client in the long run if he is compensated on performance.

  - □ *Counter-Argument A*: Without an incentive to perform, the consultant could recommend solutions that are unimplementable or ones that do not provide an adequate return on his fee. He may be motivated to make recommendations that can only be implemented by paying him another fee.
  - □ *Counter-Argument B*: If incentives are structured properly, the risk is minimal.
  - □ *Counter-Argument C*: A quality consulting firm would never recommend a quick fix that would be bad for a client, regardless of the incentive.

- **Argument 2**: No quality consultant prices this way, so it would sully our image to do so.

  - □ *Counter-Argument A*: At least one big-name firm has priced this way, and its image remains strong.

- **Argument 3**: Several low-quality consultants price this way.

  - □ *Counter-Argument A*: The pricing strategy is not what causes them be of low quality. You can find low-quality consultants who price many different ways, the same as with high-quality consultants.

I myself am neither for nor against performance pricing by consultants. The choice is a business consideration that can only be decided in a specific context. I use this example to demonstrate that sound counter-arguments can be made against most rules. Often rules are created to justify self-serving behavior. One could argue, for example, that many consultants dislike performance pricing because it would hold them to a standard they cannot meet; or, alternatively, they don't want a pricing system that will require them to monitor their clients' accounting in order to get paid. If these are the real reasons for consultants' distaste for performance pricing, the commonly cited arguments against it are nothing but sanctimonious claptrap. If you can obtain market advantage with performance pricing, following a rule against it will cost you money. If you and your client are content with the concept, it is hard to imagine why anyone else should care.

Develop the arguments and counter-arguments underlying each rule that governs your market. Do the arguments hold up? If not, what are the consequences of breaking the rule? Do the good consequences outweigh the bad? If they do, it is worth figuring out how the rule can best be broken.

Assume that you *must* break each rule. How would you go about doing so in a way that would provide you with maximum advantage and minimum disadvantage? For example, if you can't performance-price by taking a percentage of the savings you create, are there other ways? What about changes in market share or stock price?

Firms that have used telemarketers to set up cold calls provide an example of creative adaptation of a technique. The firms have succeeded by using much higher caliber people on the phones than the word "telemarketer" conjures up. These people are MBAs or the equivalent, and they perform more sophisticated screening for needs and relationship building by phone than do traditional telemarketers. If you had to make telemarketing work for your firm, what would you do? Try the same kind of thinking for each rule you consider breaking. Finally, review the rules again. What would it cost you, if you broke the rule and found that doing so didn't help you? If failure wouldn't cost very much, you have a good reason to experiment.

Imagine the future

Assume that a clairvoyant tells you that your business will double over the next two years but can give you no other particulars. Think about your current business and review the results of the previous exercises. Now make a list of those things that would have to occur for your business to grow so rapidly. Does this exercise suggest changes in markets, services, publicity, or ways you gain access to your market that you should consider especially carefully? If so you may have the basis for a breakthrough strategy.

Conclusion

In many ways, selling is more fundamental to being a professional than doing or managing the work that follows. Professionals who sell must see the client's big picture. To win they must understand how the work they are being asked to do fits into a client's larger world. The understanding you gain during a sale places you in an unequaled position to structure and oversee all work that follows. The more unusual the assignment, the more likely this is.

Those who are out in the market selling are also those most likely to see opportunities for new services and practices, because most ideas for such advances come from the market. They are the ones who most quickly pick up warnings of market changes to which a firm must adjust. They are often the visionaries of their organizations.

Professionals who sell are also primary implementers of firm plans. Decisions to expand into new markets, to offer new services, to establish strategic alliances, mean nothing by themselves. Sales give them substance. A firm's carefully developed procedures for advancing professionals up the hierarchy to partner also mean nothing if firm revenues cannot support promotions.

A professional who does a superior job of bringing in new business is seen as more than a salesperson. Her special powers make possible the way of life of the firm, the small society of which she is a part. "Rain Maker" is a fitting title for one who makes such a contribution.

The objective of this book is to give you the understanding and the tools you need to sell. If you develop the skills, if you can understand that marketing is a numbers game that requires working through many small losses to win later, if you can establish the discipline needed to keep yourself in the market, if you can cheer yourself on until you succeed, then you, too, can become a rain maker.

Introduction to Appendices

The appendices offer guidelines on how to prepare four specific kinds of marketing materials.

Appendix A covers bios, those ubiquitous descriptions of professionals' credentials. The author, Deborah Baxley, is a faculty member at IBM's Executive Consulting Institute. As a member of the faculty she has helped develop a curriculum for consulting education that accommodated over two thousand students in a two-year start-up period. Teaching students from twenty seven countries and conducting classes in North America, Europe, and Asia, she and her team have developed a variety of new approaches for teaching marketing techniques. She has personally coached over a thousand new consultants on writing their bios.

Appendix B shows how to prepare visuals to support your presentations and proposals. The author, Ralph Wileman, has written two books on the subject and consulted to Arthur Andersen, IBM, The United States Agency for International Development, and many other organizations. He is currently a professor and department chairperson of the Graduate Program in Educational Media and Instructional Design in the School of Education at the University of North Carolina at Chapel Hill.

Appendix C tells how to prepare a press release. Its author, Robin Schoen, is a public relations professional with more than ten years of experience; she is also an accomplished publicist. Her consulting practice, Robin Schoen & Associates, primarily serves professional firms.

Appendix D describes how to prepare a brochure. Its author, Michael Cucka, is a consultant whose brochures have won awards from Business/Professional Advertising Association, Print Magazine, and Champion Paper.

Appendix E lists additional readings on the subjects covered in the book.

Appendix A

Building Your Bio: Packaging Your Expertise

Deborah J. Baxley

You probably have a bio—every professional has at least one. Just having an eye-catching bio gives you some credibility as a professional. Yet many a bio is put together with little thought and then updated infrequently. With all the pressures of running a business, you're probably wondering why you should take the time to update your bio. Don't overlook its value. A well-written bio is an important yet overlooked marketing tool.

Consider this: Included in brochures and proposals, your bio will be read by every prospective client; it may be used as a primary basis of comparison between you and your competition. Like the "blurb" on a book jacket, your bio gives a thumbnail sketch of you, the professional. In a larger firm your bio can also market you internally. When it is well written and well distributed, a bio can help you carve out a niche within the firm and attract those who sell the business. Those rain makers want people on their teams who will look good to the client, and you will, if you package your expertise properly.

Never forget that your bio is a marketing document first and foremost. Early in your career you may experience difficulty in building up a reputation and selling effectively, since you lack references. Writing a bio is your chance to reflect your credentials in the most positive light. As you write, you may also notice holes in your experience, credentials, or endorsements, a help in planning your marketing strategy or personal development needs.

What about a resumé or curriculum vitae? One typically thinks of these in a job-hunting context. Potential employers don't want the same information potential clients do. Employers need dates of employment and the names of previous employers; they also want to see position titles and responsibilities. The potential client, on the other hand, wonders what you can do for him. A well-written bio answers the question, "Why are you perfect for the engagement?" A few simple techniques in constructing your bio can highlight your expertise and therefore increase your odds of winning business, or of being selected for new projects.

Wear your client's shoes

Try putting yourself in your client's shoes. What would he want to see? By framing your bio from the client's point of view, you can concisely state important facts and leave out less important information. Start by sitting down and making a list of *what your clients want to know*. Some sample questions:

- Has this person worked with or for other companies in my industry?
- What kind of benefits did the other clients enjoy? Increased profits or revenue? Favorable settlements? Reduced costs? Improved quality or productivity? Reduced time?
- How do I know this professional knows my functional area—marketing, finance, or engineering?
- Is this person a recognized expert? In what? How do I know?
- Does this he or she have hands-on experience? How much? With whom?
- Do I have anything in common with this professional?

Use the external voice

Your bio speaks about your experiences and accomplishments in the most favorable way—it puts you in the best possible light. Sometimes it's embarrassing to brag about yourself, but all of us like to be praised. How would you want someone else to describe you? An important axiom is "A humble professional is a starving professional." Remember this as you write and try writing about yourself in third person. The result will be a bio that sounds more authoritative, leaving the impression, perhaps unconscious, that a third person is talking about you and complimenting you.

Outside endorsements are powerful. Spend a few minutes jotting down all the endorsements you have received. Don't forget books, articles, papers, awards, speaking engagements, association memberships, patents, and citations. Are you an adjunct faculty member at a university? That periodicals and organizations accept you as an expert makes it easier for a prospective client to do so. Therefore, include the name of the relevant publication or school. Sometimes the caliber of publication or organization speaks louder than the content of your contribution.

Keep a library of your accomplishments

Go back to your client's point of view. Wouldn't the client want to know about projects you've worked on in his industry? Aren't descriptions of successful projects similar to your client's a good selling point?

Most professionals work in more than one industry or target area. If that describes you, you may need several bios. How do you keep track of them all? Easy.

At the end of your next project, write a new "accomplishment statement" that can be used in your bio. The complete accomplishment statement includes what kind of client you worked with, what the project was, what action you took, and the results and benefits to your client—*quantified if possible*. Get your client to agree to the benefit statement. If you do this after each engagement, you will quickly build a library of accomplishments that you can choose from in order to tailor your bio to match the precise needs of each client. Thinking from the client's point of view, sequence your accomplishments in order of importance.

What if you haven't worked on many projects but have a depth of hands-on experience from working in the industry? In this case, follow the same format. Forget job titles and ongoing responsibilities. Instead, frame your experience in terms of projects and accomplishments.

Word processors remove the only remaining excuse for static bios. With the ability to tailor your bio easily, you can precisely target the exact needs and interests of a specific client.

Test your writing—can your mother understand it?

We often fall into the "jargon" trap. By becoming so accustomed to the language and acronyms of our field, we lapse unconsciously into a kind of private vocabulary. Give your bio to relatives and friends who aren't in your business and see whether they can understand it.

In the words of William Strunk, author, with E.B. White, of the famous and durable book *The Elements of Style*, "Prefer the specific to the general, the definite to the vague, the concrete to the abstract...the surest way to hold the attention of the reader is by being specific, definite, and concrete."[1] These time-honored words from the year 1935 apply as directly to bios as to novels. Scan your bio, checking for generalities. Make sure you're using complete sentences. Specific facts are always more interesting and believable than vague generalities, and sentences are easier to read than dot-point outlines. Compare these two:

> *Worked with manufacturing company to develop information systems strategy:*
>
> ☐ *Inventory management*
> ☐ *Electronic links to suppliers/stores*
>
> *Provided the following benefits to the client:*
>
> ☐ *Competitive advantages*
> ☐ *Large cost saving*

-OR-

> *Mr. Gunther worked with a large manufacturing company to develop an information systems strategy to address the changing needs of inventory management. He and his team designed an innovative system to manage product demand by establishing electronic links between key suppliers and stores. The system provides competitive advantage and is projected to achieve a large cost saving.*

The second version sounds more professional and believable, doesn't it? But we can improve this even more:

> *Mr. Gunther worked with a large German manufacturing company developing a system that improves inventory management. He and his team designed a system, the first of its kind in the industry, to manage product demand by electronically linking 100 key suppliers and 1,200 stores. The system is projected to achieve a cost saving of at least $2 million the first year in operation, lowering retail prices by 5 percent and improving market share.*

Doesn't the final version grab your attention? The actual numbers lend the story credence.

With the content in place, concentrate on crafting your bio to be eye-catching and pleasing to read. Studies show that few people will read marketing material from beginning to end, but instead start with whatever catches their eye and then go back to the beginning if they find themselves interested. Use white space, bold type, and bullets to break up the text.

Here's one last way to test the readability of your bio. Imagine that you are to be introduced to a large client audience as the conference keynote speaker. You have butterflies in your stomach and need an injection of confidence, quick. Read your bio, or part of it, aloud. Are you proud of your introduction? Does it make you feel good about your skills and experience? Does it build any rapport with the audience? It will, if your bio tells a compelling story about your accomplishments and endorsements.

Take a fresh look

Do yourself a favor. Pull your bio out of the file and update it. Follow these techniques:

- Think about your client's point of view
- Make a list of accomplishments
- Write accomplishment statements

You can follow the format shown in the exhibits A.2 and A.3. Then, don't forget to test your readability.

What benefits will you get from your updated bio? Your clients will see the breadth and depth of your expertise. The credibility and reputation of the organizations and publications that endorsed you will reflect your own credibility. Interesting personal trivia help start interviews and begin building relationships.

Don't be afraid to display your credentials. Properly packaged, your bio will help sell you and your services.

Exhibit A.1
Bio Do's and Dont's

Do's

- Keep it to one page.
- Write in the third person.
- Use the active voice.
- Write in complete sentences.
- Specify organizations and publication names.
- Explain jargon and acronyms.
- Write in formal, crisp, professional tone.
- Include employer names.

Dont's

- Don't divulge client names if their projects were confidential. In that case, put client names in a separate client list.
- Don't use obscure job titles.
- Don't call yourself by your first name. The formal address (Mr. or Ms.) sounds more professional and authoritative.
- Don't include dates of hire, graduation, etc.

Exhibit A.2
Bio Outline

Your first paragraph is your expertise and experience statement. It summarizes your experience and accomplishments and includes:

- An introduction: name, firm name, location
- A concise statement of your expertise
- A summary of your industry and functional experience

Next, write two to four accomplishment statements. These prove what your expertise statement claims. Each accomplishment should state:

- The type of client (industry, size)
- The client's situation or issue
- Your role in helping the client
- A description of the project
- The client's results and benefits—quantified

To support your work experience from the first paragraph include:

- Your employer's name and industry
- Your position and accomplishments

Endorsements and credentials show that you are a recognized expert. Explore your options and include any of these that apply:

- Publications: articles, books
- Speeches
- University work
- Charity work
- Membership in trade or professional organizations
- Awards
- Education
- Certifications (CPA, LA, etc.)
- Patents
- Language fluency

Exhibit A.3
Sample Bio for a Litigation Expert

Marcus A. George

Marcus George is the president of Allendale Partners. He specializes in litigation support in the construction industry and provides testimony on a broad spectrum of construction issues. Mr. George has thirty-five years' experience in commercial and residential construction, with particular emphasis on the public sector. Some of his prominent clients include:

- McKinsey Breckman (New York)
- Kenge and Carboy (Chicago)
- Gumption, Gazebee and Gazebee (Dallas)

A number of Mr. George's projects in the industry highlight his expertise:

- As CEO of **First American Construction**, Wilmington, Delaware, Mr. George directed First American's successful completion of the restoration of the Delaware legislative buildings, the largest historical restoration of its kind in the industry.

- Mr. George also served as Group Executive of the **New York Construction Authority**, an agency of the New York City government. Under Mr. George's direction, the agency instituted and completed the "Grand Vision" low-cost housing project, which now houses over 1.2 million lower- and middle-income families in Harlem, the Bronx, and Brooklyn. This project, hailed as a model for the nation by the Reagan administration, saved New York taxpayers over $7 billion per year in welfare housing costs.

- Mr. George founded the **"Fulfill a Dream"** civic housing project and serves as its executive director and president. This community service project employs volunteer labor and donated materials to refurbish low-cost homes in redeveloping areas. To date, the project has restored over a thousand homes in five states.

Well known in the construction community, he has published widely on such construction issues as hiring practices, risk management, cash flow, and contract management in *National Construction Journal* and *Contract Management Weekly*. He is an alumnus of Vermont University and the Massachusetts Institute of Technology.

Appendix B

Enhancing Presentations With Visuals

By Ralph Wileman

Anyone who has ever made a presentation or a proposal knows how hard it can be to get your ideas across to your audience. One of the strongest tools to help you do this is the use of visuals—pictures, charts, graphs, and symbols that accompany your presentation and emphasize what you're trying to say. Visuals really can speak louder than words when it comes to getting your audience to buy your ideas. Don't you wish everybody would? That is the point of effective communication!

Throughout our formative years in school, the emphasis is on learning verbal communication skills. We learn that effective verbal communication is challenging and can be improved with practice. Verbal communication is closely tied to writing and involves a broad range of concepts—words, sentences, structure, tense, clarity, style, etc. Is visual communication equally complex? Read on.

Because few of us have worked on visual communications skills with the same intensity that we have given to verbal skills, we have some catching up to do. Though visual communication is as multifaceted as verbal communication, it is also natural. We see; therefore we are natural visual communication receivers. The challenge is to deliver good visual messages to our prospects and clients.

Visual communication uses pictorial and graphic symbols to represent ideas, the repertoire ranging from concrete to abstract. (See exhibit B.1.) In contemporary presentations these symbols often move (animation) and are enriched with color. Often, different kinds of symbols are combined; for instance, concept graphics are superimposed on photographs. These five kinds of symbols are evident in the world around us. We see them in videos, on computer screens, in magazines, on overhead transparencies, in brochures, in slide presentations, on signage, and so on. We can use symbols to clarify, simplify, enliven, and reinforce what we say with words.

Exhibit B.1
Kinds of Visuals

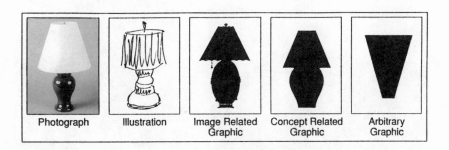

| Photograph | Illustration | Image Related Graphic | Concept Related Graphic | Arbitrary Graphic |

As you review the ideas and content of your presentation, note the places where visuals would emphasize what you have to say. Mark your outline or draft with an X at all the places where you think visuals could help communicate your ideas. Also note those ideas that are the most difficult to understand. If an idea is difficult to understand, perhaps it requires more than words to explain it. Visualizing your idea will help the audience understand. Perhaps your presentation is also complex or involved. A visual could give the audience the big picture, showing how all your points are related.

At times presentations can seem dull or predictable. In such cases, try using visuals that contrast with your text. For example, in a presentation about contemporary retail practices, use pictures of seventeenth-century retail practices. This will be even more effective if the seventeenth-century practices are related to contemporary ones. (See exhibit B.2.)

Visuals should always serve a purpose. Whether that purpose is to emphasize, clarify, illustrate the big picture, or gain attention, use them to accomplish specific objectives.

Getting your ideas across
You are communicating well when your audience pays attention, understands, and remembers. Visuals can help in all three areas. (See exhibit B.3.) *Gaining and holding attention* is fundamental. If you do not gain the audience's attention, what you do next doesn't matter. Mentally, your audience is off skiing in Colorado! We attend to things that attract our attention; our attention is attracted by how things read, how they sound, and above all how they look.

Exhibit B.2
Visuals Enliven a Presentation

Gridlock

**Point of purchase
Merchandising**

Exhibit B.3
Role of Visuals

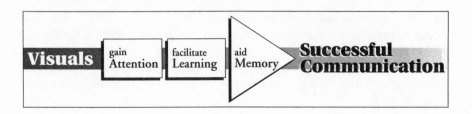

When we look at somethings in print, such as a booklet, the first thing we notice is the layout—the overall effect of the pictures, headings, and text. We have all received booklets that we discarded without reading; we were probably reacting to poor layout. Good layout may seem mysterious, but there's no real magic to it. It is characteristically simple, clear, and uncluttered. These features are basic to all presentations media.

To obtain good layout, use basic geometric shapes or letter forms such as T, H, S, or O as models for the placement of words and images. Make sure you always have some "white space" (space where there is no visual or text) to maintain viewer attention. White space keeps clutter down. Jan White's *Editing by Design* will give you an excellent short course in page layout. (See appendix E for reference.)

Another source of layout ideas can be found in the printed material we receive every day. Some materials look better than others; Save the documents, brochures, posters, and other printed matter that get your attention, without regard to content. They can be an excellent source of layout ideas for your proposals and presentations.

In addition to good layout, remember to use images that will appeal to your audience. There's plenty of scope for creativity here. If you are promoting your accounting firm, and your prospect operates a marina, put in an illustration of a sailboat with your accounting procedures as the mainsail. It should get your prospect's attention, and that is the first step in successful communication. (See Exhibit B.4.)

Exhibit B-4
Gaining Attention

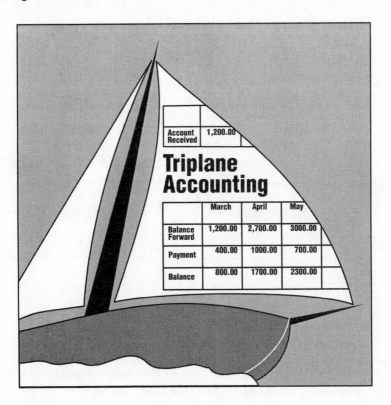

Once you have your audience's attention, the next step is presenting your message. *Visuals can facilitate learning and understanding.* This is the heart of the matter, of course: An audience who understands you is much more likely to buy your ideas than one that is not sure it knows what your message is. Pictures can bring life and meaning to your ideas. Usually unambiguous, they serve as a credible source of information. They also help communicate your message quickly.

Some messages can be conveyed far more readily through pictures than through discourse. Read your text over carefully. Are you using words to describe what would be easier to show? If so, try using pictures. Remember, you are trying to help your audience understand your message.

Visuals may also help your audience remember your ideas. Human beings have incredible powers in visual discrimination, visual storage, and visual recall. An *interesting* visual that helps your audience *understand* your message is well on its way to being *remembered*, especially if you use the visual several times. One particularly effective strategy is to relate the individual elements of a complex visual image to the elements of your proposal, product, or service. For example, use a medieval castle as a metaphor for a new information system where each part of the castle stands for a part of the system (see [a] of exhibit B.5). Later in the presentation, show the castle missing one part (see [b] of exhibit B.5) and ask what part of the information system is missing.

Exhibit B.5
Visual Aid Remembering

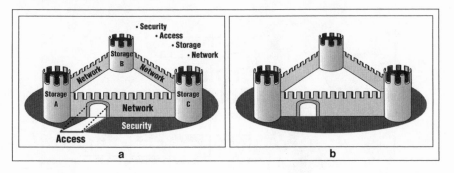

a   b

Visuals call for planning

Good visuals are the result of conscious thought, not artistic skill. You decide that a chart would help communicate your idea, or that a visual metaphor is called for. Perhaps what this presentation really needs is the realism of photographs. These kinds of intellectual decisions can be captured in quick sketches, then later rendered more elaborately. Even the most beautifully rendered visual began as an idea and then a sketch. Remember, the most important aspect of visual communication is the conceptual thought you put into the visual. Visual thinking is the ability to turn information of all kinds into pictorial or graphic images that help communicate that information. Like anything else it is a skill that needs to be practiced. The more you practice, the better your visuals.

Some people have the notion that to be a good visual communicator you must be able to draw. This is not true. Good visuals are the result of good visual *plans*. People usually plan far better than they draw. Planning starts with questions like, "Is a visual needed?" "What kind of visual would make my point?" "What purpose will the visual serve?" Answers to these questions will get you sketching an idea. Don't be alarmed; no one is going to see these sketches but you. This process can be extremely useful in helping you visualize your concepts.

If you can write with a pencil, you can quick-sketch (sometimes called "doodling"). Perhaps you get a visual idea while eating lunch in a restaurant. Sketch the idea on a scrap of paper (on a napkin, if need be), and take it back to your work station for refinement. Exhibit B.6 shows a series of refinements on a visual, from rough conceptual sketch to a finished sketch ready to be rendered in some way.

Exhibit B.6
Stages of Conceptualizing a Visual

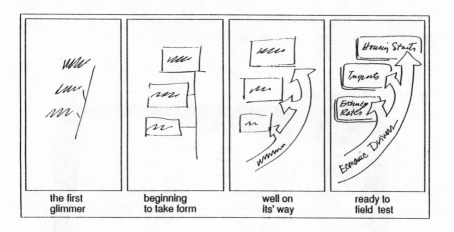

| the first glimmer | beginning to take form | well on its' way | ready to field test |

When planning a presentation that involves a series of projected visuals such as slides or overhead transparencies, try planning with storyboards. Storyboarding is to multimedia what rough drafts are to verbal communication. You can purchase storyboard pads at an art supply store or make them yourself using blank 5"x8" index cards (see exhibit B.7).

Exhibit B-7
Storyboard Card

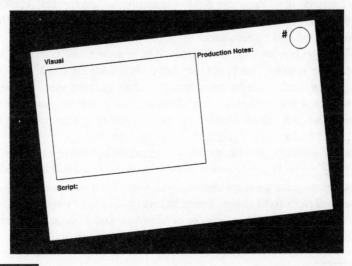

Exhibit B.8 illustrates a storyboard card that has been filled out. In the Visual area, the horizontal rectangle (2:3 ratio for 35-mm slides or a 3:4 ratio for video or a CD presentation), you sketch what you want seen on the screen. In the Script area you write the words you want heard when the visual is on the screen. Indicate in the Production Notes area how the visual is to be made.

Exhibit B-8
A Completed Storyboard

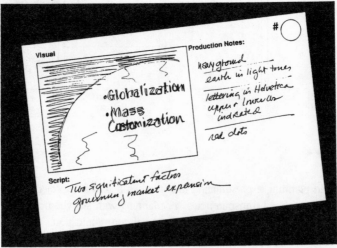

Producing visuals

Visuals can be created in four ways: stock shots, live shots, original artwork, and copy work. Stock shots are slides purchased from a vendor, called a stock photo house. A photograph of an urban area in flood, a drawing of an Olympic speed skater, and a photo montage of electronic tools are examples of slides that could be purchased from a stock photo vendor. Live shots are photos you want taken of real things or people. Photographs of a food processor, of a technician pouring chemicals on a dye-making vat, and of a prosecutor in action in front of a jury are examples of live shots. These can be taken by a photographer based on storyboard specifications. Original artwork is visual material rendered by a designer and then made into a slide. An architect's rendering of beach-front condos, a computer graphic showing a cross section of an earthen dam, and a prototype package for frozen food are examples of artwork rendered from storyboard frames. Copy work uses existing images of existing things, pictures you own, or objects you have in your possession. If you want to copy an image that you do not own, you must seek permission to use it or risk violating copyright laws.

Have a storyboard card for every visual that you will need in your presentation. Planning with storyboard cards allows you easily to add, delete, or change the order of the presentation. Carefully planned storyboards are the foundation for successful communication combining visuals and text.

Your visual ideas will improve as you practice using visuals in your presentations. Following are four guidelines that should aid your visual thinking.

1. *Information should be presented clearly and simply.*

   This simple admonition is rarely followed. It's a good rule of thumb: Have only one idea per card, and if words are to be on the screen, have no more than fifteen words per slide. (See exhibit B.9.)

2. *When projected on a screen, visuals should be readable from the worst seat in the house.*

   This is another logical admonition that often goes unheeded. Nothing is more harmful than projected images that are too small for an audience to see. Try out full-sized drafts of your images. Can you see all images and words from the back row? If you can't read a word, enlarge or delete it. *Never* project words that cannot be read! Another rule of thumb: Hold one of your slides up to a light. If you can read it with the naked eye, it will be readable when projected.

3. *The viewer's attention should be directed to the important part of your visual.*

   Just having a visual on the screen will not be enough if viewers have no idea what they are looking at. The viewer may need to be told visually where the salient information is located. (See exhibit B.10.)

Exhibit B.9
Information Clear and Simple—Which is more effective, a or b?

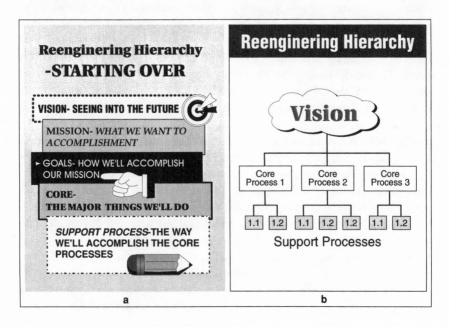

Exhibit B.10
Using an Arrow to Direct Attention

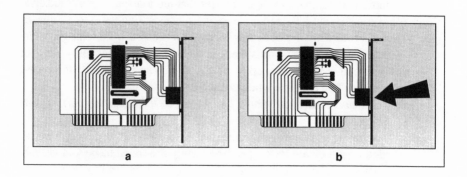

4. *Make sure it is clear which words go with which visual elements.*
When words are used to label the parts of a visual, unclear placement of labels will only confuse the viewer. Put verbal labels next to their corresponding visual elements. (See exhibit B.11.)

Exhibit B.11
Placement of Lables

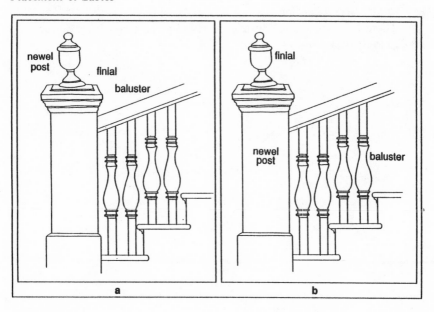

One excellent way to ensure that your visuals are serving your purpose is to field-test them before you go to press. Show a few viewers a dummied-up version of your presentation; you can use your storyboards or drafts of your visuals. Then ask your test audience questions that probe their understanding of your ideas. Also ask about what they thought of both the verbal and visual aspects of the presentation.

When you are ready to produce your work, there are many rendering tools and techniques at your call. Dover books, which are numerous, are a great source of copyright-free visuals. See appendix E for information on where to find them.

If you are doing your own desktop publishing, ask your vendor to supply you with sources of graphics and image software compatible with your work station. Many computer graphics packages include a library of visuals. Images range from fish and sun glasses to satellites and computers. Most of this electronic clip art is copyright-free, but check first before using it.

Because desktop publishing has empowered the masses to publish, some professionals can find talent in their own firm or families to help them render visuals. For a crucial presentation, however, it might be more efficient and effective to take the conceptualized dummy or storyboard to a desktop publishing house for final rendering.

An epilogue

I once helped divisions of a large religious organization petition their governing body for their respective pieces of the annual budget. Those divisions that made a visual pitch for their piece of the pie got all they asked for and, in some cases, a tad more. Those that did not make a visual pitch received, on average, half the amount they were asking for.

There is power in making a good visual presentation. May you be wise enough to use that power.

Appendix C

How to Write a Press Release

By Robin Schoen

It's impossible to think about public relations without thinking press release. Press releases are the standard, accepted mode of communicating specific kinds of information to the media. Used properly they can yield tremendous benefit to their sender by gaining media coverage, which provides powerful third-party credibility and wide exposure. Used improperly, however, they can prove a waste of time, effort, and money. The following "who, what, when, where, how, and why" of press releases is designed to help you unharness the force of press releases to benefit you and your business.

Who

Press releases are announcements understood by the media as a request to be seen or heard. Whether you are successful in your effort—that is, whether the information contained in your release is used by the media outlets to which it is sent—will largely be determined by the quality of your media list. The importance of a qualified media list cannot be overstated. If you have determined that your information is appropriate for press release format and have taken the trouble to write a strong press release, you should certainly invest the time and effort needed to create a qualified press list. A qualified press list is one in which all elements have been verified for accuracy. Here are the things you need to check.

- *Is the information appropriate to the outlet?*
- *Does the outlet you're considering have a format in which this information can be used?*
- *Is the person on your list the correct person to receive this kind of news?*
- *Are his name and the name and address of the outlet spelled correctly?*

Creation of a qualified media list protects against unnecessary mailing and re-mailing costs; helps guarantee timely delivery of time-sensitive information to the right person, thus moving you one step closer to use of your information; and provides a good foundation on which to build media relationships.

What

Press releases are the accepted means of communicating time-sensitive, "newsworthy" information to the media. Following the journalistic formula for news stories of who, what, when, where, and why, press releases present concise, factual information in a standard format. Avoid attention-grabbing ploys, which often provoke in their attempts to provide information. A truly well written press release will never earn the ire of a media contact; if appropriate to the outlet, it will more likely be appreciated, even if it is not used.

When

There are a variety of communications tools in the public relations arsenal, all of which have their most appropriate applications. You wouldn't use a letter to communicate news, anymore than you would use a press release to introduce yourself as a source for contribution to issues in your field. To be effective, press releases should be used appropriately and sparingly and sent to a qualified list of media contacts whose audience will find the information contained in your release meaningful.

Appropriate uses for press releases are to announce a new office location, executive changes, mergers, acquisitions, earnings, new services, new affiliates, performance statistics, and so on. But, you don't need to wait for a "hard news" occurrence to write a press release and gain valuable media coverage. Whether a law firm, accounting firm, or architectural firm, you probably have, or have access to, information that your target audience—clients, prospective clients, referral sources—could use or would be interested in knowing. You might conduct an informal survey of clients to learn their responses to something related to your practice—perhaps an audit to learn how clients are responding to changes in the tax laws. Or you may create "user useful" information in the form of a booklet or pamphlet that provides generic education information about some aspect of the service you provide. One example of this might be a pamphlet on criteria for selecting an elder law attorney. Once you've created your educational literature, you can write a press release announcing its availability.

Exactly when you distribute your release depends on your means of distribution—electronic, regular mail, overnight mail—and the news contained in your release. Most public relations professionals would suggest you make an attempt to get your news to the media outlet for which it is intended early in the day. If you're interested in reaching local business journals and industry trade journals, be sure to know their closing deadlines; if a publication you're hoping to reach closes on Wednesday, for example, it's useless for your material to reach them on Thursday. Mondays are busy days for daily newspapers. Depending on the importance of your news, you may find your release eclipsed by stories of greater importance if it's sent for receipt on a Monday.

The converse is also worth consideration: Many avoid sending news for receipt and publication on a Friday for fear they won't reach as many readers. Others plan to have their news received on a slow news day in order to increase their chances for "pick up." If you're announcing an event of some sort, learn the lead times for such listings well in advance of your occasion—perhaps a seminar on living wills or year-end tax planning. In general, try to send a press release as close to the actual occurrence of the new "event" as possible, while taking closing deadlines into consideration.

Where

Generally speaking, press releases are most useful to newspaper, television, and radio media. Magazines generally have longer print cycles and won't use time-sensitive material, although many local business journals and industry trade publications can and do print press release information. Where you send your release should be determined by the information you're offering, the audience you wish to reach, and the appropriateness of your information to the media outlet. For instance, although you're unlikely to reach your local business community with news of a new service via the local soft-rock radio station, you would probably be well served by your local daily newspaper or a local business journal.

How

As press releases follow a standard format and are completely factual in nature, creativity is not a must. Yes, an attention-getting headline or lead may compel the recipient of the release to read on, but what may be more important than the style in which the content is delivered is the appropriateness of the content to the person receiving the release and that person's readers, listener, or viewers. While there is no single, absolute format for press releases, the basic format elements are as follows.

- Typed, double-spaced copy with standard one-inch margins all around, on letterhead or white stationary.
- The words FOR IMMEDIATE RELEASE or FOR RELEASE AFTER JANUARY 5, if you wish the information to be held until a certain date, placed in the upper left corner of the page.
- Contact name, affiliation, and phone number in the upper right corner of the page. Be sure the contact is knowledgeable about and able to explain all the material covered in the release and that the contact is available on the day of the release.
- Concise, attention-getting headline centered beneath FOR IMMEDIATE RELEASE and contact information; subheads, if any, should also be kept brief. Where possible, eliminate articles (the, a, an) to keep the headline snappy. Although your headline probably won't be used, a strong headline encourages the reader to read on.

- Lead paragraph begun with the city, state, and date of the release's origination: New York, NY—November 5, 1994 —.

- As a vehicle for announcing news, the content of the release is organized around the journalistic formula of who, what, when, where, why, and how. Begin with the essential or most crucial information, working your way down to the supporting information or lesser points, including quotes.

  The first paragraph is a restatement of the headline or lead and contains all the pertinent facts according to the who, what, when, where, why, and how formula. To hold the reader's attention, use strong, active language, an urgent tone, and clean sentence structure.

  The second paragraph expands upon and substantiates the abbreviated version of the facts contained in the first paragraph. The remaining paragraphs provide pertinent historical information, information connecting your news to the audience you're attempting to reach, any statement from a relevant company person (your opportunity to include any subjective information you might wish to provide), any directives, and a company "boilerplate" description.

- Attempt to keep your release to one page or 250 words. Use only one side of the page. Should the release be longer than one page, end the first page at the end—not in the middle—of a paragraph, and print, in the center bottom of the page:

                              - MORE -

- Begin the second page with an identifier of some sort that links the first page to the second. This identifier should be in the upper left corner of the page, directly beneath the page number.

- At the end of the release, in the center of the page, type three pound signs, # # #, which indicate to the reader that no additional information follows. If you are attaching additional information such as a table, chart, or graph of some sort, place - TABLE FOLLOWS - centered, at the end of the release, instead of the pound signs. In this case, place the pound signs at the end of the last table.

Following are additional guidelines for ensuring the quality and favorable reception of your release.

- For best reception, releases shouldn't overwhelm with too much copy. Again, try to limit the release to one page. If the amount of information to be conveyed in the release is greater than can fit on one page, keep the individual paragraphs brief. Remember to stick to the central theme of your release throughout, keeping it concise and to the point. Where possible, use bullet points to convey information.

- Do not express opinions; a release is a factual document. Opinions are for those receiving the information to discern for themselves. Non factual information, if included at all, belongs in quotation marks.

- Where possible, link the subject matter of your release to current interest and the concerns of the media audience you're attempting to reach. As a corollary to this, shape your release to fit the needs and tone of the outlet you're approaching. This applies to the type of outlet—print, radio, television—as well as to geographical variations. Also, where possible, establish links between your news and the outlet. For instance, a business journal covering New York City business won't be interested in a New York law firm's closing its New York City office and moving to Westchester County. But the local Westchester business journal will.

- Be sure the release is absolutely accurate and error-free in every aspect. If you want your release to be received and considered, and you desire others to be received with respect at some point in the future, there is no room for error. This means accuracy of facts, correct grammar, and proper syntax.

- Be completely honest. A press release is not a place for outright fictions, truth stretching, or omission of key details. Provide only verifiable material, and avoid any unsubstantiated claims or second-hand information. Losing credibility with the media is potentially dangerous; you may forfeit your right to coverage, or worse, find yourself the subject of unflattering coverage.

- If you're sending your release to television and radio outlets, provide phonetic spelling for difficult names in order to ensure proper pronunciation.

- If you're announcing an event of some sort, inclusion of a who, what, where, and when summary at the end of your release is helpful.

- As mentioned earlier, a good media list provides a good foundation on which to build media relationships. One opportunity for furthering your relationship becomes available when your release is used. You can, if you're so inclined, call or write to express your thanks.

- While you don't wish to offend by writing down to a reader, don't overestimate your recipient's understanding of your subject matter, especially if it's technical in nature. While the local law journal may have no problem understanding legalese attached to a release about a technical matter, the local business journal might. Without patronizing, make sure your message is understandable to whomever may be receiving it, no matter what their level of education or expertise in the area of your subject matter.

Another "how" to consider is this one: "How will I know if my information was appropriate, useful, and used?" The best method for learning how well you've done your job is by following up your press release distribution with a telephone call. During this conversation you may be able to learn how your release was received, whether it will be used, and whether additional information is required. A follow-up telephone call also gives you an opportunity to begin the relationship-building process so important to all successful media relations efforts. You will also learn whether the media outlet you've contacted is responsive to follow-up telephone calls or prefers that press release senders not call.

Why

Why do you want to send out press releases? Because a well-written release with legitimately useful and interesting content can never offend the media, is a strong tool for building media relationships, and is likely to net you coverage—the most cost-effective and powerful means of communicating with your target audience.

Exhibit C-1
Sample Press Release

FOR IMMEDIATE RELEASE   Contact: Robin Schoen
                                            Robin Schoen & Associates
                                            914/948-6378

ALBERT SHILLEN & MITCHELL KARON
FORM SHILLEN & KARON

NYS Family Law Authority and Former Counsel to Charles Lamson
Meld Expertise in New Westchester Firm

Scarborough, NY — March 12, 1993 — Albert F. Schillen and Mitchell L. Karon have formed Shillen & Karon, a law firm providing family and corporate legal counsel. The firm is also the Westchester affiliate of Robins Brook Lewitt Rich Given & Glyde P.C., a 40-attorney Manhattan-based law firm primarily engaged in taxation, bankruptcy, trusts and estates, and general commercial work.

Having written practice commentaries to McKinney's New York Domestic Relations Law, Mr. Shillen is a recognized authority on New York State family and matrimonial law. He also has substantial expertise and experience in the area of litigation appeals, surrogate court matters and civil and family litigation. Mr. Karon specializes in general corporate matters, including mergers and acquisitions of businesses and professional practices, commercial real estate, and private placements.

"In addition to offering clients a superior level of family and corporate legal counsel, our relationship with Robins Brook gives our clients access to the expanded expertise and reach of a larger firm at a senior level where they would not ordinarily receive partner-level attention," stated Messrs. Shillen and Karon.

- MORE -

Shillen and Karon Form Law Firm

Mr. Shillen is an adjunct professor at Pace University School of Law teaching family law and trial practice. He has served as counsel of the New York State Commission on the Recodification of the Family Court Act, and has been an associate of New York law firms Beardsley and Bork and Manfred, Alster & Teller. Mr. Shillen began his law career as a clerk for the Honorable Martin K. Jansen, a senior associate judge of the New York Court of Appeals in Albany. A resident of Chappaqua, Mr. Shillen holds a JD from St. John's University School of Law and a BA in Economics from George Washington University.

Prior to opening the Westchester affiliate office of Robins Brook in early 1990, Mr. Karon was the only corporate partner in the New York office of Klein Marks Casper & Cohen, a firm of 300-plus lawyers based in Chicago. Earlier he was partner with Koler Hartman & Housman; an associate of Wiley Goodson & Mahler; and an associate of Hayes Busker Weiss Saltzman & Weber. His clients have included Charles Lamson; Linden, Inc., Dreyfus Baird Lindner; Part, Stein & Co.; and Omni Partners. Mr. Karon began his career as sole counsel and participant in a hostile proxy contest for control of Techtronics Associates, Inc. [TECT:NYSE]. A resident of North Tarrytown, he holds a JD from Rutgers School of Law and an AB, summa cum laude, in Political Science from Vassar College. He has also attended the London School of Economics.

Shillen & Karon is located at 26 South Highland Avenue in Scarborough. The telephone number is 914/000-0000.

# # #

Appendix D

How to Make a Better Brochure

By Mike Cucka

When I first started working on brochures, I read everything I could about them. I learned about typefaces and types of paper. I read about layout and budgets. I looked at samples from all kinds of companies. In the end, I still did not know how to develop a brochure that would *make a difference* to a business. This chapter shows what you really need to know, not the window dressing. You will learn the following.

- How to tell if you need a brochure
- What to tell about what you sell
- How to set your brochure apart from competitors'
- How to use words and pictures

How to tell if you need a brochure

There are two approaches you can use in marketing your firm: news and information. (See exhibit D.1.) Use information to explain your business. Use news to show your business in action. Too many companies rely on one of these approaches alone, providing strong information but poor news support, or poor information and strong news support. A good brochure is an information tool, but it is only one of several tools you can choose to use. How do you decide whether it will help your business? Evaluate your interactions with prospects and clients. A brochure is less useful if...

- *...the same clients come to you again and again.* If you face a long business cycle (such as a year for tax planners), you need to stay in contact with your clients. A brochure will usually not help you here. Clients will assume they know what you have to offer. Instead, provide news; for example a white paper entitled, "Ten Things You Can Do New to Lower Your Taxes Next Year." This will help people remember you as *the*

Exhibit D.1:

Information Versus News

These tools provide information. They tell what you do.	These tools provide news. They show your business in action.
Brochures Statements of qualifications Client lists Lists of services Advertisements	Newsletters Marketing letters Magazine articles Project descriptions Advertisements

source for the kind of service you supply. It can also help you change buying behavior. Your customers might come to you for assistance during the year, not just at the end of it.

The same is true of clients who buy from you often. This group has less of a need for the kind of information a brochure contains. Instead, entice them with the value you are bringing to others. Give them advice. Make yourself valuable, and they will come to you again and again.

- *...your clients provide most of your sales leads.* If this is the case, the prospect will already know something of your services. He will have learned it from the client who passed along the lead. You should meet to describe the unique benefits you provide, then help your prospect to see your service in action. Leave news of your successes and articles with advice. Your sales message is strong when you combine news and information. Show action to cause action.

- *...you rely on referrals.* If you depend on referrals from other firms, you may not need a brochure. Ask that business leads be passed to you directly; you want to control them. If you give copies of your brochure to your network contacts to distribute, you lose control of the sales process. A prospect will make a decision to call you based on what he reads. This makes it difficult for you to respond to unique needs. You should avoid using a brochure as an advertisement.

A brochure may be useful if...

- *...the market does not know about you.* If you are unknown, you have to attract attention. You have to show the people who are most likely to buy your services why they should buy from you. A brochure can help by explaining what you do better than your competitors. But do not rely on a brochure to do all your selling for you. Use other elements of the marketing mix to help stake out your position; provide news to show the benefits of your service. As the market learns about you, you will not need to use brochures as often.

- ...*your prospects frequently ask for brochures.* If they do, you can bet your competitors provide them. Match your competitors by using similar kinds of materials. Beat them on content.

- ...*you are part of a large firm.* A firm-wide brochure can help you make a sale for your practice, especially if you use it to show that you are a part of a credible organization. It can also help show resources and skills you do not have on your own, such as, "international presence." A single practice in a large firm might not need its own brochure, if a firm-wide one is available. This can save scarce marketing dollars.

- ...*you need to build credibility.* Some of your prospects may prefer brand-name suppliers. If you decide you want to sell to these kinds of customers, you should brand your service. As a first step, use a brochure and a newsletter to show you are not just a fly-by-night business. Use newsletters to draw attention to your track record; so fill them with articles covering your recent work with clients. Meanwhile, a high-quality brochure will help you make a strong first impression. This does not mean you have to spend a lot of money. To find out what it does mean, read on.

If you decide you need a brochure, you will need to consider the different brochure formats and how best to use them. How many formats are there? As many as there are ways to group five to ten pages. (See exhibit D.2.) The most common format is to fold 11" by 17" pages in half to make a booklet. Use a strong paper for a cover and then staple it and the pages together. You can also add a pocket to the inside front or back cover and use it to store other information or news you want your prospect to see. This makes your brochure more flexible, allowing you to change your material as needed.

Exhibit D.2
Representative Kinds of Brochures

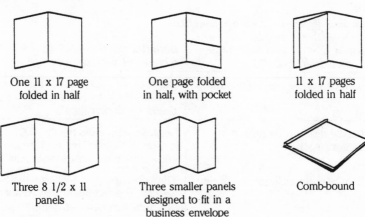

One 11 x 17 page
folded in half

One page folded
in half, with pocket

11 x 17 pages
folded in half

Three 8 1/2 x 11
panels

Three smaller panels
designed to fit in a
business envelope

Comb-bound

There are other formats to help you customize your brochure as well. Use brochures with comb or three-hole punch bindings if you expect to add or delete pages. These also help you to order pages in any sequence you like. If you constantly need to change what you want to show to prospects, this may be your best option.

How else do you decide which format to use? Ask yourself how your prospects will likely come in contact with the brochure. Will they receive it directly from you in their offices? Get it in the mail? Pick it up at conferences or trade shows? And then what—will they file the brochure or look through it quickly and throw it away? Use the format that makes your material most convenient to carry and read. This will differ according to the kinds of prospects you are trying to reach. For example, an accounting firm might keep its brochures small to encourage its accountants to carry some around with them, while an architectural firm might want a large, wire-bound brochure to show off its portfolio.

Whichever format you choose, your prospects will approach your brochure in one of four ways. They may read everything you have written. They may scan it for information they find important. They may keep it as a reference and not read it at all. Some may throw it away without looking at it. This last possibility becomes much more likely if what you have to say is dull, irrelevant, misplaced, or poorly conceived. To develop a brochure that helps sell your business, you must define *what* you are selling, to *who* you are selling it to, and *who else* in the market is selling a similar or substitute service.

What to tell about what you sell

Prospects cannot see a service before they buy it. This means they need evidence—tangible clues on which to base their hiring decision. The stronger the clues you give, the easier you will find it to make a sale. To help, you must define what you are selling by describing benefits. Make sure you avoid describing only the features of your service. (See exhibit D.3.)

Exhibit D.3
Be Sure Your Brochure Describes Benefits

Features do not show why prospects should hire you.	**Benefits** are the result of the features of your services.
We have two marketing experts on staff.	Our team of professionals helps us improve the brand awareness of our clients by 15 percent.
We handle nearly $100 million in transactions each year.	Because we handle nearly $100 million in transactions each year, we know where the best investments are.
We have been in business for fifteen years.	Through fifteen years of experience, we have created the largest database of senior executives anywhere.

Next, make sure you tell a story using these benefits. Most brochures do not. This makes it difficult to involve the reader with what you are selling. The less involved the reader, the less likely she will be to buy what you are selling. Therefore you should define your practice in a way that helps you tell a story about it. Talking to your clients and prospects can help you to do this. Ask questions like:

- *What causes you to purchase (my kind of) service?* Use this question in conjunction with the question below. Learning what motivates customers to purchase the kind of service you provide will help you appeal to sources of motivation in others. Understand the cause and you can better show the effect of your services. Answers to this question are particularly useful if need for your services is ongoing, so that hiring you means terminating some other professional. If need for your services is driven by an occasional event, the question may require restating. Then ask the client why he uses a professional instead of doing the work himself.

- *Why do you buy from us?* This will help you to show prospects why they *should* buy from you. Probe for answers that help to show the value your customers gained from your relationship with them. You may provide benefits you're not even aware of. Some of these may be highly valued by the market.

- *If you could design the ideal service, what would you offer and why?* The answers here will help you to rank benefits, they may also suggest new ways of doing things, some of which may seem impossible. Look for the reason someone would want to do things differently. You will often find that the person seeks benefits no firm currently supplies. You might reflect, too, on how well your service matches the ideal.

How do you define your business? Write down all the needs that interviewees mentioned and try to classify them. The following example comes from Executive Resource Group of Crownsville, Maryland, a firm that helps economic development organizations hire senior executives; it competes with small, regional firms. Executive Resource Group is one of the top national players. Joan Jorgenson, the firm's managing director, routinely asks clients what they need most. Recently she found that there were three major needs:

- To define the job that had to be filled. Different groups and individuals with an interest in economic development in the client communities often differed about the responsibilities and priorities of the job.

- To determine how the new hire should be compensated. The economic development boards seldom knew what salary and benefits would be required to recruit and retain the talent they needed.

- To find a highly skilled executive with ten to fifteen years of economic development experience.

Executive Resource Group had two strengths: It could develop a community consensus around the job to be filled, and it could find better people. Recognizing these strengths helped it define the business in two ways, as shown in exhibit D.4.

Exhibit D.4
Define Your Business

Market Need	Benefit	Potential Business Definition
Help in defining the job that needs to be filled.	We develop community consensus around the job's responsibilities.	We sell diagnostic ability. You get a clearly defined job that can and needs to be done.
Help in determining how it should be compensated.	We recommend what you should pay to hire and retain superior talent.	
Help in finding highly skilled executives with 10 to 15 years of economic development experience.	We provide the skills to help you build your economy.	We sell market knowledge. You get the right person for the job.

Incidentally, be sure not to confuse how you *define* your business with how you *label* it. Use labels to briefly introduce what you do, as shown in exhibit D.5. They can be used, for example, when you are networking or speaking to the press. Then it is perfectly all right to say, "I am in the executive search business."

Exhibit D.5
Don't Confuse Definitions with Labels

Company	Label	Definition
Executive Resources Group	Executive search	Market knowledge
Supreme Accountants	Accounting	Financial security
Your firm	Use two or three words to describe what you do.	Show the main benefit you provide to all clients.

The next challenge is to decide which definition to use. Pick the definition that best matches the needs of the group of people you want to reach. Pick the definition that sets you apart.

How to set your brochure apart from competitors'

You probably compete with many firms similar to your own. Others may be much larger, or they may do more things or sell substitute services. How does this affect how you produce your brochure? Imagine that your prospect receives brochures from three of your competitors. What you can do to make *your* brochure attract his attention? What do you want to say? What do you want to show? If you say what everyone else is saying, you stay with everyone else. There is only one way to make yourself known, and that is to make yourself unique.

There are three ways to do this. You can develop a unique message, you can develop a unique presentation, or you can develop a unique message and present it uniquely. The last method is the most powerful. To use it you need to know what your competitors are doing. Read their material to see what benefits they are highlighting. You will find there are three kinds of brochures:

- *Those that define a service but do not describe its benefits.* These brochures focus on the seller rather than the buyer by describing what the former sells instead of the benefits that the latter will receive. A competitor who does this has clearly misplaced his emphasis.

- *Those that describe benefits but do not define the business.* These brochures provide a list of benefits but no story to tie them together. They can leave a prospect wondering what point the brochure is trying to make.

- *Those that tell a story to help the prospect see the benefits.* Few competitors will reach this ideal, but those that do have a powerful presentation. If a firm does this, its prospects will see both what it is offering and why it is different.

After you read your competitors' brochures, talk to your clients (and those who have hired someone else) and your prospects. Ask them these questions.

- *What kinds of sources do you turn to for the kind of service I offer?* Here you want to assess who you are competing with. The answers may surprise you. For example, a financial adviser may find that it competes not only with other similar firms but also with published investment surveys. Make sure you define your business so that customers see they gain more value from it than from substitute products.

- *What do my competitors do better than I do? What do I do well?* These questions will help you see what you need to do to offer a unique service. Do not promise what you cannot provide. Use your brochure to highlight your strengths. Pick strengths that differ from the strengths of your competitors.

- *How are my competitors not meeting your needs?* It is often easier for people to explain what they did not like about a service than what they did like. Use this question to find out where your competitors are weakest. The answers here will also help you to meet the needs of your market better than other companies do.

Once you see where you stand, you are ready to develop your unique story. Build from the way you have chosen to define your business; then develop a premise. This shows the specific advantages customers gain by using your service. The format is, "Use (your company) to gain (unique benefit)." For example, a New Jersey law firm has specialized knowledge of the ins and outs of the court system in a particular county. It sells the increased probability of obtaining favorable rulings and decisions, and it can prove its effectiveness by showing results obtained for past clients. The premise is, "Use our firm to gain favorable legal results in XYZ County." Larger competitors lacked the specialized knowledge of this one county's courts, and no local firm could match its track record of wins.

A firm premise becomes the underlying theme of a brochure. Elaborate on it using pictures and words. As you develop these, have clients review the material for you. Ask them to tell you what they think. Always look to improve what you have.

How to use words

At this point you need to decide how you will write your brochure. Freelance copywriters usually charge fifteen cents per word. You'll pay more if you use an advertising agency; however, the agency will also help you with production work. In general, although outside professionals can be helpful in shaping your brochure and making it as professional as it can be, it pays to do as much as you can yourself. For example, you can hire a freelance writer to edit copy you have written.

Pay attention not only to what you say but also to how you say it. Dull writing will not help you entice readers. Here are some rules to make your writing effective.

- *Keep your writing simple.* You do not want to put your reader to sleep. Do no write like this:

  > By comparing your organization's core competencies within the rubric of best practices or "world-class" competitors (those corporations and institutions that are effectively leveraging their competitive strengths across the value chain), our service will implicitly help to identify your leverageable assets and strategies to drive to rightsizing excellence.

  > What is simple writing? Look in the children's book section of your local bookstore and leaf through picture books that have won Newbery awards. These books tell stories using pictures and simple, elegant language. They are good models for brochure writing.

- *Write only as much as you need to,* to tell prospects what you want them to know. Casual readers will scan the text for the information they want. Headlines will help to attract attention: Write them so that they move people to read more. For example, "We reduce medical benefits costs by

25 percent" is better than "Medical Costs." Don't err by being overly explicit or the reader may feel patronized.

- *Use action words.* Say "We improve productivity" rather than "Productivity improvement is our specialty." "Improve" expresses action; "is" does not.

- *Show what you mean.* Most brochures tell readers what they need to know about a service. It is better to *show* them what they need to know and then tell them about it. What is the difference? *Telling* explains ideas. *Showing* brings ideas to life. I can *tell* you that Quirk Factory helps toy companies design unique toys or I can *show* you Quirk Factory by using an example.

> A toy company wanted to develop a line of metal wind-up toys. Its executives had worked for months to come up with a theme for the new product. The toys had to be quirky and imaginative. For help, the company called Quirk Factory. Our team of designers went right to work. Within a week we presented three concepts..."

When you *show* advantages, you involve the reader in what you are saying.

If you choose to have your brochure written for you, keep these rules in mind as you evaluate your final copy. The next step is to integrate pictures with your words. This helps you show your story better.

How to use pictures

Most books will tell you about the different kinds of graphics you can use in a brochure: photographs, illustrations, graphs, etc. There are really only two: ones that help you show the benefits of your service and ones that do not. Avoid the latter. How? Imagine that you have only one piece of paper to use to tell your story to your prospects. What graphics would you use if you had to tell your story using pictures alone?

This exercise is not as farfetched as it may sound. You cannot know what part of your brochure will interest a prospect. You have to make all parts work for you. Do not include graphics if they do not help you support the story you are telling. There are some simple tests you can use to see if your graphics are effective.

- *Are they relevant?* This does not mean relevant to *you.* Your graphics must be meaningful to your buyer. A brochure is not the place to show pictures that make you feel good. Show pictures that make prospects feel good about buying your service. Make your pictures tell a story. Avoid placing them as if they were in a museum display, with few links connecting them. Client feedback is particularly helpful in judging relevancy.

- *Do they make you curious?* The cover of your brochure should cause prospects to want to read what is inside; the graphics you use inside your brochure should make them want to read further. Achieve this by keeping your images original and new. Show action. Link pictures to words and to the story you are telling.

- *Do they show comparisons?* Comparisons can help to show prospects what they gain by using your service. Charts and graphs are the most commonly used tools, but photographs and illustrations can work just as well. You must show what came before and what happened after the use of your service.

- *Do they tell too much?* This is a common problem with charts, graphs, and tables. Keep your comparisons simple. The more you clutter your graphics with information, the more difficult they are to read. Few people will spend the time to find out what point you are trying to make. Use color coding and labels to show the reader what you want him to see. Use a heading above the graphic to emphasize your point. For example: "We can cut six months off the design and construction of your new office." As you develop your graphs, you should ask yourself whether a twelve year old child would understand them. If the answer is no, see whether there is a simpler way to present your idea.

In your text, be sure to reference, directly or indirectly, any graphics you have included. Refer to tables or graphs that show improvements. These are graphics with messages you want your reader to see. Use a caption under your graphic to quote from your text.

You must also pay attention to the design of your brochure—how you arrange your words and pictures on the page to make them interesting to a reader. The better you design, the easier you will find it to capture readers. Dull design will send your prospects running. Hire a graphic artist if you can; otherwise use desktop-publishing software. Read the manual that comes with such programs for suggestions on how to make things easy for people to see and read. Here are a few tips to get you started.

- Use typefaces that are easiest to read. Times Roman is best for small type; Helvetica for large-type headlines.

- Do not print your text using all capital letters. WRITING IN CAPITAL LETTERS WILL MAKE YOUR BROCHURE DIFFICULT TO READ.

- Have a consistent look. Trying to see the relationship in "Make everything **look** as if it is part of the *same* thing" is more difficult than "Make everything look as if it is part of the same thing."

- Keep your choice of paper simple. This makes it easy to find. You need to match paper to make other materials or to add pages to a flexible brochure. The heavier the paper, the better it will bear up under frequent use. Use paper that weighs more than sixty pounds.

■ Do not forget to note your firm name, address, and telephone and fax numbers somewhere on the brochure. You can also add a space for your business card. You want to make sure your prospects know where to find you.

Choose how you will produce your brochure

Know what you want and about how much you want to spend. You will find your printer more than eager to develop a budget with you. There are two printing processes you can use: xerography and offset printing. Depending on which you chose, you can spend one day or up to a month getting your brochure printed. Each process has strengths and weakness. (See exhibit D.6.) Use quick printers for xerography work and commercial printers for offset printing.

Exhibit D.6
Weigh the Merits of Different Printing Processes

Process	Advantages	Disadvantages

Xerography	Quick turnaround
	Lower cost
	Affordable short runs
	Reasonable color
	  capability
		Lower quality resolution
		More limited paper
		  choice, especially if
		  you use color

Offset Printing	Excellent color quality
	Excellent resolution of
	  words and pictures
	Broad paper choice
		Higher cost, especially
		  for short runs
		Longer turnaround

If you wish to print in color, the options remain the same. Offset printing provides high quality, but you pay for it. You may find that high-quality color xerography will do for your project. Color xerography technology is improving rapidly; in fact, you should not assume that the quality you see at your local copy service is the best available. Some printers have equipment that will produce a quality most untrained eyes would confuse with offset printing. Each year the quality gets better and costs drop.

To keep your costs low, provide camera-ready work. This includes text printed on a laser printer and formatted to the size of your brochure with graphics included. Many printers can take your work off computer disks if you use standard programs. Some quick printers also provide computer work stations so you can work on this software right in the shop. The more camera ready work you supply, the faster the job will be finished. When you visit the printer...

■ ...*know how many copies you want.* How many copies will you need? If you think you will need to make changes to your brochure, produce fewer of them, with a more flexible format. Otherwise, print enough to last six months. The exception is four-color brochures. They are expensive to produce; you may want a year's supply or more.

- *...know what kind of paper you want.* If you are not using a designer, ask your printer to help you select the best paper for your job. For most businesses, something simple and standard is best. Quick printers seldom stock a wide variety of paper; don't let them persuade you that what they have is necessarily best. Also avoid direct-mail supply houses. Their designer papers are over-used and may cheapen your image. Commercial printers usually have more paper from which to choose. They will also order paper for you. This can add a week or more to the time it takes to produce your brochure, so order paper as early as you can and work on the text and graphics while you wait for it to arrive.

- *...have your layout ready.* Even if you are just shopping for estimates, your layout (or draft of it) will help the printer see what you want to do. If you use graphics, be sure to indicate where they fit. Number the backs of your pictures and match these to spaces on your layout.

When you work with offset printing, you should ask to see the mechanical. This is the proof copy of the brochure prior to printing. Proofread it by reading text backward word by word. This helps you spot letters that are out of place. Otherwise you can look at the text and see what you expect to see instead of any mistakes that might be there. Then have one or two people who have some stake in seeing your firm succeed look it over. You will save time and aggravation.

Stand apart
The way to be noticed is to be different. Your brochure must be different in a way that means something to your prospects. Use the guidelines given here to help you create a brochure that tells a story. You will attract the curiosity of those who see it and those who read it. A brochure will not close a sale for you; it can and should help you make one.

Appendix E

Further Readings and Information

Article writing and writing in general

Strunk, William, Jr. and E. B. White. *The Elements of Style*. New York: Macmillan Publishing Co., Inc., 1979
> If you follow the guidance given in this eighty five-page book, your English composition will improve noticeably. It has become the standard source on the subject, recommended by teachers and writers because its advice is so sound and readable.

Bacon's Magazine Directory. Chicago: Bacon's Information Inc. Published annually.
> This directory provides the most complete listing of magazines available. It will give you basic information on what publications are available in a particular field and tell you what they cover and how to reach them. Too expensive for most people to buy and not carried by all libraries, you may have to use a copy at a public relations firm or department.

The Chicago Manual of Style. Chicago: The University of Chicago Press, 1982.
> This is one of several style manuals (others are produced by the *New York Times* and the U.S. Government Printing Office) used by editors and publishers to ensure consistency in punctuation, abbreviations, reference formats, and other details. You will find it useful if you write a lot.

Public speaking, seminars, and presenting

Axtell, Roger E. *Do's and Taboos of Public Speaking*. New York: John Wiley & Sons, Inc., 1992.
> Any business bookstore will offer several titles on public speaking. This one is better than most.

Jolles, Robert L. *How to Run Seminars and Workshops*. New York: John Wiley and Sons, Inc., 1993.
> Oriented toward training, this book provides useful guidance for speakers and trainers at seminars.

Preparing visual aids and graphics

Wileman, Ralph E. *Visual Communicating*. Englewood Cliffs, New Jersey: Educational Technology Publications, 1993.
> The helpful 147-page book is the reason I asked Professor Wileman to write an appendix for this book.

White, Jan V. *Editing by Design: A Guide to Effective Word-and-Picture Communication for Editors and Designers.* New York: Bowker, 1982.

Robertson, Bruce. *How to Draw Charts and Diagrams.* Cincinnati: North Light Books, 1988.

Networking and relationship marketing

Boe, Anne, and Bettie B. Youngs. *Is Your "Net" Working?* New York: John Wiley & Sons, Inc., 1989.

Roane, Susan. *How to Work a Room.* New York: Warner Books, Inc., 1988.

Cathcart, Jim. *Relationship Selling.* New York: Perigree Books, 1980.
This book deals with face-to-face selling more than with lead generation. It is more relationship-oriented than other books on sales.

Stanley, Dr. Thomas J. *Networking with the Affluent and Their Advisors.* Homewood, Illinois: Business One Irwin, 1993.
This book is clever and should be read by anyone selling directly to high-income individuals. I find its tone to be mercenary in a way inconsistent with good relationship marketing, but the concepts are sound.

Encyclopedia of Associations. Detroit: Gale Research Inc. Published Annually.
This directory is the standard reference for associations and can be found in most libraries. It gives the size, interests, publications, location of annual meetings, and other useful information about thousands of associations and trade associations.

Cold calling and selling

Miller, Robert B., and Stephen E. Heiman, with Tad Tuleja. *Conceptual Selling.* New York: Warner Books, 1987.
The guidance in this excellent book on face-to-face selling can easily be adapted to the professions.

Rackham, Neil. *SPIN Selling.* New York: McGraw-Hill Book Company, 1988.
This is another good book on face-to-face selling.

Miller, Robert B., and Stephen E. Heiman, with Tad Tuleja. *Strategic Selling.* New York: Warner Books, 1985.
This book provides valuable insight into complex sales, sales that must be made to several people or a committee. It also will help you manage multiple sales simultaneously.

Schiffman, Stephen, *The Consultant's Handbook: How to Start & Develop Your Own Practice.* Holbrook, Massachusetts: Bob Adams, Inc. Publishers, 1988.
Because it is directed at professionals, this book provides good commentary on the numbers-game and time-management aspects of cold-call selling.

Shafiroff, Martin D., and Robert L. Shook. *Successful Telephone Selling in the Nineties.* New York: Harper and Row, 1990.
This book will help you develop the telephone skills needed to get a meeting.

Proposals and fees

Shenson, Howard. *The Contract and Fee-Setting Guide for Consultants & Professionals.* New York: John Wiley & Sons in association with University Associates, Inc., 1990.

Notes

Introduction

1. Wittreich, Warren J. "How to Buy/Sell Professional Services." *Harvard Business Review*, March-April 1966. p. 129.

2. Dennett, Tyler (ed.), *Lincoln and the Civil War in the Diaries and Letters of John Hay*, New York: DaCapo, 1988. p. 179.

Chapter 1

1. *Bacon's Magazine Directory*. Chicago: Bacon's Information Inc. Published annually. Not all libraries have this book. If yours doesn't, try your firm's public relations director or public relations firm.

2. Westlake, Donald E. "Champing at the Bar." *New York Times Book Review*, 12 December, 1990.

3. Rose, Mark. *Shakespearean Design*. Cambridge, Massachusetts: The Belknap Press of Harvard University Press, 1972.

4. Branch, Taylor. *Parting the Waters: America in the King Years, 1954-63*. New York: Simon and Schuster, 1988, pp. 76-77.

Chapter 2

1. Branch, Taylor. *Parting the Waters: America in the King Years, 1954-63*. New York: Simon and Schuster, 1988, pp. 76-77.

2. Toastmaster International is an international organization with many regional affiliates. To find one near you, contact Toastmasters International, P.O. Box 9052, Mission Viejo, California 92690-7052. Telephone: (714) 858-8255.

3. *Encyclopedia of Associations*. Detroit: Gale Research Inc., Published annually. Most libraries have this useful reference.

Chapter 4

1. *Encyclopedia of Associations*. Detroit: Gale Research Inc., Published annually. Most libraries have this useful reference.

Chapter 5

1. Cathcart, Jim. *Relationship Selling: The Key to Getting and Keeping Customers*. New York: Perigee Books, The Putnam Publishing Company, 1990, pp. 25-40.

Chapter 9

1. Blumberg, Donald C. "Getting Customers to Ask for Your Services." *IMCommunicator*, January 1994. p. 3.

2. *Bacon's Magazine Directory*. Chicago: Bacon's Information, Inc. Published annually. Bacon's also publishes directories of other media.

3. Hiaasen, Carl. *Tourist Season*. New York: Warner Books, 1986, p. 371.

Chapter 10

1. I have adapted the typology from Raymond L. Gordon and his book *Interviewing: Strategy, Technique and Tactics* Homewood, Illinois: The Dorsey Press, 1975.

2. *Ibid.*

Chapter 20

1. Caplan, Lincoln. *Skadden: Power, Money and the Rise of a Legal Empire*. New York: Farrar Straus Giroux, 1993, pp. 52-53, 78.

2. *Ibid.* pp. 84-85.

Appendix A

1. Strunk, William, Jr., and E. B. White. *The Elements of Style*. New York: Macmillan Publishing Co., Inc., 1979, p. 21.

Index